SYLVIA PLATH AND THE SUPERNATURAL

Sylvia Plath and the Supernatural brings a fresh and interdisciplinary perspective to the reading of Plath. Following recently published new material, this book offers a novel approach to the re-examination and celebration of supernatural themes in Plath's writings. It expands Plath studies by establishing Plath's creative and intellectual interests in early modern literature about witches and demonology, knowledge of the legacies of the Salem witch trials during McCarthyism, and her depth of understanding of the complex relationship between gender and magical powers. The book also demonstrates how Plath and her contemporaries responded to post-war American and British politics through employing and repurposing supernatural concepts while engaging with popular culture, atomic warfare, and colonialism. This book provides a systematic overview of Plath's materials, from draft manuscripts to *The Bell Jar*, and a unique analysis of post-war literature and culture through the lens of the supernatural.

DR DORKA TAMÁS is a researcher and academic with an interest in Sylvia Plath, the legacies of early modern witch-hunt, twentieth-century women's writing, ecocriticism, and post-1945 American culture. She is the editor of *The New Sylvia Plath Studies*, published by Cambridge University Press and co-founder of the Sylvia Plath Society.

SYLVIA PLATH AND THE SUPERNATURAL

DORKA TAMÁS

CAMBRIDGE
UNIVERSITY PRESS

CAMBRIDGE
UNIVERSITY PRESS

Shaftesbury Road, Cambridge CB2 8EA, United Kingdom

One Liberty Plaza, 20th Floor, New York, NY 10006, USA

477 Williamstown Road, Port Melbourne, VIC 3207, Australia

314–321, 3rd Floor, Plot 3, Splendor Forum, Jasola District Centre, New Delhi – 110025, India

103 Penang Road, #05–06/07, Visioncrest Commercial, Singapore 238467

Cambridge University Press is part of Cambridge University Press & Assessment, a department of the University of Cambridge.

We share the University's mission to contribute to society through the pursuit of education, learning and research at the highest international levels of excellence.

www.cambridge.org
Information on this title: www.cambridge.org/9781009575515

DOI: 10.1017/9781009575539

When citing this work, please include a reference to the DOI 10.1017/9781009575539

First published 2026
Cover image: Courtesy Lilly Library, Indiana University, Bloomington, Indiana.

A catalogue record for this publication is available from the British Library

A Cataloging-in-Publication data record for this book is available from the Library of Congress

ISBN 978-1-009-57551-5 Hardback

In loving memory of my caring and supportive father, György Tamás, who passed away while I was completing this book, and to those who believe in the power of poetry, the magic we make, and life from the ashes.

Contents

Acknowledgements

I am deeply grateful for all the support from my friends and colleagues: Dr Julie Irigaray and Kitty Shamburov, Dr Madeline Potter, Dr Roslyn Irving, and Dr Giulia Champion. My sincere thanks go to Professor Heather Clark for her brilliant Plath biography, *Red Comet*, and advice, Peter K. Steinberg for his assistance in my research project regarding the Sylvia Plath archives and bringing together Plath's prose and letters, and Dr Amanda Golden, co-editor of Plath's new poems collection, with whom I had fruitful conversations and lunch at Smith College. Thank you for reading an earlier version of this book. I am thankful for the help I received from the librarians and archivists in the Smith College Special Collections at the Neilson Library, both during the pandemic and during my visit to the Plath archives in person. Special thanks to Karen V. Kukil, Research Affiliate in English Language & Literature, for her important work on Plath's letters, archives and for the support. Thank you to Kate Long, Research Services Archivist at Smith College, for the help. I am grateful for the assistance of the librarians and archivists at the British Library; Stuart A. Rose Manuscript, Archives, and Rare Book Library at Emory University; Lilly Library at Indiana University; and BBC Written Archives Centre, who helped me with archival research essential to this book.

I appreciate the support from my colleagues at the University of Groningen, particularly from Dr Pauline McGonagle, Dr M. Pilar Milagros, and Professor Julia Kühn. I am grateful for the guidance of Professor Marion Gibson and Professor Jo Gill during my doctoral degree at the University of Exeter and beyond. Thank you for the interest in my work from Plath scholars: Professor Anita Helle, Dr Di Beddow, and Catherine Rankovic. Thank you for the support and friendship from Olivia Foster, Dr Betty Doyle, Dr Iona Murphy, Dr Maria Rovito, and Anna Dykta. My thanks go to the recurring participants of the Sylvia Plath Society and members of the Plath community with whom I interacted over the years. My sincere thanks go to the organisers, volunteers, and participants of the 2022 Sylvia Plath Festival, especially Dr Sarah Corbett and Ian Humphreys.

My gratitude goes to my students at the University of Exeter and the University of Groningen, who showed enthusiasm about Sylvia Plath and my book. Thank you to my former employer, Nick Sheppard and the University of Leeds Library, for their support and help in expanding my knowledge of research culture. Thank you to the brilliant Plath critics with whom I corresponded and inspired my work. A special thanks to Dr Christina Britzolakis, literary scholar, who passed away in 2023, whom I never met nor with whom I talked, but who influenced my work. I am grateful to Claire Mitchell QC and Zoe Venditozzi for their ongoing work and conversation about the witch trials in the *Witches of Scotland* podcast. Thank you to Ash Caton and his *Edinburgh's Most Powerful Book Podcast* for conversations on Plath. My deepest gratitude goes to the readers of my publications and audiences of conferences who took the time to engage with my research. Thank you to the editors, peer reviewers, and conference organisers for allowing me to share my ideas in public forums.

My deepest appreciation goes to Cambridge University Press, the syndicates for their approval of my monograph, and the editorial and management team, including Ray Ryan whose support and enthusiasm for this research project was essential. Thank you to the external readers for their valuable feedback that shaped this book. I appreciate the hard work and interest in my book from my indexer, Paula Clarke Bain.

I am grateful to the Sylvia Plath Estate for granting me access and permission to quote from the archives. The cover of *Sylvia Plath and the Supernatural* is a reproduction of a photograph from the Gordon Lameyer Collection from the Lilly Library, courtesy of the Lilly Library, Indiana University, Bloomington, Indiana.

My deepest thanks go to my partner and my family who supported and encouraged me while writing and editing this monograph. I dedicated this book to my father whose loving presence will always accompany me. Thank you to my friends and acquaintances from Hungary who showed their ongoing support and enthusiasm for my work regardless of the language barriers.

Thank you to the reader who picked up this book.

Abbreviations

AR	Plath, Sylvia. *Ariel: The Restored Edition*. London: Faber, 2004.
BL	Hughes, Ted. *Birthday Letters*. London: Faber & Faber, 1998.
CP	Plath, Sylvia. *The Collected Poems*. Ed. Ted Hughes. New York: HarperCollins, 2008.
J	Plath, Sylvia. *The Unabridged Journals of Sylvia Plath*. Ed. Karen V. Kukil. New York: Anchor Books, 2002.
L1	Plath, Sylvia. *The Letters of Sylvia Plath Volume I: 1940–1956*. Ed. Peter K. Steinberg and Karen V. Kukil. London: Faber, 2017.
L2	Plath, Sylvia. *The Letters of Sylvia Plath: Volume II: 1956–1963*. Ed. Karen V. Kukil and Peter K. Steinberg. London: Faber & Faber, 2018.
LH	Plath, Sylvia. *Letters Home: Correspondence 1950–1963*. Ed. Aurelia Plath. New York: Harper & Row, 1975.
MS	Manuscript from Sylvia Plath Collection, Smith College Special Collections
Prose	Plath, Sylvia. *The Collected Prose of Sylvia Plath*. Ed. Peter K. Steinberg. London: Faber & Faber, 2024.
SCSC	Smith College Special Collections
TBJ	Plath, Sylvia. *The Bell Jar*. London: Faber & Faber, 2001.
THCP	Hughes, Ted. *Collected Poems*. Ed. Paul Keegan. London: Faber & Faber, 2005.
THL	Hughes, Ted. *Letters of Ted Hughes*. Ed. Christopher Reid. New York: Farrar, Straus and Giroux, 2008.
TS	Typescript from Sylvia Plath Collection, Mortimer Rare Book Collection, Smith College Special Collections
WCD	*Webster's New Collegiate Dictionary*. Springfield, Massachusetts: G. & C. Merriam Co., 1949.

Introduction

In the Preface of *The Collected Prose of Sylvia Plath* (2024), the editor Peter K. Steinberg highlights that Plath's short stories 'have concerns with material wealth, poverty, depression, loneliness, and magic' (*Prose* xvii). Steinberg's acknowledgement of magic as a significant theme in Plath's prose demonstrates the importance of revisiting and carefully considering the supernatural in her work. Magic was also one of the main themes of the Sylvia Plath Literary Festival in October 2022, celebrating Plath's ninetieth birthday with events across Hebden Bridge and Heptonstall, and a topic of the poetry and essay collection *After Sylvia* (Nine Arches Press, 2022), edited by Sarah Corbett and Ian Humphreys. The present book, *Sylvia Plath and the Supernatural*, is the outcome of the recent and long history of public and scholarly attention to theorising Plath's engagement with magic. I approach the subject with critical, literary, cultural, political, and gendered perspectives, passion for the subject, and consideration for Plath's published and archival writings. This book brings an interdisciplinary approach to Sylvia Plath and the supernatural themes and retracts previous reductionist narratives on her engagement with the occult. The critical examination of Plath's poetry, prose, and private writings demonstrates the influence of historical, cultural, political, and literary discourses and texts on the supernatural in Plath's carefully crafted language. My study of the subject is centred on those aspects and interpretations of the supernatural that are central to Plath's understanding and deployment of the concept within the cultural, historical, political, and gendered framework in which she lived – in post-war America and during the Cold War.

Throughout the seven chapters, I investigate what Plath might have meant by invoking or exploring the supernatural and the ways in which she employed its related concepts to articulate political and personal matters in her poetry, fiction and non-fiction and personal writings. This book is interested in the cultural models Plath draws on in her poetry and prose when she deploys concepts such as the witch, sympathetic magic, black magician, and a witches' sabbath. For example, the concept of witchcraft – one of the several subcategories of the supernatural – is rooted in the early modern witch-hunt and its literature, which she was familiar with through her education in American literature and Elizabethan and Jacobean plays. Plath had a varied and often contradictory engagement with the supernatural across different historical periods, classical to contemporary literature, and cultural frameworks. My close reading of her works also relies on the drafts of her poems and other writings from archives to further illustrate her extensive knowledge and deep interest in the supernatural and its themes. Yet Plath is not the only poet of her generation who utilised supernatural themes in her poetry: along with Plath's writings, I examine the works of post-war poets who have been affiliated with Plath, such as Anne Sexton, Ted Hughes, and writers who are compared less often to Plath, such as Karl Shapiro, Elizabeth Bowen, Arthur Miller, John Berryman, John Ashbery, and Robert Graves, demonstrating the cultural, poetic, and political discourses and texts from which Plath sought inspiration.

In her often-used 1949 *Webster's New Collegiate Dictionary* (*WCD*), held at Smith College Special Collections (SCSC), Plath frequently underlined entries. Amanda Golden argues that 'by considering Plath's library and those of other writers, we learn that their annotating can be a means of engaging in larger conversations, responding to critical contexts and writers' own social and political landscapes' ('Sylvia Plath's Library' 111). Thus, my focus on Plath's annotations and marginalia reveals not only her knowledge of and emphasis on certain topics but also the cultural context in which she encountered texts and terms and responded to them in her writing. Plath's dictionary defines the supernatural in three ways, of which I quote the first two relevant definitions:

> *adj.* 1. Of, or proceeding from, an order of existence beyond nature, or the visible and observable universe. 2. Ascribed to agencies of above or beyond nature; miraculous. – ***n.*** With *the*, divine operation, intervention etc. hence something miraculous or marvellous. ('supernatural')

The entry outlines the supernatural as a phenomenon beyond the human material world across different beliefs, cultures, and times. The second definition connotes a religious understanding of the supernatural in Western history and culture, mainly Christianity. I use the supernatural as an umbrella term, which covers wide-ranging topics from spectrality, religious miracles, and magic to witchcraft in Western thoughts. This book is interested in those interpretations and aspects of the supernatural that Plath engaged with in her prose and poetry and in the broader literary and cultural discourses and discussions. In colloquial speech, the lines between magic and witchcraft are often blurred. In the *WCD*, witchcraft is further defined as a 'practice of witches', a 'power more than natural'; and magic is described as 'the art which claims or is believed to produce effects by the assistance of supernatural beings or by a mastery of secret forces in nature' ('witchcraft', 'magic'). Like the dictionary definitions, Plath's interpretation of these concepts was diverse. This book differentiates between the supernatural (meaning all that is beyond our perception of natural occurrences), witchcraft (the supernatural power associated with witches and the Devil), and magic (as a learnt supernatural power associated with magicians). These concepts, defined in *WCD*, are rooted in the vocabulary and history of the early modern witch-hunt, which provides a historical and theoretical framework for this book.

One of the objectives of *Sylvia Plath and the Supernatural* is to move away from the narrow understanding of Plath's engagement with the supernatural, which has often focused on a sensationalised understanding of witchcraft, ignoring her well-informed knowledge of the broader subject. Biographers, such as Edward Butscher and earlier critics like M. L. Rosenthal, frequently labelled her poems witchy, diabolical, or occultist without unpicking these concepts. Recent critics, such as Heather Clark, draw attention to the fact that when women poets such as Sylvia Plath are writing about supernatural themes, they are often labelled as playing with 'witchcraft, or quasi-occult practices' ('An Iconic Life' 3). Clark adds that the posthumous identification of Plath with the figure of a priestess or witch is patronising and sexist. Emily Van Duyne likewise affiliates the supernatural with Plath's posthumous life, originating the labels in trauma and misogyny:

> When yet another young woman is haunted, or hunted, by a danger so keen she dies of it, what story do we tell ourselves about it so that we can move on? The house killed her. The devil made her do it. What stories do we still tell about Sylvia Plath? It was Yeats's house. It was black magic. Her poems killed her in the end. (106)

Van Duyne suggests that the supernatural has been weaponised against Plath and her work, concealing her authentic self and narrative. However, there is also textual evidence among the published and archival materials, drafts, correspondences, and journals that Plath engaged with the supernatural in various ways. This book unearths Sylvia Plath from the careless employment of demons, devils, witches, black magic and more, and contextualises concepts associated with the supernatural within their historical and cultural framework. I closely examine terminologies that critics, biographers, and non-specialist readers have equally deployed superficially on Plath for over six decades. Plath's writings provide evidence of her broad understanding and knowledge of the history of witch-hunts, supernatural beliefs, religious terminologies, and the political rhetoric of the supernatural. The foundation of my analysis, subcategories of supernatural, and how I employ these terms is the well-defined and well-researched field of witchcraft and demonology, which comprises historical, textual, and discourse analyses interpreting the witch-hunt and its causes and outcomes. By relying on an interdisciplinary framework, I provide a new historical and cultural context for Plath studies and the broader field of twentieth-century literature.

The period of the great witch-hunt covers approximately three centuries; across Europe, it lasted roughly from 1450 to 1750. During this time, communities within most European countries and New England participated in prosecuting alleged witches. The emergence of a system to criminalise witchcraft was a long process, which developed from the religious fight of the Catholic Church against pagans and heretics. Inquisitorial punishments and prosecutions of heretics defined the medieval Crusades. In the early modern period, the crime of witchcraft was said to be characterised by *maleficium*, that is, harmful acts such as cursing and blaspheming and pacts with the Devil, who, according to contemporary Christian beliefs, gave magical powers to witches (Levack, *The Witch-Hunt* 7–8). The fight against witches became more widespread after the Bull of Pope Innocent VIII issued in 1484, which called for the establishment of an ecclesiastical inquisition for the elimination of witchcraft. The Pope's main advocates, Heinrich Kramer and Jacob Sprenger, wrote the infamous *Malleus Maleficarum* (1487), in which the Bull is reprinted. The misogynistic text codified the belief that midwives, and more generally women, were witches who killed infants and harmed men's fertility. While historians remain critical of the status of *Malleus Maleficarum*, for example, J. A. Sharpe argues that the influence of the text has been overestimated (180), it resurfaced in twentieth-century feminist interpretations of the witch-hunt like Barbara Ehrenreich and Deirdre English's *Witches, Midwives, and Nurses* (1972) and in the works of second-wave radical feminists, such as Mary Daly in *Gyn/Ecology* (1984), as a key source describing witches and their crimes. My book considers the religious and political context of the early modern witch-hunt and its interpretations in the post-war era – before the feminist reclamation of witches – to pin down Plath's well-informed readings of the history and literature of witchcraft and its role in the political discourses of the post-war era.

The Salem witch trials were the most influential mass execution of witches in New England, which started in 1692 and ended in 1693. Plath knew of the witch trials from American literature and historical sources, while she also lived in close proximity to Salem village. During the series of trials, more than two hundred people had been accused of practising witchcraft, and nineteen were executed who lived in Salem village and neighbouring places. The mass accusation started with the fits, delusions, and convulsions of children who accused Samuel Parris's slave Tituba who was from Barbados. Tituba confessed to being a witch but denied hurting the girls, snowballing a series of accusations, especially among women of the village community. Many of the accused were hanged or died in prison. More than four hundred years after the trials, there are still numerous questions about what could have happened with the children and why so many people were accused and executed. The Salem witch trials became part of national memory in America, often evoked during times of moral and cultural dilemmas, and represented a line between the superstitious, colonial past and the rational, modern, and independent America (Adams 4–6). While historical studies originate the witch trials in community tensions, such as Stephen Nissenbaum and Paul Boyer's *Salem Possessed: The Social Origins of Witchcraft* (1974), Salem remains a symbol of mass hysteria, delusion, and the abuse of institutional power. Such interpretation appealed to Plath who often sought inspiration from historical injustices and grew up in the 1950s in Massachusetts where the concept of the witch-hunt not only experienced a return in political discourses but the geography evoked the haunting parallels between anti-communism and the execution of witches.

As the fear of witches heightened across North America and Europe, the early modern period, magicians who practised 'white magic' – regarded as helpers and healers – could also be accused of performing diabolical magic (Levack, *The Witch-Hunt* 11). They were often known as 'cunning men', 'wizards', or 'wise men/women' (Thomas 210). The Protestant Reformation also wanted to eliminate Catholic protective magic, such as miracles, the canonisation of saints, and magical attributions to prayers, which increased the fear of magic among the peasant society (Levack, *The Witch-Hunt* 118). The popularity of cunning folk in the villages suggests that magic was perceived by ordinary people as fearful only when it was linked with the Devil and demonic activities. In early modern plays, we often see the opposition between the 'good' white magic, associated with the intellectual abilities of the magus, and 'evil' magic, related to a feminised understanding of witchcraft, as in Shakespeare's *The Tempest* and *Macbeth*. While it would be an overstatement to say that magic and witchcraft reflect the gender binary in Western history and culture, the former is often linked to the male magus and the latter to the female witch. Chapter 3 and Chapter 4 unpick the different references to the gendered elements of witchcraft and binary perception of good vs. evil magic in Plath's writings and contextualise their meaning in the historical period in which they originate.

Despite the evidence of gendering witchcraft, most (male) historians during the twentieth century avoided analysing the gender power dynamics of the witch-hunt period, such as Hugh Trevor-Roper's *The European Witch-Craze of the Sixteenth and Seventeenth Centuries* (1969) and Keith Thomas's *Religion and the Decline of Magic* (1971), which focused on the social-economic and religious context of the witch-hunt. Studies of the witch-hunt, which engaged with gender imbalances, such as Christina Larner's *Enemies of God* (1981), Carol Karlsen's *The Devil in the Shape of a Woman* (1987), Diane Purkiss's *The Witch in History* (1996), and Silvia Federici's *Caliban and the Witch* (2004), became more widespread with the second- and third-wave feminist movements and the establishment of women's and gender studies as an interdisciplinary academic field. The witch figure also emerged as a metaphor for women's oppression during the second half of the twentieth century: in the late 1960s, the organisation W.I.T.C.H. (Women's International Terrorist Conspiracy from Hell) was founded, which drew on popular beliefs about and imagery of witches as powerful, wicked women who are part of a secret organisation (Purkiss 8–9). As highlighted, radical feminists like Mary Daly and Andrea Dworkin reworked some unsubstantiated claims about the witch-hunt; they echoed the earlier sentiment that 'wise women' were regarded as the enemy of the Church because they healed while Christianity advocated suffering and emphasised the guilt of humanity, particularly of women (Gage 74). Indeed, many women accused of committing witchcraft were midwives or healers; however, Daly and Dworkin overstated their persecution; rather, women were often victims of witch accusations due to their limited professional options (Levack, *The Witch-Hunt* 147). Plath's writing alludes to these stereotypes, yet her knowledge of the witch-hunt shows a more nuanced understanding of the historical, literary, gender, and political aspects that constitute the witch.

Feminist revisionist mythology encouraged an interpretation of Plath's use of witch imagery that focuses on the hierarchical gendered power dynamics. Writing about Plath's and Sexton's use of supernatural female figures, Alicia Ostriker argues that 'when they traffic in the demonic, women poets have produced some of the most highly charged images' (221). Poems like 'Lady Lazarus' and 'Witch Burning' reference witches and present a similar narrative of rebirth through burning and transcendence in which the objectified and tortured female body is a central spectacle. The feminist interpretations of the poems tend to concern themselves with the socio-political context in which we read the poems and less with how Plath employed the witch imagery in her poetry of the 1950s and early 1960s when such concepts were diversely used and understood. As Susan Van Dyne highlights, Plath had conflicting ideas about gender, art, and embodying female personae in her poetry: 'to become a poet, for Plath, means to resist becoming her gender' (*Revising Life* 85). A central argument of *Sylvia Plath and the Supernatural* is that Plath's portrayal of the witch is as a layered and multidimensional figure who embodies martyrdom, modern scapegoating and societal injustices, and maternal malice – more often than a proto-feminist sorceress. She often relied on her substantial knowledge of the witch-hunt, political rhetoric, and literary sources rather than a straightforward feminist stance.

Plath's dictionary is one of the key sources in tracing her knowledge of the concepts of the witch and witchcraft. Below is the *WCD*'s definition of the witch, in which the underlining replicates Plath's annotation:

> **witch** *n.* [AS. *wicce*, fem., *wicca*, masc.] 1. One who practices the black art, or magic; one regarded as possessing supernatural or magical power by compact with an evil spirit, esp. with Devil; a sorcerer or sorcerers; – now applied to women only. 2. An ugly old woman; hag; a crone 3. *Colloq*. One who exercises more than common power or attraction; a charming or bewitching person. — *v.t.* 1. To work a spell, esp. an evil spell, upon by sorcery. 2. To effect by sorcery, or witchcraft 3. To bewitch; fascinate. – **witch**. *adj*. ('witch')

Her highlights demonstrate that she emphasised the negative connotations of the witch figure, such as her association with black magic, her haggish look, and her ability to bewitch with spells. On the same page, the dictionary also included entries on 'witch broom', 'witchcraft', and 'witches' Sabbath'. *WCD*'s definition contextualises the concepts in the early modern witch-hunt and shows the highly gendered and sexist perception of witchcraft. The gendered portrayal of the witch, particularly as an old maternal figure, still defines our cultural representation of this supernatural figure. Plath's depiction of witches in her poems like 'Witch Burning' and 'The Disquieting Muses' draws on varied sources, such as the historical witch-hunt, the literature of witchcraft, and political discourses, which I discuss in detail in Chapters 1, 2, 3, and 7. My book shows that witch figures and witchcraft are not employed as trans-historical symbols of female oppression by Plath, but she recognised the complex histories of the concepts rooted in the political and cultural frameworks of the European and New England witch-hunts, the McCarthyist witch-hunt, and literature concerned with witches and their powers.

Plath's references to the supernatural in her poems, *The Bell Jar*, short stories, correspondence, journals, and archival materials frequently interrogate the relationship between gender and magical power. The majority of Plath's archives are kept either in Smith College Special Collections (SCSC) or in the Lilly Library, Indiana. Critics such as Marjorie Perloff in 'The Two Ariels: The (Re)making Of The Sylvia Plath Canon' (1984), Lynda K. Bundtzen in *The Other Ariel* (2005), and Susan Van Dyne in *Revising Life: Sylvia Plath's Ariel Poems* (1993) studied Plath's manuscripts, particularly her *Ariel* poems. This book benefits from the handwritten drafts (holographs) and typewritten drafts (typescripts) of Plath's poems: I examine the manuscripts to identify Plath's deep-rooted poetic allusions to supernatural themes and employment of the vocabulary of the witch-hunt. Plath's early manuscripts are often undated, however, as her writing process developed, she dated the poems, frequently adding her name on the top of the page. *The Bell Jar* and several of her later poems were written on the pink Smith memorandum paper Plath seized while teaching at Smith College in the 1957/58 academic year. Her journal entry from March 1958 suggests that she considered the pink paper inspiring and full of life, as opposed to the blankness of white paper (*J* 344). This book pays attention to the pattern in Plath's creative writing process and interrogates her repeated erasures of expressions that directly deploy the imagery of witch prosecutions, sympathetic magic, diabolism, or reference the magic powers of spoken or written words. While Plath's archives reveal a narrative of her knowledge of and interest in the supernatural, the Harriet Rosenstein Research Files on Sylvia Plath 1910–2018 at Emory University, opened in 2020, exposed controversial discussions on Plath's alleged sorcery and apparent witchy poems in interviews five decades earlier. The archives constitute correspondences, audio files, and interview transcripts from Rosenstein, who was working on a Plath biography in the early 1970s; however, she abandoned her project, and her research materials were unseen until recently. The interview tapes and notes with Plath's friends, neighbours, and acquaintances provide rich perspectives on how the discourse of Plath's engagement with the supernatural emerged and shifted over the decades. The over-emphasis on her 'witch' identity, involvement in witchcraft, and rumoured practice of magic in the research files demonstrate that, in one way or another, the supernatural has always been an underlying theme in understanding Plath's life and work. The critical examination of the discourse on Plath and the supernatural and the close reading of her personal, poetic, and discursive engagement with the topic is not only timely but needed to untangle what is being said and meant in these interview files, and what kinds of historical and cultural frameworks influenced Plath's associations with popular ideas of witchcraft.

This book would not be a wide-ranging study of Sylvia Plath and the supernatural without the publication of new materials and the expansion of Plath studies. Most importantly, *The Letters of Sylvia Plath* vol. 1 (2017) and vol. 2 (2018), edited by Karen V. Kukil and Peter K. Steinberg; *The Collected Prose of Sylvia Plath* (2024), edited by Peter K. Steinberg, containing many of Plath's non-fiction and journalistic writings; and the forthcoming *The Poems of Sylvia Plath* (2026) edited by Amanda Golden and Karen V. Kukil. Without question, Heather Clark's monumental biography *Red Comet: The Short Life and Blazing Art of Sylvia Plath* (2020), shortlisted for the Pulitzer Prize, had a great influence on reevaluating Plath's place both in the wider public and academia, encouraging scholars to reexamine Plath's life, work, and legacy. Recent edited publications reflect on this turn in Plath studies, including *Sylvia Plath in Context* (2019), edited by Tracy Brain, and *The Bloomsbury Handbook to Sylvia Plath* (2022), edited by Anita Helle, Amanda Golden, and Maeve O'Brien. In the latter collection, Katherine Robinson's chapter, 'The Law of Similarity and the Law of Contact: Sylvia Plath, Ted Hughes, and Sympathetic Magic', signals the timely reconsideration and scholarly interest in Plath and the supernatural. Forthcoming edited collections, *The Routledge Companion to Sylvia Plath*, edited by Emily Van Duyne, Janet Badia, and Julie Goodspeed-Chadwick, and *The New Sylvia Plath Studies*, under my editing with Cambridge University Press, offer new critical pathways, intersectional and interdisciplinary approaches, and popular reading practices of Plath's work in the twenty-first century. *The New Sylvia Plath Studies* also includes my chapter, 'Plath and the Diabolical Atomic Age', an expansion of Chapter 4 of this book, focusing on an interdisciplinary study of Plath's writings on the Cold War in which politics, science, and black magic were intertwined.

Sylvia Plath and the Supernatural parallels the scholarly activities and critical reassessment of supernatural themes, magical histories, and

Western esotericism in literary studies and the humanities, such as Amy Hungerford's *Postmodern Belief: American Literature and Religion Since 1960* (2010), Leigh Wilson's *Modernism and Magic* (2013), and *Revisiting the "Nazi Occult": Histories, Realities, Legacies* (2015), edited by Monica Black and Eric Kurlande. My book explores key concepts associated with the supernatural, which I read within the broader framework of post-war culture and politics. The seven chapters study how supernatural concepts have been deployed in literary, cultural, and political discourses and popular culture to establish Plath's perception and employment of them in her writings. Apart from closely reading Plath's writings, I look at the broader cultural conversations in, for example, newspapers and magazines. The media archives, read along with Plath's non-fiction and journalistic writings, demonstrate that supernatural themes were embedded in the language, culture, and politics of post-war America and Britain and, more broadly, the Cold War. Plath's education in classical myths and early modern plays, contextualised within the cultural framework in which she encountered them, gives evidence of her knowledge of the literature of witchcraft, supernatural beings, and magical powers. My book also deemphasises the role of Ted Hughes as an initiator and influence on Plath's writings about the supernatural and considers the broader context of post-war American poetry, particularly the Boston poets such as Anne Sexton and Robert Lowell, who are regularly read along with Plath's confessional-style poems. From *Macbeth* and *Doctor Faustus* to demonic possession and Nathaniel Hawthorne's Salem writings, post-war writers were interested and invested in the intersections between gender, magic, and power at larger societal levels and in interpersonal relationships. They engaged with the literary and political discourses and shared an intellectual interest in the supernatural.

The chapters of this book follow a thematic structure, moving from politics to literary discourses, examining the different geographical and historical discourses and cultural frameworks with which Plath engaged. Chapter 1 contextualises the socio-political framework in which Plath encountered the concept of the witch-hunt, particularly focusing on the legacies of the Salem witch trials in American history, politics, and literature. Late 1940s and early 1950s America was characterised by McCarthyism, which revived the concept of the witch-hunt, describing the prosecution of 'witches associated metaphorically with communists and subversion of other kinds' (Gibson, *Rediscovering Renaissance Witchcraft* 99). Discussing the deployment of the witch-hunt in post-war America as an abuse of institutional power, this chapter discusses Plath's poems and prose on surveillance during the Cold War and reads *The Bell Jar* in conversation with Arthur Miller's drama *The Crucible* (1953) in their shared interest in nonconformist women during the different witch-hunts in America. I also assess Plath's extensive knowledge of the witch trials and the influence of Nathaniel Hawthorne's *The Scarlet Letter* and *The House of the Seven Gables* in her writings. Some of Plath's poems, such as 'Witch Burning', explicitly draw on the early modern witch-hunt and demonstrate her well-informed knowledge of the literature of witchcraft and the way in which the concept of witch-hunt informed political debates in mid-twentieth-century America.

Moving on from the historical witch-hunt, Chapter 2 centres on Plath's metaphorical employment of the concept for which I close read two *Ariel* poems and short stories from the late 1950s. Plath's poems reveal her distrust in male authority figures, from clerics to doctors, building a parallel between the power dynamics of religious and political persecutions of the medieval and early modern periods and the authoritarian politics of World War II and the Cold War. While Plath was aware of the explicit gender element of the witch-hunt, for her, the historical witch figure functions as an embodiment of the marginalised and prosecuted groups with whom she expressed sympathy. This chapter discusses Plath's engagement with martyrdom and religious prosecutions during the Cold War in her short stories, such as 'Johnny Panic and the Bible of Dreams' and poems like 'Lady Lazarus'. Looking at the early drafts, this chapter reveals the expressive language and metaphor of witch prosecutions in 'Lady Lazarus' and 'Fever 103°', which she later abandoned or deleted from her manuscripts. Plath's poetic language mimics the rhetoric of the Cold War, where references to the witch prosecutions were frequent: even Ethel Rosenberg, the victim of McCarthyism, compared herself to the martyr Joan of Arc who is often evoked in Plath's late poetry. Looking beyond the feminist interpretations of the witch, this chapter establishes Plath's Cold War poetics and politics as a metaphorical deployment of the witch prosecutions. Plath uses the gendered body as a site of the institutional and authoritarian violence of World War II and the Cold War, seeking inspiration from the power imbalance of the witch-hunt period and Joan of Arc's martyrdom.

Chapter 3 moves to the literary influences in Plath's writings, focusing on the gendered understanding of the witch and the magician, which often aligns with her portrayal of parental relationships. The chapter traces Plath's employment of maternal and paternal magic influenced by Shakespearean supernatural figures. *Macbeth*'s Weird Sisters appear in Plath's writings as sinister, hag-like figures whose inescapable presence influences the speaker's fate, originating their power from mythological female figures. In some of her writings, the trio of supernatural female figures materialise as spectral maternal figures and a sinister hag-head with paralysing powers. In 'The Disquieting Muses', she merges the fairy-tale witch into the Weird Sisters as a representation of maternal malice to express ambiguous feelings towards her mother. In contrast to *Macbeth*'s witches, the influence of *The Tempest* has been highlighted by previous criticisms of Plath's poetry, which I discuss in more detail later. I establish a parallel between Prospero's magical power and the father figure's beekeeping: some of Plath's bee poems and short stories, such as 'The Beekeeper's Daughter' and 'Among the Bumblebees' express her likening of her father's beekeeping to a magical power. In other poems, like 'Full Fathom Five', Plath draws on the larger-than-life presence of the father-magician whose power is desirable yet inaccessible to the speaker. The chapter demonstrates that for Plath, *The Tempest* functioned as a metaphor for her childhood seascape in which the Prosperoean father is exiled to the island where his power and knowledge are represented by magic. The supernatural figures from Shakespeare's plays express a gendered binary understanding of magic and power, which influenced Plath's writings on her ambiguous parental relationship.

Alongside Shakespeare's plays, Marlowe's *Doctor Faustus* functioned as an early modern literary influence on Plath's writings. Chapter 4 centres on the concepts of demonic possession and demonology portrayed in Marlowe's play and Goethe's *Faust* as retellings of the Faust legend. Building on Golden's interpretation of marginalia in *Annotating Modernism* (2021), I look at Plath's annotations of the plays in her books and read them along with her poems that reference the plays. The supernatural concepts from *Doctor Faustus* and *Faust* aided Plath with a vocabulary to articulate ambiguous feelings about romantic and parental relationships, such as the demon metaphor in 'On Looking into the Eyes of a Demon Lover'. This chapter likewise looks at the broader post-war discourse, from Freudian psychoanalysis to politics that borrowed the themes from the well-known legend about a black magician and Mephistopheles. I revise over-simplified narratives around Plath's use of diabolical language to show her knowledge of the subject that influenced her and demonstrate that American poets, such as Anne Sexton, Karl Shapiro, and John Berryman, whom I read in conversation with Plath, employed Faustian vocabulary in their poetry. The post-war deployment of the themes of diabolism and demonology reveals that Plath is not the only poet who linked diabolism with Nazism in 'Daddy', alluded to demonic possession in *The Bell Jar*, and associated dark imagery with violence in 'Man in Black', but that the Faust legend provided a metaphor for world politics through the themes of evil, redemption, and morality. This chapter discusses the re-interpretation of *Doctor Faustus* in post-war discourses, carefully unpicking the references to diabolism and demonology in the works of Plath and her contemporaries.

Continuing the theme of magic and/as power, Chapter 5 discusses Plath's poems that directly engage with the ways in which the language of magic operates. I introduce the concept of ritual magic, which is a formal or informal performance that employs ritualistic, incantatory language, such as chants, spells, and ritualistic acts. Ritual magic has a set intention to create a physical change by supernatural means, for example, by conjuring, excorcising spirits, or using magical objects. I draw on the medieval and early modern understanding of ritual magic and development in the contemporary trends in the performative reading of poetry to demonstrate that 'Daddy' and 'Burning the Letters' engage with the idea of poetic spellcasting. My analysis relies on the drafts of the poems, highlighting Plath's attribution of magical powers to poetic language, which she often erased from the final versions of her poems. Plath had substantial knowledge of the way in which the language of magic functions and her letters give accounts of her practice of informal and spontaneous ritual magic, often used as poetic inspirations. The chapter draws attention to Plath's poems that interrogate what constitutes ritual magic: by transforming everyday objects into magical aids, for example, the boot in 'Daddy', she engages with the blurred boundaries between mundane and magical rituals, exploring the powers of poetry as spellwork.

Continuing the examination of how supernatural vocabulary and narratives operate in poetry, Chapter 6 discusses supernatural transformations in Plath's poems that interrogate questions about women's bodily autonomy and magical power. This chapter introduces two concepts associated with supernatural transformations, metamorphosis and shapeshifting, which express different narratives of transformations. Plath explores women's powerlessness regarding their bodies, sexuality, and reproductive choices through the concept of metamorphosis associated with Ovid's *Metamorphoses*. In the poem 'Virgin in a Tree', referencing Daphne's myth, the female body transforms into a vegetal form, which is a violent and forceful process. One of Plath's last poems 'Edge' likewise narrates the violent metamorphosis of the female body. In contrast, shapeshifting is a voluntary transformation from human to animal form, which traditionally has been regarded as a power of magical women, such as witches. Shapeshifting grants women autonomy who find power and liberation in their animal (often flying) form, which Plath alludes to in, for example, 'Goatsucker', and is paralleled by female poets, such as Anne Sexton and Margaret Atwood. Plath also experiments with the fluid borders between the human and the nonhuman in 'Ariel', which shows an imaginative flying motion as transformation. My close reading of the drafts of 'Ariel' further pays attention to the supernatural aspects of the relationship between the rider and the horse. Plath's employment of the concepts of supernatural transformations questions normative ideas about gender, agency, and the boundaries between the human and the nonhuman. Her creative and personal writings reach back to mythology and folklore on supernatural transformations examining women's gendered existence and struggle for autonomy in the mid-twentieth century.

The last chapter circles back to Plath's engagement with political exploitation of the rhetoric of witchcraft and looks at the discourses of modern witchcraft in the 1950s–60s Britain. Chapter 7 introduces the post-war British political landscape and the way in which English nationalism and Cold War anxieties corresponded with the association of witchcraft with the dark other. I look at Plath's narratives about England in her short stories like 'Mothers' and 'Charlie Pollard and The Beekeepers', which demonstrate her awareness of the intertwined relationship between the Anglican Church, English nationalism, and British colonialism that contributed to the revival of racial rhetoric of witchcraft. My chapter also brings attention to Margaret Murray's witch-cult hypothesis that became a foundation for Wicca and discusses the perception of witchcraft in post-war British literature and politics. I argue that the dark, racialised, and female bees in Plath's bee sequence interrogate the binary between self and the other and challenge ideas about magical and racialised power. She draws on post-war politics on the racial rhetoric of witchcraft, literature on the witches' sabbath, and dark magic in *The Tempest* in comparing the bees to diabolical flying women. Plath's poems correspond to the view that the fear of the other and the fear of witchcraft originate from the same sources. The drafts of the bee poems reveal her explicit association of the bees with diabolical foreign creatures whose ability to fly makes them similar to witches. While this chapter also addresses concerns about Plath's engagement with the racist and colonial rhetoric of witchcraft, I emphasise her understanding of the witch-hunt as a metaphor for twentieth-century racial injustices and her empathy towards marginalised communities.

Plath's bee metaphor simultaneously challenges and reinforces the identification of the dark other with fearful magical power.

This book benefits from the attention paid to the rich resources from the archives, including drafts of Plath's poems in which the supernatural imagery has previously been overlooked. I look closely at Plath's drafts, annotations, and marginalia that inform us about her writing and editing process. In addition to the manuscripts, I consider Plath's annotations in books and additional memorabilia kept at SCSC and interview files from the Harriet Rosenstein research papers, Plath's high school paper from the Lilly Library to reexamine narratives on her engagement with and interpretation of the supernatural. What all chapters share is the reading of Plath's poetry, prose, and supplementary personal writings from an interdisciplinary approach, which centres supernatural themes, vocabulary, and narratives on gender, power, and magic. I offer a series of chapters focusing on a set of key concepts and themes that illuminate Plath's varied engagement with the supernatural to interrogate gender, power, and magic, offering pathways for new scholarship. This book is a celebration of everything magical in Plath's writings: it recentres discussion around Plath and the supernatural, pivoting it to her well-informed knowledge of the history and literature of witchcraft, the political and cultural framework in which she encountered these discourses, her poetic craft, and the curiosity and empathy that allowed her to create such rich work.

CHAPTER 1

Sylvia Plath and the American Witch-Hunts

The historical, political, and literary discourses Plath encountered during the early Cold War regarding the concept of the witch-hunt demonstrate her broad knowledge of witch prosecutions and the nuanced employment of the witch trials in her writings. Plath's writings about McCarthyism also give evidence of her knowledge of the New England witch trials, particularly of Salem, as understood within the post-war political and literary landscape. This chapter discusses Plath's encounters with American literature on the Salem witch-hunt and her reflections on the historical witch trials, poems, and short stories about post-war surveillance culture, and offers a comparative reading of Arthur Miller's *The Crucible* and Plath's *The Bell Jar* on nonconformist women and witches. Plath's historical and literary engagement with witch-hunts in America develops a foundation for the following chapters, particularly Chapter 2 on the metaphor of religious persecutions for her Cold War poetics and short stories. Her political, personal, and literary engagements with the early modern and post-war witch-hunts in American history express the parallels she makes between persecuted witches and political victims.

In a letter sent on 24 October 1952, before Eisenhower was elected to be the next president of the United States, Plath debated with her mother on voting choices. Here, she directly referenced the red scare as a witch-hunt:

> Really, I can't see why you don't vote for him [Adlai Stevenson II]. Do you think the change of administration, which of course is partially desirable if only to make the opposition party more responsible – is worth the power it will give to the red-witch hunts of McCarthy, the southern snobbery of Jenner, the reactionary foreign policy of Taft??? (*L1* 516).[1]

[1] William E. Jenner, state Senator of Indiana (1934–42) and Republican Senator (1944–45, 1947–59), supported McCarthyism and probably Robert Alphonso Taft, a Republican politician, who also sought the presidential nomination in 1952.

Plath's view recalls the newspaper articles, which argued that Eisenhower made an immoral pact to secure his win ('Eisenhower Is Assailed'). In the same year, Plath wrote several political reports for the Smith College Press Board, such as 'Marxism Seeks to Replace God, Lecturer Says' in March 1952. Even in April 1952, Plath saw Joseph McCarthy giving a lecture that took place at Smith College (*L1* 436), demonstrating her political interest in the election and the McCarthy witch-hunt. Her opposition to the Communist witch-hunt was a personal matter: during her years at Smith College, several professors were called in for hearings; in 1954, a letter was even sent to alumni asking them not to donate to the college 'whilst it employed Communists' (Ferretter 95). In 1953, Robert Gorham Davis, Plath's writing teacher, was investigated for allegedly committing 'Un-American Activities' (Clark, *Red Comet* 191). Margaret Shook, a student at Smith during the 1950s who also returned to teach there, disclosed in a lecture about *The Bell Jar* that Smith's college paper conducted a survey that revealed three-quarters of the undergraduates supported Eisenhower; among the faculty, however, it was 'of course, the opposite' ('Shook, Interview'). Though Plath was never interrogated as some of her teachers were, she had first-hand exposure to McCarthyism and articulated her disapproval of the political witch-hunt and Republican scaremongering. While Plath was well informed about the political discourses of the early 1950s, she also gained extensive knowledge of the witch-hunt in New England through her education in American history and literature.

1.1 Hawthorne and Salem Witch Trials

The Salem mayor Charles W. Upham's two-volume book *Salem Witchcraft* (1867, 1869) was one of the first interpretive accounts that criticised the witch trials for the abuse of institutional power embodied by the Puritan ministers, judges, magistrates, and legislatures. Throughout the nineteenth century, changing perspectives also affected the new spiritualist movements, including mesmerism and hypnotism, which provoked hostility and scepticism from Puritans, fearing another 'delusion' or religious fanaticism similar to the Salem witch trials (Adams 68–69). Matilda Joslyn Gage was the first to take a feminist stand on the witch-hunt in *Woman, Church and State* (1893), in which she argued that if we read 'witches' as 'women', we gain a better understanding of the cruelties of the Church and its institutional abuse of power (90). Gage claimed 'that women accused of witchcraft had in fact been early scientists, mesmerists and workers with plant extracts' (Gibson, 'Retelling Salem Stories' 88). In contrast, George Miller Beard's

1882 study argued that the fits of many of the victims of witchcraft were a form of nervous and mental 'exhaustion' (Gibson, *Witchcraft Myths* 103–4). By the mid-twentieth century, the Salem witch trials became an often-used metaphor for the abuse of power and public disorder reimagined in literature and exploited in political debates.

Plath encountered the various interpretations of the early modern witch-hunt through her education in American history and literature. In Nathaniel Hawthorne's *The House of the Seven Gables* (1851), Matthew Maule, who is executed for witchcraft, is suggested to have practised mesmerism or animal magnetism on Alice Pyncheon, who 'awoke from her strange trance. She awoke, without the slightest recollection of her visionary experience' (155). Plath underlined the definition of the devil in her *WCD* in which one of the definitions highlights the links to mesmerism: 'a belief in sin, sickness, and death; animal magnetism or hypnotism' ('devil'). Plath worked on a project on Hawthorne's *The House of the Seven Gables* in her senior high school year (1947/48). Her 41-page-long high school paper, kept in the Lilly Library at Indiana University, starts with a biography of the novelist, showcasing her knowledge of Hawthorne's family connection to the Salem witch trials. The report also includes a detailed analysis of the short story 'Rappaccini's Daughter' (1844) – a story she also taught – and *The House of the Seven Gables.* Plath carefully researched the history of American witch-hunts, particularly the Salem trials; she quoted from the *Encyclopaedia Britannica* on witchcraft laws: 'The fear of witchcraft, again impels men at all stages of culture to purify their spiritual surroundings by wiping out the witch' ('Lawes'). The dictionary understands the witch-hunt as a 'cleansing', meaning a spiritual purification, which echoes the imagery of her late poems such as 'Fever 103°'. Plath's essay gives evidence of her knowledge of the witch trials, including that there were nineteen people hanged as witches. She mentions Tituba, the slave who was the first to be accused by name and shows familiarity with the writings of Puritan clergyman Cotton Mather and his belief in witchcraft. The most interesting part of the paper is when Plath gives her personal opinion: at the end of her essay, she likens the prosecution of witches to 'the race riots' in post-war American society ('Essay: Seven Gables' 18). She equated the Salem witch trials to the persecution of racial minorities under Jim Crow, showing her understanding of the ways in which the witch-hunt became a metaphor for twentieth-century political debates. In the essay, Plath also notes the disenchantment of modern society and compares the beliefs about witchcraft to the juvenile magic of fairy tales.

Plath read several of Hawthorne's short stories and heavily underlined and annotated them in her copy kept at the Smith. Among them, 'Young Goodman Brown' (1935) narrates Goodman Brown's attendance at the dream-like witches' sabbath, which becomes 'the most agonizing spiritual crisis imaginable for a Puritan' (Eberwein 23; 26). When our protagonist meets with a fellow traveller in the forest, who later turns out to be the Devil, he ensures Brown that he knows his family well as well as all the Puritans, alluding to Hawthorne's criticism of New England Puritanism. In Chapter 7, I further demonstrate the short story's influence on Plath's poetic imagination of witches, such as 'The Bee Meeting', in which critics named 'Young Goodman Brown' an influence. When Plath returned to Smith College as a teacher in the 1957/58 academic year, she was teaching Hawthorne's short stories (*L2* 182n1). Golden argues that Plath's copy of *Hawthorne's Short Stories* shows the way in which she used the student practice of annotating in her teaching ('Sylvia Plath's Library' 111). In February 1958, Plath noted that she knew *The Scarlet Letter* 'by heart', which demonstrates that she re-read the novel several times for her teaching (*J* 338). *The Scarlet Letter* is centred on Puritan ideas about sin, and gender particularly plays a role in the fictional public's perception of Hester's adultery. Her scarlet letter, which is subject to the Puritan gaze throughout the novel, becomes the main symbol of the psychological and moral crisis in the Puritan community. Plath's poems, such as 'Witch Burning' and 'Lady Lazarus', often seek inspiration from the novel in staging the female body to highlight power dynamics between the spectators and the scrutinised woman. Plath made an early connection to the novel's portrayal of Puritanism and her experience in post-war America: in 1954, after returning to Smith College, Plath wrote to Jane Anderson that she was feeling 'sure that my scar was glowing symbolically, obvious to all (the way Hester's scarlet letter burned and shone with physical heat to proclaim her default to all)' (*L1* 694–95). While here Plath refers to her suicide attempt as a scarlet letter, her wording anticipates the themes of post-war surveillance, the private versus public debates, and voyeurism in her poems inspired by the persecuted witches. Plath's rich, repeated encounters with Hawthorne's writings show that her knowledge of the early modern witch-hunt was rooted in the portrayal of the Salem witch trials in American literature. She read Hawthorne at a time when McCarthyism and the red scare revived the concept of the witch-hunt, which became a symbol of the institutional power abuse of the post-war American political landscape.

Plath also grew up near Boston and later lived in the city, which is only a thirty-minute train ride from Salem where the most renowned witch trials of the country took place, suggesting the importance of geographical proximity to the village haunted by the violent history of executions. In 1957, Plath returned to the United States after studying in Cambridge, England. During her relocation to her homeland in the late 1950s, her engagement with witches frequently shows the influence of Ted Hughes, who also grew up close to a significant place during the English witch trials, which I discuss further later. In April 1958, Plath mentioned in her journal a book she encountered on the witch trials, linking it to a fight with Hughes: '[H]e accusing me of throwing away his awful old cufflinks "as I had done away with his coat", and, for that matter, his book on Witches, since I never could stand the torture parts' (*J* 372). The book in question is not found or identified in the Hughes archives; however, Plath likely refers to a historical overview of the witch-hunt period, as she alludes to the torture of witches. Her phrasing suggests an emotional resonance to the witch-hunt, particularly the violence and torture of the witch prosecutions she links to the authoritarian politics of the twentieth century in her late poems, as she did in her high school essay on Hawthorne's novel. Plath's poetic engagement with witches is likewise demonstrated by an anecdote when the couple were residents at the Yaddo in New York, at a writers' retreat in 1959: Hughes wrote down topics on a piece of paper for Plath as poetic inspirations, which included the theme for Plath's 'Witch Burning' (Clark, *Red Comet* 577). While Plath knew of the Salem witch trials and showed interest in the subject, Hughes instigated the subject as a poetic inspiration for Plath, which corresponds to his lending a book to her about witches.

Just as much as the Salem witch trials influenced and guided Plath's poetic exploration of witches and the New England witch-hunt, Hughes's poetry and views on witches were rooted in the history of the most renowned witch trial in England, known as the trial of the Pendle witches, which took place in North West England close to his birthplace at Mytholmroyd. The Pendle trials occurred in 1612, during which ten people, mostly family members, were executed, with the majority of accusations relying on a child's statement, paralleling the young accusers of the Salem witch trials. The alleged gathering at Malkin Tower was a central accusation in the Pendle trials, which has been regarded as a witches' sabbath (Millar 147–48). The Pendle witch trials also fit into the conspiracy narrative of secret meetings of witches (Sharpe 72). The fear of conspiratorial secret societies resurfaced in the twentieth century, demonstrating the influence of witchcraft beliefs in modern politics. Hughes's poetry often portrays the mystic countryside, and he draws on his experiences of being brought up in a small Yorkshire village near the most significant place of the English witch-hunt. Plath and Hughes were locals of important places in the history of witch-hunts in their respective countries, influencing their engagement with narratives of witchcraft.

In 1958, Plath wrote the short poem 'The Times Are Tidy', which is one of the most significant accounts of her poetic representation of the witch-hunt period. The speaker is positioned as a storyteller who evokes the witch prosecutions as the 'Burning Times'. The first stanza of Plath's poem starts with the portrayal of contemporary society as one in which heroes are not needed anymore. While the first two stanzas describe the dullness of contemporary life, the last stanza centres on the hazardous past, alluding to the witch-hunt period: 'The last crone got burnt up / More than eight decades back / With the love-hot herb, the talking cat' (*CP* 107). Plath contrasts the crone with the male hero who appears in the first stanza, alluding to the gender roles and expectations of post-war American culture. The male, like the soldiers, is the saviour of the country, whereas the crone, the woman, is the dangerous figure of the past. Plath's portrayal of gendered places and spaces is embedded in the sexist rhetoric frequently employed in the early 1950s. Jo Gill suggests that the association between 'the city, rationality, masculinity and the public world of work and the suburbs, irrationality, femininity and a privatised domestic sphere' pervaded the post-war era; further, it was adapted by Betty Friedan's *The Feminine Mystique* ('"Quite the Opposite of a Feminist"' 431). Plath reflects on the misogynistic ideas of post-war America by evoking the early modern witch-hunt, during which the feminised figure of the witch embodied irrationality and danger. In the poem, the witch is burnt – an expressive image she returns to in 'Witch Burning' a year later – even though, in New England, witches were hanged. Only in countries such as Germany were the prosecuted witches burnt in public before being executed (Roper, *Witch Craze* 64–65). In 'The Times Are Tidy', Plath references an actual witch trial: she keeps the historical accuracy of the date ('More than eight decades back'), which she reimagines as a metaphor for the misogynistic post-war American culture.

The witch trial in 1878, which happened exactly eight decades before Plath wrote the poem referencing the trial, grasped the public's attention and was famously named 'the second Salem witch trial': it took place at the Supreme Judicial Court at Salem (Davies 96). Yet, the incident happened in Ipswich, a town close to Salem, in which several of the victims of the 1692 Salem witch trials lived (Larner 138). The 'charge reads remarkably like the indictments for witchcraft two centuries earlier, and the trial's location' further linked this dispute to Salem (Davies 96). In the trial, Daniel H. Spofford, a Christian Scientist, was accused of committing harm with malignant animal magnetism on Lucretia Brown, a disabled woman whom he treated as a patient for her spinal injuries. Animal magnetism was believed to give 'its possessor the ability to hypnotize victims and compel them toward their doom', linking witchcraft to nineteenth-century interest in spiritualism (Gibson, *Witchcraft Myths* 107; 111). The trial of 1878 frames the historical reference in Plath's poem; it also demonstrates the shifts in the concept of witchcraft in America and how such changes shaped the understanding of the Salem witch trials.

'The Times Are Tidy' alludes to the beliefs about witches and their craft, such as the herbal knowledge and healing powers attributed to witches in the popular imagination. Likewise, her reference to the cat shows her knowledge of the animal as the most well-known familiar spirit of a witch (Thomas 530). Plath saw the comedy play *Bell, Book, and Candle* in 1953, writing to her mother that it was 'a heavenly humorous tale of modern witchery' (*L1* 553). The film adaptation was released in 1958 in which the modern witch Gillian has a cat as her familiar (Gibson, 'Retelling Salem Stories' 92–93). The poem also references the imagery of fairy tales, which is supported by the light verse and playful rhyme scheme. The allusions to popular beliefs about witchcraft demonstrate Plath's knowledge of folk and literary representations of the witch figure, which point to a highly gendered understanding of the witch, associating the crone with the 'wise woman'. The last line of the poem refers to the beliefs about witches' power to transform milk or even steal it, as during the early modern period, it was commonly believed that witches attacked farmers (Hutton, *The Witch* 250). Plath's allusion to superstitions around witches' powers further references their hazardous character. Lyndal Roper argues that witch accusations often 'rested on a whole economy of bodily fluids', evoking beliefs and fears about the mother's breast milk and her inability to feed her child (*The Witch* 5). 'The Times Are Tidy' portrays the witch-hunt as a poetic inspiration for Plath and her deployment of the concept as a metaphor situated in post-war American culture. Though she takes liberties with depicting the nineteenth-century trial, the poem opposes the crone – who suffered from accusations throughout history – with the contemporary 'unlucky' male hero, demonstrating Plath's early engagement with the gendered power dynamics of the witch-hunt. The tone remains light and nursery rhyme–like, which is a significant distinction from Plath's later poems.

Plath wrote her next 'witch-hunt' poem a year later. In 'Witch Burning', she uses the figure of the executed burning witch as an alter ego of the tortured poetic self. As in many of *The Colossus* poems she wrote at that time, the poetic voice remains distant. 'Witch Burning' is the sixth poem of the 'Poem for a Birthday' sequence and is centred on the images of burning. Some of the themes of the sequence are central to 'Witch Burning', such as the process of rebirth and recovery, which reflect Plath's horrifying experience of undergoing electroshock therapy (Rose 57). Plath brings the electric burning into parallel with the fiery burning of a witch through the metaphor of torture. In the poem, the witch's burning also alludes to the understanding of witch-hunt as purification or cleansing, similar to the *Britannica* definition Plath used in her high school paper. Like 'The Times Are Tidy', in 'Witch Burning' she deploys an image from the popular imagination: the burning woman. Plath's reference does not accurately portray the witch prosecutions in America: she alludes to the European witch-hunts in places such as Germany and Scotland, where, as clarified earlier, they burnt witches. Her blending of the imagery of the witch-hunt is notable regarding her American and German national affiliations. 'Witch Burning' likewise draws on Hughes's 1957 poem, 'The Martyrdom of Bishop Farrar', which tells the story of the ancestor of Hughes who was burnt in a marketplace. Plath wrote about Hughes's interest in writing this poem in her fragment 'Afternoon in Horncastle Crags' written in 1956: '[H]e sat tousled in his mother's parlour in his old RAF [Royal Air Force] sweater, writing poems about water drops and martyred bishops' (*Prose* 746). Hughes's poetic imageries of martyrdom, public execution, and fire that 'come from Hell even, / [. . .] As he fed his body to the flame alive' are mimicked in Plath's poem (*THCP* 48–49). Jonathan Bates suggests that 'The Martyrdom of Bishop Farrar' is reminiscent of 'the tradition of Protestant brimstone sermon' (30). There is a parallel between Hughes's and Plath's poetic retellings of witch-hunt histories: they both build on their own cultural and national histories of religious and witch persecutions.

The narrative of 'Witch Burning' moves from the marketplace to the speaker's psychic landscape, putting the female body on display. The market alludes to the public space where witches were burnt and hanged. It is also the centre of Hester's public shaming in Plath's beloved *The Scarlet Letter*. Sarah Burton notes that the poem expresses 'female bodily fragmentation' and wants to 'inscribe the witch's fate of pain, death and suffering, rather than reveal any of her historical subversion' (133–34). 'Witch Burning' likewise compares to Anne Sexton's 'Her Kind', written around the same time, in which the speaker takes up the persona of a witch who is isolated and alienated from her environment (Gill, *Anne Sexton* 25).

I discuss further Sexton's and Plath's shared imagery in their poems in Chapter 6 on the supernatural transformations and beliefs about shapeshifting of witches. In Plath's poem, the speaker distances herself from her body by calling it a 'wax image' and a 'doll's body' (*CP* 135). The expressions allude to the popular witchcraft belief that witches made wax images or dolls as a form of sympathetic magic and pierced needles into them to harm others (Gibson, *Rediscovering Renaissance Witchcraft* 9). Plath's imagery shows that she was familiar with the wax doll as a tool of malicious magic. The speaker becomes both the perpetrator (witch) and the object used for magical harm (wax figure), which suggests her ambiguous identity. The metaphor is particularly noteworthy since wax melts under the fire and changes shape, which anticipates the speaker's transformation at the poem's end.

In 'Witch Burning', black is a dominant yet ambiguous colour, which evokes danger and the unknown. In the first and second stanzas, the speaker perceives confinement both as physical ('cellar', 'cage') and mental imprisonment ('sickness'). In the poem, the redness of fire symbolises rebirth and freedom, but it is also a danger – paradoxically, the cause of death. Plath's imagery of fiery burning, particularly her deployment of the female body as the site of gendered struggles, features in her mature poems. From the third stanza, the narrative shifts from the external to the internal world of the speaker. Plath highlights the speaker's bodily experience of torture. She is subject not only to being burnt but also to being confined, even shrinking. The stanza ends with growth and self-development, which is described as a painful process: 'It hurts at first. The red tongues will teach the truth' (*CP* 135). The short sentences highlight the stages of growth. The line, 'They are turning the burners up, ring after ring' (*CP* 135), evokes a cooker's electric rings, suggesting an association between the domestic space and the burning imagery. The speaker identifies with starchy rice grains, indicating that while the fiery burning is painful, it is necessary for growth. By contextualising the witch-burning within the feminine-coded kitchen, the poem engages with the conflicted place of the kitchen in the domestic ideology of post-war America. 'Witch Burning' was written a few months after the infamous Kitchen Debate between Nixon and Khrushchev.[2] In the poem, fire is both a restrictive and a

[2] In May 1956, while studying at Cambridge, Plath met Nikita Khrushchev and Nikolai Bulganin at a diplomatic event at the Soviet Embassy where she went to write an article about it. Her report 'B. and K. at Claridge' appeared in the *Smith Alumnae Quarterly* in May 1956 (*Prose* 568–73).

torture device and a means to be born again. The fiery aids the speaker to reach the authenticity of the self; Vincent Balitas calls this the '*process of becoming* a witch' (28). However, the speaker does not embrace it as her power, as we see in the later poetic persona of 'Lady Lazarus'. 'Witch Burning' demonstrates that Plath employs similar vocabulary on the burning of a female poetic persona throughout her work: the expression 'red tongues' from 'Witch Burning' is evocative of the 'tongues of hell' from 'Fever 103°' (*CP* 135; 231). The last lines allude to a flight similar to the metaphorical ascending of the poetic persona in 'Fever 103°'. However, at the end of the poem, we do not know whether she is reborn from the painful burning or escapes by flying away.

'Witch Burning' demonstrates that burning often signifies both rebirth and torture, and this ambiguity is a significant characteristic of Plath's late poetry. The poem expresses Plath's empathy towards the victims of torture, as identified earlier in a journal entry on Hughes's book on witches, by associating her experience of electroconvulsive therapy with the early modern witch-hunt. 'The Times Are Tidy' and 'Witch Burning' exhibit Plath's poetic engagement with the burning witch figure and the politics of the witch prosecutions. In the poems, Plath's voice remains descriptive; she narrates mainly an external, not an internal, struggle of the speakers, the latter of which defines her mature poetry. She transforms, exaggerates, and reimagines the historical witch-hunt period. The poems embrace the witch-hunt as a historical event that corresponds to aspects of Plath's political, personal, and gendered experiences. The historical and political significance of the Puritan witch-hunt in New England was developed further by its metaphorical and literary revival during McCarthyism, which influenced Plath's association between the witch figure and persecuted groups.

1.2 Salem and McCarthy Witch-Hunts

Writers and poets of the post-war era often employed the history and literature of the American witch trials to reflect on the politics of fear and surveillance. In Reed Whittemore's poem 'Hester Prynne' (1945), inspired by Hawthorne's *The Scarlet Letter*, the window appears as a metaphor for blurred boundaries between the private and the public, which gives opportunities for voyeurism (Gill, *The Poetics* 134). In her review of *Contemporary American Poetry* in 1962, Plath mentions Whittemore as one of the significant contemporary poets, demonstrating her familiarity with his work (*Prose* 698). In his poem, Whittemore parallels seventeenth-century Salem to the post-war American suburban landscape:

> [. . .] In Salem now
> The just are just the weekday men
> Too old and wise to measure out a row.
> But at that time – yes, the suburbs came;
> And all the earth (and Hawthorne saw one more). (449)

In the poem, the suburbs symbolise the loss of privacy in which 'the weekday men' stand for the judgemental Puritan community. By directly naming Salem and Hawthorne, Whittemore compares the post-war surveillance culture and the public harassment of citizens, particularly women accused of witchcraft. The Salem village, haunted by the memory of the trials, becomes a geographical and metaphorical site of the affluent suburban landscape with its lack of privacy and judgmental community. Voyeurism also defines Robert Lowell's poem 'Hawthorne' (1964), written for the centenary anniversary of the novelist's death year. Lowell's poem guides the speaker's gaze through the village of Salem to Hawthorne's birthplace: 'Follow its lazy main street lounging / [. . .] You'll walk to no purpose / in Hawthorne's Salem'; 'Hawthorne's picture, / however, has a blond mustache' (38–39).[3] By employing the possessive pronoun, Lowell suggests a personal closeness to the place and the objects that bear witness to time. While the poem does not directly allude to the Salem witch trials, the references to the village and Hawthorne's 'disturbed eyes' (39) imply the spectral presence of the witch trials during McCarthyism.

Plath's poems written in 1962, such as 'Eavesdropper', 'The Detective', and 'The Other' are often preoccupied with the question of privacy and surveillance in the Cold War: she 'registers the pervasiveness of surveillance in ordinary life and links it to a transformation of confession' (Nelson, *Pursuing Privacy* 80–81). In particular, 'Eavesdropper' presents images similar to Whittemore's suburbs in which neighbours (instead of the political power holders) become each other's judges:

> Do not think I don't notice your curtain—
> Midnight, four o'clock,
> Lit (you are reading),

[3] Salem has a Hawthorne museum, however, the house of his birthplace was moved in 1958, the year Plath and Hughes lived in Boston, to the estate where the building that inspired *The House of the Seven Gables* is found (Nathaniel Hawthorne's birthplace).

> Tarting with the drafts that pass,
> Little whore tongue. (*CP* 260)

The speaker calls the watcher 'Sister-bitch! Sweet neighbor!' (*CP* 261), presenting the ambiguous perception of the neighbour in public and private spaces. The poem's engagement with the female spectatorship compares to *The Scarlet Letter*, in which Hester's onlookers are mainly women who express the desire to be the judge of her crime. 'Eavesdropper' not only reflects Plath's understanding of the post-war American domestic ideology, but it also seeks inspiration from Hawthorne's novel and the early modern witch-hunt in which the politics of fear was created by heightened tensions and surveillance among community members.

In the poem, Plath recycled materials from her short story 'Shadow Girl' (1961) about a girl, Jenny, whose father works in book publishing. She struggles to find autonomy and voice among the men in positions of power and resorts to eavesdropping:

> All at once, she saw the absurdity of her position. There she was, in the hall of the one man in the world she loved and trusted, listening in to his phone conversation like some brazen lady spy. Not listening. *Eaves*dropping. (*Prose* 458–59)

Here, Plath calls her protagonist not only an eavesdropper but a 'lady spy', arguing for the gendered dynamic of surveillance in interpersonal relationships – as opposed to the patriarchal institutional surveillance – similar to her poem 'Eavesdropper'. Plath's writings show her clear understanding and poetic distinctions between the early modern witch prosecutions and the McCarthy witch-hunt. Her poems and personal writings demonstrate interest and awareness of metaphorical and political relations between the two witch-hunts: the early modern one linked to Salem, martyrdom, burning, and Hawthorne's name and the post-war red scare associated with McCarthy's name, surveillance, and interpersonal conflicts. The links between the metaphorical and historical witch-hunt were further reinforced by fictionalised accounts of the Salem witch trials published during the 1940s–50s, most notably by Arthur Miller in *The Crucible*. Plath's *The Bell Jar*, which narrates her experience of the oppressive culture of McCarthyism, shares similarities to Miller's play: they both portray nonconformist women and institutional punishment contextualised in the witch-hunt and sexual containment of the early Cold War.

The Crucible debuted on Broadway on 22 January 1953, during the peak of the trial of Ethel and Julius Rosenberg, who were electrocuted on

19 June 1953 for allegedly giving out information on American nuclear weapon design to Russia. Miller's play brought the witch-hunt into parallel with the anti-communism of McCarthyism, though Miller himself acknowledged that 'there never were any witches but there certainly are Communists' ('Why I Wrote The Crucible'). In the same interview, he also noted the influence of Charles W. Upham's writings on his portrayal of the role of institutional authorities in the prosecution of witches. In May 1953, a month before the Rosenbergs were executed, Plath saw *The Crucible* on Broadway while travelling with her friends. She reported to her mother that it was '[a] very good play about the witch hunt in Salem' (*L1* 610). In her journals, Plath shows awareness of the parallels between the Salem witch trials and the Communist witch-hunt. Her emotionally charged journal entry written on the day Julius and Ethel Rosenberg were electrocuted, likens their prosecution to the public executions:

> The execution will take place tonight; it is too bad that it could not be televised [. . .] so much more realistic and beneficial than the run-of-the mill crime program. Two real people being executed. No matter. The largest emotional reaction over the United States will be a rather large, democratic, infinitely bored and casual and complacent yawn. (*J* 541)

The descriptions prefigure her interest in public voyeurism, spectacle, and tortured bodies in her later writings. Clark suggests that for Plath, the Rosenbergs' death sentence was about making an example of them 'like the women in the Salem witch trials' (*Red Comet* 253). Though Clark does not represent the fullness of the Salem trials – not only women were executed – she notes a significant parallel between the Salem and McCarthy witch-hunts. Ann Burnside, who also partook in the *Mademoiselle* Guest Editorship in June 1953, claimed that while 'Sylvia was agonizing over the execution of the Rosenbergs and McCarthyism, others were delighting to dream over trousseau lingerie at Vanity Fair's showroom' (Winder 148). Burnside's phrasing frames the electrocution of the Rosenbergs in the gender politics of the Cold War, in which women's bodies functioned as a site of the public versus private debate (Nelson, *Pursuing Privacy* 116). *The Bell Jar* famously starts with the public prosecution of the Rosenbergs, which Esther associates with her private agony: 'It was a queer, sultry summer, the summer they electrocuted the Rosenbergs, and I didn't know what I was doing in New York' (*TBJ* 1). Deborah Nelson argues that in the novel, Plath links Esther with Ethel Rosenberg; 'she casts Esther's rebellion against 1950s codes of femininity in Cold War terms' ('Plath, History, and Politics' 24–25). Plath's preoccupation with the Rosenbergs' trial alongside her encounter with *The Crucible* prompted her to engage with the witch-hunt metaphor, particularly with the witch as a gendered figure who stands for the marginalised and persecuted groups. *The Crucible* further prompted Plath to relate the witch prosecutions to McCarthyism.

Miller's play was not the only fictionalised account of the Salem witch trials during the McCarthy era: William Carlos Williams's play *Tituba's Children* (1948), Ann Petry's children's book *Tituba of Salem Village* (1956), Marion L. Starkey's historical fiction *The Devil in Massachusetts: A Modern Inquiry into the Salem Witch Trials* (1949), and Shirley Jackson's *The Witchcraft of Salem Village* (1956) stressed the slave Tituba's role, who was the first to be accused at the trials. Indeed, Tituba 'appears in the overwhelming number of narrations as the central figure in the genesis of the witch trials' (Rosenthal 10). By centring the witch accusations on a racially othered woman, the writers reinterpret the Salem witch trials within mid-twentieth-century American society, which saw significant protests against racial segregation, such as the Montgomery Bus Boycott.[4] Further, several fictionalised accounts changed Tituba's representation from Native American to half to fully black, which expressed an 'involuntary lapse into racism' (Gibson, *Witchcraft Myths* 131). The shifts in her representation mean that in American witchcraft history, the witch is not only gendered but a racially marked figure, which runs in parallel with the history of racism in the United States. In Europe, popular beliefs about the crimes of witches originate from antisemitism, such as ritual murder, blood sacrifice, the killing of infants, and cannibalism (Owens 75–76). In Chapter 7, I return to the racial rhetoric of witchcraft in post-war Britain to discuss Plath's imagery of the dark bees and the politics of exclusion in her writing about the English community in Devon. As my earlier analysis showed, Plath's high school essay on *The House of the Seven Gables* also reveals her contextual reading of the witch-hunt, likening the persecution of witches to the twentieth-century oppression of racial minorities.

While Tituba's example demonstrates that the fear of witchcraft and the fear of the other originate from the same racial stereotypes, the Salem witch trials also put young women at the centre of witch accusations (Norton 305). By focusing on the girls' accusations, hysteric attacks, fits, and delusions, the Salem trials show the preoccupation of the strict Protestant community with the behaviours of women. Miller's play also

[4] Witchcraft beliefs in early modern New England were also embedded in racial stereotypes (Purkiss 253).

'ascribed this misogynistic sexualization of the story' by making Abigail Williams the promiscuous antagonist (Gibson, *Witchcraft Myths* 64). *The Crucible* is critical of Cold War politics and openly condemns McCarthyism, yet it likewise reinforces sexist post-war views on women's sexuality and continues to associate promiscuity with witchcraft: 'Sex, sin, and the Devil was early linked, and so they continued to be in Salem, and are today' (*Crucible* 250). In the early modern witch-hunt, several beliefs about witches were associated with sex and sexuality, for example, the witches' sabbath was considered a sexual rite, and, in the case of female witches, the pact with the Devil was regarded as a result of their sexual desires (Levack, *The Witch-Hunt* 145–46). In Puritan New England, witchcraft meant 'a conception of femininity tied to the Puritan image of the Devil's constant, present temptations of body' (Reed 210–11). Therefore, witchcraft was often understood as a sexual crime of women, which Miller's drama reinforces by his portrayal of the adolescent accusers as sexually promiscuous girls who 'emerge as the play's real witches' (Gibson, 'Retelling Salem Stories' 93). In the 1692 Salem trials, Abigail was only eleven or twelve years old; in Miller's play, she is aged up to seventeen to become 'a vicious wench who not only exploits her chance to supplant Elizabeth Proctor [. . .] but also sets the entire cycle of accusations in motion for selfish reasons' (Levin 540). Miranda Corcoran also argues that in 'post-war literature, the metaphor of teen girl as witch enabled writers to bring the unfamiliar (the adolescent girl) into the realm of the familiar by couching her in the recognisable language and iconography of witchcraft' (55–56). More than four decades after writing the play, Miller noted that his relationship with Marilyn Monroe, whom he married in 1956, influenced his portrayal of Abigail: 'I had not approached the witchcraft out of nowhere, or from purely social and political considerations. My own marriage of twelve years was teetering and I knew more than I wished to know about where the blame lay' ('Why I Wrote The Crucible'). Thus, anxieties about young womanhood and female sexuality took the centrepiece of post-war containment culture, for which the witch figure served as an easy shorthand and embodied nonconformist women.

In the play, both Elizabeth and John Proctor use sexist language to describe Abigail's promiscuous behaviour who, upon being rejected by John, accuses the couple of committing witchcraft:

ELIZABETH : John – grant me this. You have a faulty understanding of young girls. There is a promise made in any bed –

[. . .]

PROCTOR : How do you call Heaven! Whore! Whore! (*Crucible* 269; 304)

While Abigail 'bewitches' John with her alleged sexual power, the group of girls also persuade and manipulates the judges, suggesting that female sexuality is dangerous. *The Crucible* portrays the hysteria, fits, and delusions of teenage girls as a malicious act, yet they do not get punished for their 'witchcraft'. Abigail and her friends are questioned about their dancing in the forest, which is 'highly sexualized and resembles the witches' sabbat' (Tunc 268). Miller was highly influenced by Starkey's *The Devil in Massachusetts*, originating the Salem witch accusations in the fears and fantasies about adolescent female sexuality (M. Corcoran 66–67). In the play, the girls blame Tituba for making them 'drink blood' and speaking to the Devil 'in Barbados', which perpetuates racist stereotypes about witches in New England (*Crucible* 255–56). Miller's play draws on the association of witchcraft with the subversions of gender and race in the historical and fictionalised account of the Salem witch trials. Plath's encounter with the play mirrored some of her experiences with Puritan morals and sexual double standards in the post-war era and thoughts on racism and witch-hunt. Telling her mother about seeing Miller's play, Plath noted that she stayed up until 5 am with her friends 'talking long about Communism, racial prejudice, and religion' (*L1* 610). Plath's interest in the gendered and racial abuses in American history is undeniable. The return to Puritan morals, particularly on female sexuality during the McCarthy era, reflects the similarities between post-war politics and seventeenth-century witch persecutions.

In the year *The Crucible* debuted and the events of *The Bell Jar* took place, the Kinsey Report on *Sexual Behavior in the Human Female* (1953) was published. The report increased the moral panic on sexuality, particularly on the sexual behaviours of white middle-class young women whom the study exclusively focused on (Reumann 115). During the *Mademoiselle* internship, Plath and the other guest editors had to write a report on the Kinsey study. The article, however, did not appear in print due to the magazine's fear that it would reduce advertising revenues (Bren 240–41). Plath wrote in February 1954 to her boyfriend at the time, Gordon Lameyer, that she 'heard a fine Unitarian "sermon" on marriage and the Kinsey report' (*L1* 688), suggesting that *Sexual Behavior in the Human Female* was a subject of discussion in religious groups and communities. In *The Bell Jar*, Plath reminisces of her experiences of the moral panic on female sexuality in the 1950s: in chapter 7, Esther Greenwood reads an article her mother gave her titled 'In Defense of Chastity', encouraging young women not to have sex. Catherine Rankovic notes that the actual article in question was published in *Reader's Digest* in 1937 titled 'The Case for Chastity' ('The Case'). In the novel, Esther mocks the article and feels angry over the gendered and sexual double standards:

> Of course they [men] would try to persuade a girl to have sex and say they would marry her later, but as soon as she gave in, they would lose all respect for her and start saying that if she did that with them she would do that with other men and they would end up by making her life miserable. (*TBJ* 77)

The Bell Jar's portrayal of young women's sexual behaviours – or the expected lack of it – echoes *The Crucible*'s vilification of female promiscuity. While Esther Greenwood struggles with the sexist post-war culture and her lack of sexual freedom, Abigail, however badly, articulates her sexual desires. The two young women can be read as the different sides of the same coin in their experience with oppressive Puritan morals: whether it is a seventeenth-century Salem or 1950s New York, female sexuality is regarded as dangerous, and women who express sexual desires are vilified. Beatrice Hitchman notes that Joan's lesbianism in Plath's novel reflects the Cold War paranoia, linking homosexual desire with Communism (171). While Esther expresses lesbophobia in the novel, *The Bell Jar* portrays the social control of female sexuality and erotic desires and the women who express them are punished.

In the novel, Esther's depression is a symptom of the oppressive atmosphere of the Cold War: when she undergoes electroshock therapy, which she perceives as torture, it is foreshadowed by the electrocution of the Rosenbergs:

> It had nothing to do with me, but I couldn't help wondering what it would be like, being burned alive all along your nerves. I thought it must be the worst thing in the world.
>
> [. . .]
>
> Then something bent down and took hold of me and shook me like the end of the world. Whee-ee-ee-ee-ee, it shrilled, through an air crackling with blue light, and with each flash a great jolt drubbed me till I thought my bones would break and the sap fly out of me like a split plant. I wondered what terrible thing it was that I had done. (*TBJ* 1;138)

Plath uses the metaphor of torture and capital punishment to link Esther's psychological trauma with the public and political execution of the Rosenbergs. During the post-war era, Ethel Rosenberg represented not only a political but a gender nonconformity for many, she was a traitor but also a woman and a Jew, while her husband was also a second-generation

Russian (Knox 32). President Eisenhower saw Ethel Rosenberg as 'stronger' and 'worse', the supposed leader of the alleged spying (Ashe 218). In *The Bell Jar*, Plath creates a double between her protagonist and Ethel Rosenberg whose full maiden name was Ethel Esther Greenglass similar to Esther Greenwood (Nelson, 'Plath, History, and Politics' 25). Plath associates in the novel the torturous treatment of the male-dominated medical profession with the abuse of power by political institutions, which is evocative of the Salem witch trials. The metaphor of torture suggests that Esther Greenwood and Ethel Rosenberg are punished for their subversion of sexual and gender roles as the witches of the early modern period were. The comparative reading of *The Crucible* and *The Bell Jar* shows their shared interest in the oppression and vilification of women's sexual behaviours and desires by patriarchal institutions. The return of Puritan morals in 1950s America symbolically reinvented witches in the Cold War, not only regarding McCarthy's Communist witch-hunt but in persecuting nonconformist sexuality, particularly among women. Esther Greenwood shares her discontent with post-war gender and societal expectations for which she feels punished; Ethel Rosenberg was perceived as both a gender and political rebel; even for Abigail Williams, who is an accuser, her promiscuity and malicious behaviour make her the real villain of the play. While these historical and fictional women were not labelled as actual witches, their gender nonconformity and transgression of societal boundaries demonstrate shared associations and parallels to accused witches of early modern New England.

Plath's knowledge of the Salem witch trials and witch-hunt period originates in American literature and the history of the United States, which directly influenced her writing. Her poems from the late 1950s studied in this chapter recall the witch-hunt history of the United States: 'The Times Are Tidy' alludes to the afterlife of the Salem witch trials and contrasts post-war gender roles with the early modern prosecution of witches, and 'Witch Burning' uses imagery from Hawthorne's *The Scarlet Letter*. Despite writing them in the late 1950s, the poems lack any direct reference to McCarthyism. 'The Times Are Tidy' and 'Witch Burning' demonstrate Plath's interest in the history and literature of the witch-hunt and they employ the imagery of the burning witch, which becomes more significant and metaphorical in her later poetry. Plath's writings express her awareness of the connotation of the Salem witch trials and her knowledge of the politics of the witch-hunt in New England. Fictionalised accounts of Salem from Hawthorne's prose to Miller's play further demonstrate the significance of the witch trials in American history and their employment in political discourses, such as the critique of extreme Puritanism, gender and racial inequalities, and McCarthyism. While Plath's condemnation of the McCarthy witch-hunt and sympathy towards the Rosenbergs have been at the forefront of the critical interpretations of her *The Bell Jar*, looking closely at her encounter with Miller's drama demonstrates her engagement with the parallels between the Salem witch trials and McCarthyism. Reading *The Bell Jar* in parallel with *The Crucible* reveals their shared critique of Puritan morality, abuse of institutional power, and portrayal of subversive female sexuality. Esther Greenwood is an outcast in McCarthy's America, like Ethel Rosenberg: metaphorically speaking, they are the witches of the early Cold War.

CHAPTER 2

Religious Prosecutions in Plath's Cold War Poetics

Plath's poems written in the early 1960s in England take a new turn in their political engagement and reliance on historical and religious iconography of burning and martyrdom. In the autumn of 1962, Plath's poetry developed its distinct voice, characterised by the themes of domestic surrealism, violence, and the strong presence of disfigured bodies and body parts, marking her political/poetic engagement with the Cold War. In an article Plath wrote in November 1961 for the *London Magazine*, she noted that the subjects that concerned her at the moment

> are the incalculable genetic effects of fallout and a documentary article on the terrifying, mad, omnipotent marriage of big business and the military in America [. . .] My poems do not turn out to be about Hiroshima, but about a child [. . .] They are not about the terrors of mass extinction, but about the bleakness of the moon over a yew tree in a neighbouring graveyard. Not about the testaments of tortured Algerians, but about the night thoughts of a tired surgeon. (*Prose* 601–2)

Though in the article Plath does not admit the explicitly political character of her writings, she notes that world politics is a backdrop of her poetry. Plath's statement also reflects her conversations in her correspondence with family members and friends. During the week when she wrote 'Lady Lazarus', 23–29 October 1962, she criticised her mother for finding her daughter's poems too disturbing: 'but you have always been afraid of reading or seeing the world's hardest things — like Hiroshima, the Inquisition or Belsen' (*L2* 888). Plath's wording highlights the significance of political themes in her writings; she makes a parallel between the political crimes of the twentieth century and the inquisitorial executions. This chapter discusses the metaphors of religious prosecutions and martyrdom in Plath's late poems, in particular 'Lady Lazarus' and 'Fever 103°', as well as in her short stories from the late 1950s in which Plath borrows elements from the Christian rhetoric of the Cold War. Expanding on

Plath's engagement with the supernatural, I argue that short stories like 'Johnny Panic and the Bible of Dreams' and the drafts of poems like 'Lady Lazarus' demonstrate the parallels she drew between early modern religious prosecutions and martyrdom and modern political horrors, which establish Plath's Cold War poetics.

In an interview with Harriet Rosenstein, Plath's friend and poet Ruth Fainlight highlighted that the images of war were an obvious topic of poetry for her generation (Fainlight). Elizabeth Sigmund, Plath's neighbour in North Tawton, also noted that Plath often criticised American nuclear warfare and capitalism, and she was happy to find another 'committed woman' in the village ('Sigmund, Part Two'). Influenced by World War II and the Cold War, Plath's writings often express sympathy towards marginalised groups, such as Jews, heretics, witches, and abuse victims, and condemn the authoritarian politics personified by the priest, God, doctor, Führer, executioner, and male lover alike. Plath discussed her interest in political themes in an interview with Peter Orr in 1962: 'I'm very interested in battles, in wars, in Gallipoli, the First World War and so on, and I think that as I age I am becoming more and more historical. I certainly wasn't at all in my early twenties' (169). Many of the *Ariel* poems bear the direct influence of political events of their times, such as the intensified Cuban missile crisis, Eichmann's trial, Hiroshima, and the Holocaust (Peel, *Writing Back* 183–86). While Plath makes several direct references to contemporary politics, the metaphor of witch prosecutions links the horrors of the past and present. Her short stories and poetry show a preoccupation with institutional violence and torture across historical periods and victims of inquisitorial and ecclesiastical punishment alike. Plath's Cold War poetics is characterised by the imagery of the burning of heretics and witches of the medieval and early modern period, framing them as a gendered power struggle between an authoritarian male figure and the female speaker that she compares to modern political warfare.

Religious themes were part of the larger political conversations of the Cold War: in his infamous speech delivered in West Virginia in 1950, Senator Joseph McCarthy claimed that 'we are engaged in a final, all-out battle between communistic atheism and Christianity' ('Enemies from Within'). He equated Communism with atheism, against which the only hope was the (capitalist) Christian democracy of the United States. However, it was not only McCarthy who employed biblical narratives. In 1954, the Evangelical preacher Billy Graham called Communism 'Satan's religion', in a publication in which he asked, '[w]hat does Communism have that would make Ethel and Julius Rosenberg go to death rather than confess?' (42). For Graham, the Rosenberg couple were the devil-worshipping Adam and Eve. Newspapers, such as *The Washington Post*, also partook in the religious rhetoric ('Christianity vs. Communism'). The biblical language of the early Cold War was present in popular culture: Hollywood films, such as *Red Planet Mars* (1952), acted as propaganda, opposing Christian America with atheist Russia: 'Holy men [. . .] popped up in a variety of cinematic settings in the 1950s, affirming the Church's protective role either in the Cold War specifically or more generally in Western society' (Shaw 218). The vocabulary of Christianity attributed religious connotation to the Cold War and empowered American militarism and patriotism. In a letter sent to her mother in 1961, Plath expressed her worry about the union between the Christian religion and nuclear warfare in the United States:

> One of the most distressing features of about all this is [. . .] ministers & and priests preaching that it is all right to shoot neighbors who try to come into one's bomb shelter. Thank goodness none of this idiotic shelter business in England. (*L2* 697)

Plath's wording foreshadows the imagery of many *Ariel* poems where she compares the horrors of the twentieth century with the burning of a heretic and witch prosecutions, subverting the religious rhetoric of the Cold War in the United States.

In England, anti-communism and religion were not as intertwined as in the United States, yet 'Cold War rhetoric was fundamentally bound up with clergy efforts to rebuild the unity and purpose of their congregations after the war' (Jones 194). Plath's encounter with the Anglican rector in the village of North Tawton suggests that the spreading of Cold War rhetoric was common among small religious communities. She told her mother in March 1962 that the rector was not the religious leader she was looking for:

> I honestly dislike, or rather, scorn the rector. I told you about his ghastly H-bomb sermon, didn't I, where he said this was the happy prospect of the Second Coming & and how lucky we Christians were compared to the stupid pacifists & humanists & "educated pagans" who feared being incinerated (*L2* 738).

Plath's description of the cleric's language is reminiscent of the rhetoric of McCarthyism. Her account of the rector's sermon, which argued that nuclear warfare was a 'Second Coming', anticipates the religious and political vocabulary in her late poems, such as the fiery annihilation, priest as the prosecutor, and burning in 'Lady Lazarus' and 'Fever 103°'.

Elizabeth Sigmund described an anecdote when the rector went to see Plath after her separation from Hughes: Plath reported to Elizabeth that the rector was talking about such 'monstrous things; she said, "I became so angry that I chased him out of the house waving my broom like a witch"' ('Sigmund, Part Five'). Plath's 'self-identification' with a witch figure who stands up against religious authority echoes the power dynamics of the witch prosecutions, which she draws on in her writings about the Cold War. The imagery reappears in short stories, such as 'Johnny Panic and the Bible of Dreams', 'Tongues of Stone', 'Stone Boy With Dolphin', and the poems 'Lady Lazarus' and 'Fever 103°' in which the speaker attempts to defy religious and medical authorities.

Plath not only condemned the rector's political views but ridiculed his religious teaching: 'When he talks of sinfulness, I have to laugh' (*L2* 669). The reversal of religious morality is a central motif in 'Fever 103°'. Plath drew on her personal experiences with the religious authority figure and her opposition to the Cold War to merge the near-present political events with religious persecutions. In her poems, the tortured female body is a central metaphor embodying the gendered power dynamics between the marginalised and persecuted groups, such as witches and Jews, and the authority in the figure of a torturer, God, and priest identities. Clark also originates the 'ultimate spectacle – her own death' in 'Lady Lazarus' from Plath's interest in female martyrs, such as Joan of Arc (*Red Comet* 787). Plath often links the medieval and early modern Christian prosecutions with the Cold War by alluding to Joan of Arc. The martyr's ambiguous characterisation as a saint and witch demonstrates a pattern where the female poetic persona manoeuvres between sainthood and heresy, such as 'Lady Lazarus' and 'Fever 103°'.

Early on, Plath showed interest in Joan of Arc: when she visited Paris in 1955, she saw a French play by Charles Peguy, 'Joanne D'Arc', by which she was tremendously moved (*L1* 1068). Earlier the same year, Plath watched the silent film *The Passion of Joan of Arc* (1928) at the Museum of Modern Art, which left her feeling 'shocked and sickened' and said that she would always remember 'the final scene at the pyre [which] was perfect and terrible' (*L1* 870). Her descriptions are evocative of the burning and martyrdom in poems, such as 'Witch Burning' and 'Lady Lazarus', particularly in the draft, linking the politics of exclusion to religious persecution. Clark likewise notes the influence of the film on the themes of martyrdom, torture, and fire in Plath's late poetry (*Red Comet* 355). Anne Sexton's 'Her Kind' makes a similar connection between the gender politics of the Cold War and the prosecution of witches, alluding to Carl

Dreyer's *The Passion of Joan of Arc* film (Alkalay-Gut 52): 'I have ridden in your cart, driver, / waved my nude arms at villages going by, / learning the last bright routes, survivor / where your flames still bite my thigh' (16). Here, Sexton portrays the ambiguities of the martyr-witch figure as an outcast who, despite the social sanctions, survives. *The Passion of Joan of Arc* functions as a significant influence for both Sexton and Plath to interrogate the gender politics and religious rhetoric of the Cold War.

In her journals, Plath reflected on her personal affiliations with the martyr, logging her nightmare in an entry in 1958: 'Joan of Arc's face as she feels the fire and the world blurs out in a smoke, a pall of horror' (*J* 386). The citation anticipates her comparison of the horrors of nuclear annihilation to religious burning in 'Lady Lazarus' and 'Fever 103°'. Peel likens Plath's journal entry to Ethel Rosenberg's identification with Joan of Arc upon the judge dismissing her request for the ease of the death sentence ('The Problem of the Enemy Within' 208). He frames Plath's allusion to the burning martyr in the politics of the Cold War. Within the arts, the celebrated modern dancer Martha Graham developed the choreography about Joan of Arc in *Seraphic Dialogue* (1955). While Graham claimed she was not making a political statement, the rhetoric of the Cold War implies otherwise; her choreography 'told a story of religious persecution, drawing on the idea of a universal human narrative; that of the righteous being victimized' (Phillips, 'Cold War Modernist Missionary' 54; 58). Victoria Phillips argues that 'Joan's story became compelling in the post-Holocaust atomic age' for which freedom of religion 'was a central Cold War propaganda trope because it had infused the language of the myths of the men of the *Mayflower* landing' (*Martha Graham's Cold War* 82–83). The role of Joan of Arc, along with the religious vocabulary of the period, influenced Plath's allusions to martyrdom, torture, heresy, burning, and the prosecution of witches in her writings, interrogating the entanglement of religious rhetoric and authoritarian politics during the Cold War.

2.1 Torture and Prosecution of the Female Body

In her earlier prose, Plath reveals a preoccupation with the suffering body and the power dynamic of religious prosecutions. In the short story 'Tongues of Stone' (1955), Plath included several themes and images that anticipate both *The Bell Jar* and 'Lady Lazarus', particularly in her portrayal of the body and suffering. In the narrative, Debby (similarly to Esther Greenwood) undergoes insulin and electroshock treatment in a mental hospital. Plath's protagonist laments the exploitation and abuse of her body by medical professionals.

> There was nothing to her now but the body, a dull puppet of skin and bone that had to be washed and fed day after day after day. And her body would live on for sixty-odd years or more. After a while they would get tired of waiting and hoping and telling her that there was a God or that someday she would look back on this as if it were a bad dream.
>
> [. . .]
>
> I felt the subtle slow inevitable corruption of her flesh that yellowed and softened hour by hour. She imagined the waste piling up in her, swelling her full of poisons that showed in the blank darkness of her eyes when she stared into the mirror, hating the dead face that greeted her, the mindless face with the ugly purple scar on the left cheek that marked her like a scarlet letter. (*Prose* 253–54)

The use of the third-person narrator demonstrates her wanting to detach herself from the experience of the mental hospital that she had only two years before writing the short story. Plath's reference to God – or the lack of spiritual relief – signals the disillusionment with religious authorities that her speaker defies in 'Lady Lazarus'. The slow decomposition and torture of the body suggest Plath's early engagement with ideas of martyrdom, sacrilegious suffering, and institutional punishment. Plath seeks inspiration from one of her favourite authors at the time: the references to the scar as a scarlet letter and the feeling of being poisoned allude to Hawthorne's *The Scarlet Letter* and 'Rappaccini's Daughter'. In Chapter 1, I highlighted the personal and poetic significance of the imagery of the scarlet letter in Plath's writings. Plath revisited the Hawthornean references later, which show their influence in 'Lady Lazarus' (Clark, *Red Comet* 109). In a later part of 'Tongues of Stone', Plath writes that the doctors and nurses 'raised her up like Lazarus from mindless dead, corrupt already with the breath of the grave' (*Prose* 256). The juxtaposition of the gothic decay of the body and the divine spirit anticipates the imagery of the suffering and mistreated female speaker in her later poems. Plath draws on her personal experience to make a political statement about the worst of humanity.

In 'Johnny Panic and the Bible of Dreams', written in December 1958, she seeks inspiration from her experience as a secretary at the adult psychiatry clinic of the Massachusetts General Hospital. Just like in 'Tongues of Stone', in 'Johnny Panic', Plath centres the narrative on the institutional punishment of the female narrator by the medical professionals, whom Plath likens to the clergymen. The short story is primarily concerned with the theme of good and evil and the boundaries between reality and dream, in which she questions the 'spiritual purity of doctoring' (*Prose* 359). Luke Ferretter compares the themes of 'Johnny Panic' to Plath's poetry sequence 'Poem for a Birthday' in which Plath articulates the torturous experience of ECT treatment through the metaphor of rebirth (76). In Plath's short story, the narrator is called a witch by the male Clinic Director, which further engages with the gendered power dynamics of witch prosecutions: '"Here she is." "The little witch!"' (*Prose* 368). Plath's speaker is hunted and tied down by the nurses and doctors of the clinic who want to punish her with electroshock therapy:

> Then, from the four corners of the room and from the door behind me come five false priests in white surgical gowns and masks whose one lifework is to unseat Johnny Panic from his own throne [. . .] The masked priests move to their posts and take hold: one of my left leg, one of my right, one of my right arm, one of my left. (*Prose* 369)

Plath's description of the narrator's physical abuse and restraint shows a similarity to crucifixion; further, the priest-like doctors allude to the religious execution of witches and heretics. Plath's long-standing distrust of medical and religious authority figures was further reinforced by the 'marriage' between Christianity and American militarism during the Cold War. Her writings about institutional punishment and oppression during the decades after World War II build on the religious prosecutions of the early modern period.

Among Plath's 1962 poems, 'Lady Lazarus', particularly its holograph held by Smith, expresses Plath's condemnation of Cold War politics: she draws on the religious rhetoric of the era and identifies the speaker with marginalised groups from martyr, witch, and Jew, as she attempts to defy various patriarchal institutional powers. The poem has several characteristics that define Plath's *Ariel*, such as tercet form, repetition of sounds words, and structures, and frequent enjambment and full stops. Plath's holograph, an undated manuscript, was written on pink memo paper on the back of pages from *The Bell Jar*, which lacks a consistent narrative. The six-page-long manuscript includes several revisions, which are the most noticeable in Plath's uncertainty about the speaker's identity. On the second page, she calls herself a saint, a virgin, and a parent of two girls, then on the third page, she rather resembles a prosecuted witch. The draft reveals Plath's struggle with ending the poem: she was uncertain whether the speaker was a human, superhuman, or nonhuman after her rebirth.

The holograph employs imagery similar to 'Witch Burning', however, Plath's allusions to witch prosecutions here are violent and expressive. In the revised typescripts, Plath crossed out some stanzas, but the narrative is consistent with the final version of the poem.

Though the poem often employs religious language, Plath subverts biblical narratives like the resurrection of Lazarus. Crowther argues that Plath's regendering of the resurrection story has one aim: to 'eat men like air' ('Religious Context' 216–17). Yet the retelling of the biblical story as a narrative of torture, resurrection, and revenge not only portrays gendered power dynamics but also aims to relate the poem to broader political struggles between the powerful and disempowered. Rather, the speaker rejects and mocks the religious authorities. For example, she describes her return from the dead as 'A sort of walking miracle' (*CP* 244). A miracle is a supernatural phenomenon that has religious connotations. In the Bible, the resurrection of Lazarus is considered a miracle (John 12:17–18). In 'Lady Lazarus', the speaker dismisses her comeback as a 'miracle', which expresses her rejection of being an object of doctors ('Herr Doktor') who are often called 'miracle workers'. Plath uses a similar narrative in the poem 'Surgeon at 2 a.m.': 'The body is [. . .] / a statue the orderlies are wheeling off. / I have perfected it' (*CP* 171). Clark notes that 'Lady Lazarus' was likely influenced by news articles circulating during the period Plath wrote the poem, which commented on 'unethical drug experiments on humans' (*Red Comet* 788). The poem echoes Plath's critical view of Christianity, particularly the rejection of the male deity, whom she merges with the authoritarian Doctor and executioner figures, where she also draws on her encounter with the unsympathetic rector in the Devon village.

The repeated references to the number three express Plath's allusions to Christianity: the tercet form and the three times repeated 'ash' accentuate the supernatural rebirth of the phoenix-like speaker. The number three is not only a symbol of the Trinity but also of magic, frequently referenced in fairy tales. The poem names three enemies (Doktor, Lucifer, God), while unlike the resurrection of Lazarus, the speaker's comeback happens three times: 'And like the cat I have nine times to die. // This is Number Three' (*CP* 244–45). Here, the number is deployed as her 'lucky charm'. In the fifteenth stanza, the speaker mocks the biblical narrative on resurrection by bringing attention to her own death, which she does 'exceptionally well' (*CP* 245). The adjective highlights that she 'can take care of herself and furthermore boasts about her ability to cheat death' (Crowther, 'Religious Context' 217). While Crowther deems the speaker's rejection of the male-focused resurrection 'secular', the poetic persona rather subverts and ridicules those concepts of Christianity that are associated with male supernatural powers, such as miracles and the Holy Trinity. She is positioned as a heretic or witch who is burnt because she has powers more majestic than the Christian idols. Mark Ford notes that by referencing the number three, the speaker 'predicts, she will again emerge like the phoenix from the ashes, though this time as a vampiric, female avenger' ('Lady Lazarus'). By resurrecting her body three times, the poetic persona defies the male authorities, which signals her greater supernatural abilities.

In Plath's poetry, the imagery of the persecution of heretics, witches, and Jews is often intertwined, which complicates the way in which gender, race, and identity are portrayed in the poem. In the draft, Plath also taps into awkward Orientalism, alluding to the victims of the nuclear bombing in Hiroshima and Nagasaki, as she does in 'Fever 103°'. Jerome Ellison Murphy argues that in 'Plath's work, race operates within her system of associative logic, so that races become a lexicon of "code words" for the speakers' interior conditions' (95). Plath's references to Jews and Japanese appear similar to the heretics and witches as victims of political persecution. In 'Mary's Song', written some weeks after Plath completed 'Lady Lazarus', she likens the burning of heretics to the massacre of Jewish people during the Holocaust:

> The fire makes it precious,
> The same fire
> Melting the tallow heretics,
> Ousting the Jews. (*CP* 257)

Similar to Plath's other poems, here the imagery of the burning appears ambiguous. The fire is both sacred, sacrificial, and violent. While heresy is a religious concept, Plath was aware of its political salience during Cold War McCarthyism. In 1952, Plath listened to a lecture by the Dutch mathematician-Marxist theorist Dirk Jan Struik titled 'Academic Freedom and the Trend of Conformity'. She wrote the article 'Heresy Hunt' to the Smith College Press Board, noting that the lecture identified the heresy hunt as a menace to academic freedom and physical and spiritual well-being. Her article drew on the vocabulary of the 1950s: newspaper articles occasionally called McCarthyism a 'heresy hunt' ("Communists Decry 'Hunt'"). Arthur Miller also noted that during McCarthyism, Communism was identified as heresy ('Are You Now?'). In 'Lady Lazarus', the Jew-prosecutor power dynamics accentuate the similarities between the Holocaust of the twentieth century and the religious prosecutions of the medieval and early modern periods. By placing the suffering, resurrected, and wounded female body in the centre of the narrative, Plath acknowledges the gendered body politics of persecution, evoking the imagery of the witch-hunts and the metaphorical figure of Joan of Arc.

In 'Lady Lazarus', the female body is disassembled, bruised, buried, and eventually transformed through rebirth, which shows similarities to 'Witch Burning' covered in Chapter 1. Plath depicts the body as tortured and gruesome: 'The nose, the eye pits, the full set of teeth? / The sour breath / [. . .] I may be skin and bone,' (*CP* 244–45). Instead of being a victim, the speaker deploys her alienated body to create a terrifying effect. She knows this torturous performance has a charge. Tracy Brain suggests that the speaker positions herself as a stage magician who is selling her body while performing the 'magic trick' of her resurrection ('Sylvia Plath and You' 88). The poetic persona turns away from conventional feminine sex appeal to perform this bizarre strip tease: 'The peanut-crunching crowd / Shoves in to see / Them unwrap me hand and foot' (*CP* 245). The speaker shows off her scars, bones, hands, and knees to mock the staging of the female body. Ann Keniston argues that Plath's presentation of the body parts in the poem 'evokes the Catholic relics worshipped as a representation of the intact saint' (50). Plath's speaker is an ambiguous figure: holy, witchlike, and a martyr at the same time.

In the holograph of 'Lady Lazarus', Plath includes a highly revised stanza on the second page, where she explicitly names her capital punishment. The references to executions and martyrdom are reminiscent of the film *The Passion of Joan of Arc* in which Joan is confined to a torture chamber before being burned at the stake. In the draft, the speaker is more passive than in the final version of the poem: she is chosen by the crowd, which redefines the power dynamics between the poetic persona and her enemies. At the bottom of the third page of the holograph, Plath alludes to religious prosecutions by attributing a greater presence to the clerical figure and crowd that watches her execution: 'And there's always a mob & an executioner / A priest & and a torturer' (MS 'Lady Lazarus,' undated). In the lines, Plath links torture and public execution across historical periods. As the poem's narrative progresses, the speaker's opponents materialise from the lower case enemy to 'Herr Doktor. / So, Herr Enemy' and 'Herr God, Herr Lucifer' (*CP* 246). Plath adds the German honorific 'Herr' to each figure, suggesting an explicitly patriarchal force behind religious and medical authorities. The draft likewise introduces the speaker's promiscuous sexuality, suggesting that she is prosecuted for sexual crimes. During the medieval and early modern period, witches and heretics were believed to be sexually transgressive and promiscuous, 'a stereotype of the heretic as a secret, nocturnal, promiscuous devil worshipper'; likewise, 'it was believed that the witch often made a pact with the Devil because of sexual temptation and then engaged in promiscuous sexual intercourse at the sabbath' (Levack, *The Witch-Hunt* 43; 145–46). The explicit references to the priest, executioner, torturer, and mob allude to the public prosecution of witches and heretics and evoke the imagery of the tortured Joan of Arc. Plath's metaphor of witch prosecutions highlights the murder committed in the name of the religious rhetoric of patriarchal authorities, which brings attention to the politics of the Cold War.

Plath further employs violent imagery in the draft to convey the speaker's horrific objectification by others who touch her wounds. The holograph stresses the ecstasy she experiences through this performance: she gets excitement from her pain and is even willing to monetise it. Van Dyne argues that while the lines portray the 'mob's voyeurism', the speaker finds enjoyment in this ('Fueling the Phoenix Fire' 416). During the torture, the speaker 'turns and burns', which echoes the line 'They are turning the burners up' from 'Witch Burning' (*CP* 135; 246). We see another resemblance between the two poetic personas whose portrayal was influenced by the torture and prosecution of witches. However, unlike the speaker of 'Witch Burning', who ascends during the burning, Lady Lazarus 'melts to a shriek' (*CP* 246). The imagery suggests a painful and torturous burning. It echoes *The Passion of Joan of Arc*, which ends with a long torturous scene of the burning Joan, who twists and turns her face away from the smoke as she takes her final breath. In the poem, the speaker describes the invertebrates feeding from her body: they 'pick the worms off me like sticky pearls' (*CP* 245). During the pyre scene of *The Passion*, Joan looks at the ground filled with ash and bones; including a human skull that has worms coming out from its eye socket. The film's imagery suggests its strong impression on Plath and influence on 'Lady Lazarus', which has an uncanny resemblance to Joan of Arc's death.

For the poetic speaker, torture is necessary for her transformation, which Plath highlighted in her radio reading of the poem: she 'has the great and terrible gift of being reborn. The only trouble is, she has to die first. She is the Phoenix, the libertarian spirit, what you will. She is also just a good, plain, very resourceful woman' (*CP* 294n198). Plath's wording focuses on the speaker's identity: she refers to her as a woman and a phoenix, evoking the merging of human and nonhuman subjects in 'Ariel', discussed further in Chapter 6. In the drafts, Plath freely shifts between the different identities: she attributes a greater power to the speaker who deploys the fire as her supernatural power by consuming fire. She is also portrayed as phoenix-like with flaming feathers instead of hair. The poetic persona rises with her powers like 'an avenging female who was both erotically tempting and fearsomely destructive' (Van Dyne, 'Fueling the Phoenix Fire' 409). The adjectives Plath uses to describe the speaker's hair create the lively and fearless persona of a heroine ready to defy death, as opposed to the initial martyr figure. Plath's earliest childhood poems, such as 'Angelic Girls', foreshadow her association of long and wild hair with rebellion (Clark, *Red Comet* 57). The manuscript of 'Lady Lazarus' demonstrates the instability of the identity: she could be a woman, a witch, or a shapeshifting being who can change into a phoenix form. There is a pattern in Plath's portrayal of the fluid transformation of nonhuman and human identities, particularly in the *Ariel* poems. In the later typescripts, Plath somewhat reduces the uncertainty of her persona. Instead of the fire, she only consumes men – her torturers. The published version retains the speaker's resistance to male authority figures: 'I eat men like air' (*CP* 247), overcoming suffering. The end of the poem is not a mere reflection on female victimhood and survival but it expresses a political statement on defying tyranny. Plath associates the speaker's freedom not only with the rising defiance of authority but her red hair becomes the source of female autonomy.

In the holograph, Lady Lazarus is a martyr, a witch, a phoenix, and a femme fatale, and a mother with two daughters. She is a proud and caring maternal figure, who is concerned with the future of her children. In her private writings, Plath often expressed her anxieties about the uncertainties of the future due to nuclear warfare. Peel brings attention to Plath's female-only family system, which stands opposite to the patriarchal authorities of the God/Führer/Doktor (*Writing Back* 192). The draft echoes the female-only colony in the bee sequence, in which the speaker relates her identity to the maternal queen bee, which I discuss in Chapter 7. In a letter written in 1960, Plath wrote that 'Frieda is my answer to the H-bomb' (*L2* 520), which anticipates the juxtaposition between motherhood – a metaphor for life – and the patriarchal authoritarian politics of the Cold War, representing death.

Plath's writing process reveals that 'Lady Lazarus' is a complex political poem that uses the metaphor of religious prosecutions to condemn the Cold War. The holograph centres on a struggle between the speaker and the doctor/priest/torturer, which draws on the power dynamic between the prosecuted female witch or heretic, alluding to Joan of Arc and the male institutional power. 'Lady Lazarus' strongly critiques the religious institution of Catholicism and deploys the rhetoric of nuclear war and religious prosecutions to condemn these institutions. The poem suggests that faith and religion do not provide shelter from the horrors of the Cold War, on the contrary, they participate in the persecution of marginalised groups and punish those that oppose the status quo. The poem interrogates body politics and autonomy by portraying the speaker's torture as a striptease. Her staged body is perceived as an object, a wonder, even a miracle in the eyes of the doctors, priests, and the crowd. 'Lady Lazarus' is a poem about a public execution and torture where the male authorities 'see', 'touch', and 'unwrap' the female body.

2.2 Nuclear Burning and Martyrdom

Plath's early opposition to and fear of nuclear warfare is evident early on from her letters and journalistic writings, such as her article about a lecture 'The Atomic Threat' (1948) and a co-written piece with Perry Norton to the *Christian Science Monitor* 'Youth's Plea for World Peace' (1950). Her political actions became more direct in the early 1960s: she attended the 'Ban the Bomb' march in London in April 1960 (*L2* 461). Plath's preoccupation with the nuclear threat is notable in the poem 'Fever 103°' in which the imageries of religious martyrdom, heretical burning, and sin critique the hellish reality of the Atomic Age. She introduced her poem 'Fever 103°' in her script she wrote for the BBC's 'New Poems by Sylvia Plath' reading: 'it is about two kinds of fire – the fires of hell, which merely agonise, and the fires of heaven, which purify' (*AR* 194). Her wording expresses the ambiguous narrative of burning, which alludes to religious purification. In the poem, Plath merges Catholic imagery, the fear of nuclear annihilation, and feverish hallucinations to narrate the speaker's burning, which is both torture and ecstasy. Plath's poem subverts the biblical rhetoric of McCarthyism and the Cold War by focusing on the sinfulness of religious figures. Purkiss argues that in several of Plath's poems, 'being burned is a metaphor for a caress that accepts the body's responsiveness, and pain a symbol of passion' (23). The ambiguities between burning as ecstasy and torture are present equally in 'Fever 103°' and 'Lady Lazarus'. However, the erotic passion is not in the poem's focus; rather, it questions the concept of purity and sainthood. In the 'Fever 103°', the speaker 'embarks on a spectacular display of physical suffering, disease and immolation all serving to purge the woman/artefact/patient/burlesque/performer/saint of her inessential identities as she ascends, theatrically, to paradise' (Tunstall, 'Plath and the Lyric' 95).

In another publication, Tunstall further suggests that the aforementioned *The Passion of Joan of Arc* highly influenced the poem with its close shots and disruptive visuals ('Vision and Visual Art' 146). The speaker navigates the blurred boundaries of heresy to sainthood, evoking the burning of Joan of Arc.

Plath drafted an earlier undated poem titled 'Fever' and its variant 'Fever in Winter', likewise inspired by her fever, which she did not finish. The drafts, written on the back of *The Bell Jar*, suggest that Plath did not yet find a coherent narrative. This poem is heavier on autobiographical elements, however, one of the typescripts, numbered 4–6, also includes images of the nuclear destruction of the natural environment and additional allusions to Joan of Arc and her heard voices and visions of angels and saints who instructed her to go to war. Plath abandoned 'Fever' and composed 'Fever 103°' on 20 October 1962, in which she repurposed several ideas from 'Fever'. Despite some similarities, they are treated as two separate and different poems. The drafts of 'Fever 103°' include a three-page-long holograph that has a clearer stanza structure; it is dated 20 October 1962 and written on the pink Smith memo paper. There are also four revised typescripts of 'Fever 103°' with handwritten corrections: the first is written in dense handwriting and includes heavy revisions; it comprises two pages, numbered 2 and 3. In each draft, the narrative and structure remain similar.

Plath starts 'Fever 103°' with a question, doubting religious purity: 'Pure? What does it mean?' (*CP* 231). The poem understands burning as a purification, recalling *Britannica*'s definition of witchcraft laws that define the witch-hunt as a spiritual cleansing from the sin of witchcraft referenced in Chapter 1. She uses the adjective 'dull' for the hellish fire, implying that it does not affect the speaker as she burns stronger than Hell. In the poem, Plath employs the symbolism of the number three, similarly in 'Lady Lazarus'. Karen V. Kukil argues that Plath's poem was influenced by 'the three realms, the Trinity, and the number three [which] are prominent in *The Divine Comedy* like the tercet structure' ('The Fires of Heaven and Hell'). Indeed, the first part of the poem frequently references the inferno: the second stanza evokes the triple-tongued mythological dog, Cerberus, who is the guardian of the gates of the Underworld, as Plath underlined in her *WCD*. The number three also reappears in the second half of the poem, suggesting the speaker's purgatory: 'Three days. Three nights. / Lemon water, chicken / Water, water make me retch' (*CP* 232). The stanza alludes to a religious ritual in which water counteracts the fiery burning. The purifying water references baptism and blessing conducted by clergy with the Holy Water. In the stanza, the repetition of the number three resembles the third-day resurrection of the speaker in 'Lady Lazarus', highlighting the significance of the number in Plath's Cold War poetics. However, as opposed to 'Lady Lazarus', which scrutinises the male figures of Christianity, in 'Fever 103°', Plath subverts the religious rhetoric of the Cold War employed by clerics who also supported nuclear warfare. Her poem expresses the sinfulness and immorality of modern-day politicians, whom she compares to the inquisitors who burnt heretics and those that prosecuted witches.

The poem deploys varied imagery to describe burning, calling it 'hell', 'fever', 'radiation', 'lantern', and 'candle' (*CP* 231). One of Plath's main inspirations for the poem was the 103° fever – close to 40° Celsius – and flu she experienced in September 1962 (*L2* 821). She parallels the private agony of the illness with the public suffering of burning and death, alluding to the Cold War. In the poem, the smoke foreshadows the mass death of nuclear annihilation that chokes 'the aged and the meek' (*CP* 231). Here, Plath evokes the process when the bomb fuses into a 'mushroom' shape, and yellow smoke appears with other toxic elements. She portrays the fears of nuclear annihilation from which there is no escape. The atom bomb is described as transforming from a mushroom shape into a 'Devilish leopard! / Radiation turned it white' (*CP* 231). The lines imply that the atomic bomb is diabolical and is an act of *maleficium*, linking the vocabulary of the early modern witch-hunt to the Cold War. There is also a contrast between the dark imagery of the bomb and the whiteness of the radiation. Peel notes that 'Fever 103°' recalls Plath's early political opposition to the atomic bomb and the Korean War, which she could respond to in her poetry once she had 'a global perspective offered by her late experience' ('Political Education' 40). For the young Sylvia Plath, the nuclear bomb could only be a sin: 'That the A-bomb was ever dropped seems like a sin to me' (*L1* 168). The citation from her letter from 1950, written to her German pen pal, anticipates Plath's provocative imagery in 'Fever 103°'. For Plath, the political and religious authority figures are guilty of sin – not witches or heretics. Her disapproval of the 'ghastly H-bomb sermon' of the rector in Devon, which I highlighted at the beginning of this chapter, shows her awareness of the union between Christianity and the Cold War. After this sermon, Plath wrote to her mother: 'I've not been to church since. I felt it was a sin to support such insanity even by my presence' (*L2* 738). Her condemnation of the rector alludes to the Original Sin, subverting the religious rhetoric of the Cold War. In Chapter 7, I further discuss Plath's critique of the Anglican clergy and the politics of exclusion in post-war Britain in relation to her writings about beekeeping in the Devon village.

In 'Fever 103°', the speaker explicitly asserts the sinfulness of the nuclear bombing: 'Greasing the bodies of adulterers / Like Hiroshima ash and eating in. / The sin. The sin' (*CP* 231). The stanza references the film *Hiroshima, Mon Amour* (1959), which Plath saw in the cinema (Steinberg, 'Sylvia Plath: Film Buff'). Tracy Brain notes that the images in the stanza 'come straight from the film's opening scenes': the ash from the nuclear bomb falls on the two naked bodies of the lovers (*The Other Sylvia Plath* 118). Further, Plath's poem parallels the monologues of the film's heroine, for example, they both allude to the meek victims of the bomb, sexual desire and adultery, and interrogate what is considered a sin. Laura Perry notes that Plath's engagements with purity and cleanness in her poems 'emerge from sexual, racial and national containment during the Cold War years' (191). The poem interrogates the ambiguities of purity and sin with the imagery of fiery burning, contextualised within the Cold War. It questions what is considered a sin, sexual desire or the bombing of Hiroshima, and who are the sinners, witches, heretics, adulterers, or the politicians and clergy with the power to execute and murder.

The speaker is purified not by an inquisitorial fire but by sexual burning. Purkiss notes that in the poem, 'only fire can affirm the sexuality of the female body' (23). The speaker describes herself as camellia, 'Glowing and coming and going, flush on flush' (*CP* 232). Her sexuality is not a sin but signifies spiritual purity as she transcends into the divine, suggesting that she is purer than God. The speaker condemns God, whom she makes responsible for the sins of humanity, such as nuclear warfare. In the short story 'Stone Boy with Dolphin' written in March 1958, Plath references Joan of Arc's martyrdom and the burning of witches to suggest the sexual frustration of the protagonist Dody: '[S]he listened [...] to witches on the rack, to Joan of Arc crackling at the stake, to anonymous ladies flaring like torches in the rending metal of Riviera roadsters, to Zelda enlightened, burning behind the bars of her madness' (*Prose* 337–38). The merging images of the roadster car, a symbol of American dating culture in the 1950s, Zelda Fitzgerald, and the burning Joan of Arc anticipate the sexual encounter; at the same time, it warns of the dangers of burning passion. Jessica McCort argues that '[f]or Dody, as for many of Plath's speakers (especially, as we will soon see, in the early 1960s), the active, plotting, intelligent witch offers possibilities' (168). In 'Fever 103°', the ambiguities of sexuality and purity recall Joan of Arc's martyrdom, who refused to obey the clergy and was condemned for disobeying strict societal, religious, and gender norms. Plath experiments with the blurred boundaries between burning sexual desire, the threat of fever, and nuclear death to critique the politics and religious rhetoric of the Cold War. In both 'Fever 103°' and 'Lady Lazarus', the female body is not only the site of torture, suffering, and sin, but of sexuality, transformation, and power. The poetic personae clash with the religious and political male figures for bodily autonomy. Like 'Witch Burning', 'Fever 103°' portrays the female figure torn between agonising torture and ascending, reinforcing the imagery of witch executions as Plath's poetic response to purification.

In an earlier version of her poem, Plath directly references inquisitorial punishment and the witch-hunt, which further critiques the ecclesiastical authorities and their support of the Cold War. Plath read the poem for an interview at the British Council with Peter Orr in October 1962, where she included the lines that are not in the published version. Here, she explicitly references martyrdom and heretical burning: 'O auto-da-fé! / The purple men, gold crusted, thick with spleen // Sit with their hooks and crooks and stoke the light' ('Fever 103°' audio). Brain notes that the concept of auto-da-fé is present in Plath's *WCD*, in which she underlined the definition; and she kept the lines in her poem until the fourth typewritten version (Brain, *The Other Sylvia Plath* 28). The dictionary defines heretical burning as the 'ceremony accompanying the pronouncement of judgment by the Inquisition, followed by the execution by the secular authorities, hence, the execution, esp. the burning of a heretic' ('auto-da-fé'). The uncertain status of the lines in 'Fever 103°' continues the pattern that Plath frequently erased from the final version of her poems emotionally charged and expressive imagery and the vocabulary of the supernatural. The direct reference to the ritualistic burning of a heretic in the poem critiques the inquisitorial past of Christianity and highlights the influence of Joan of Arc's martyrdom as a recurring symbol in Plath's Cold War poetics. In the second deleted line, the speaker references 'purple men'. Purple has been associated with power, both as a royal colour – because it was hard to produce – and the high-ranking Christian clergy (Elliott 183; 192). The powerful clergy 'thick with spleen' implies their anger, who 'Sit with their hooks and crooks and stoke the light'. Here, Plath describes the violence of the ecclesiastical authorities by alluding to the expression, 'by hook or by crook', which means by any means necessary. The stanza evokes the burning of heretics and witches, like Joan of Arc, continuing the poetic imagery of religious purification associated with the martyr figure.

Plath also drew a parallel between inquisitors and the perceived sinfulness of her characters in some of her prose and used a vocabulary similar to 'Fever 103°'. In 'Johnny Panic and the Bible of Dreams', she employs the same expression as the deleted lines from the poem to identify the medical professionals with clergy who take any measures to be part of the religious congregation: 'What's worse: day by day I see these psyche-doctors studying to win Johnny Panic's converts from him by hooks, crooks, and talk, talk' (*Prose* 364). Here, Plath makes a parallel between the doctors and clergymen who want to please their superior. In *The Bell Jar*, Esther evokes inquisitorial punishment and sinfulness to question her guilt in the oppressive social and political climate that wants to torment her:

> Of course, I didn't believe in life after death or the virgin birth or the Inquisition or the infallibility of that little monkey-faced Pope or anything, but I didn't have to let the priest see this, I could just concentrate on my sin, and he would help me repent. (*TBJ* 158)

In the passage, Esther mocks the clerical authority and considers lying to the priest just to get her desired salvation. The institutional and religious authorities have the power to decide who and what is considered morally and spiritually pure and punish those that they deem sinners.

In 'Fever 103°', the speaker is in a feverish delirium and imagines herself as a victim of Hiroshima and inquisitorial burning as well as a purified virgin who rises to Heaven. Like Joan of Arc, who was burnt as a witch but became a saint, the speaker's identity shifts between heretic, witch, and holy saint, who overcomes the morality and power of religious and political authorities. The last lines of the poem express a complete annihilation and ascension, which is neither a positive purification nor destruction. It is a rejection of male authorities. The poem ends with the speaker's metaphorical and literal flight from the lover/God/inquisitor. She is dissolved in the process of burning-as-purification, which questions the positive connotations of ascending to Paradise. By becoming 'too pure' (*CP* 232), the speaker suggests subtler revenge than the poetic persona of 'Lady Lazarus'. She exceeds the ecclesiastical and political male authority figures – even God – who do not have the power to make her a heretic or a saint. 'Fever 103°' challenges the binary system of purity and sin prescribed by the religious teaching and the rhetoric of the Cold War through the metaphor of inquisitiorial punishment, thereby subverting the rhetoric used by political and clerical figures during the Cold War who compared the 'hell' of nuclear warfare to a Second Coming. Her speaker rejects the moral superiority of the patriarchal figures and follows the rebellious heretics, witches, and martyrs who were prosecuted for standing up against institutional power, similar to the political nonconformists during the Cold War.

Plath's employment of the medieval and early modern religious prosecutions in some of her *Ariel* poems and short stories shows her engagement with the religious rhetoric of the Cold War, in particular, she plays with the witch-prosecutor power dynamics and questions martyrdom and inquisition through allusions to Joan of Arc. The writings discussed in this chapter are characterised by an anticlerical attitude influenced by her hostile encounters with religious figures who spoke positively about nuclear warfare. While 'Lady Lazarus' and 'Fever 103°' centre on gendered power dynamics between the speaker and the male figures embodying authoritarianism, they also articulate her broader employment of the metaphor of the witch-hunt and religious prosecutions that describe the horrors of World War II, the early Cold War, and nuclear warfare. The manuscripts directly connect fear of nuclear annihilation to the horrors of being burnt alive as a heretic in 'Fever 103°' and equate the witch prosecutions with the Holocaust, McCarthyism, and the Cold War in 'Lady Lazarus'. In her short stories such as 'Tongues of Stone' and 'Johnny Panic and the Bible of Dreams', Plath builds on the religious rhetoric of the McCarthy era, which prompted her to draw parallels between victims of war and medical experimentation and the martyrs of inquisitorial punishment. As opposed to the writings I discussed in Chapter 1, these poems and short stories frame the early modern witch persecution not exclusively within the history of the United States and the Salem witch trials but it materialises as a metaphor for the Cold War. Plath employs emotionally charged imagery, such as heretical burning and public executions, along with the prominent figure of Joan of Arc, responding to the fears and anxieties of the Cold War and critiquing the leaders of both state and ecclesiastical institutions.

CHAPTER 3

Shakespearean Maternal and Paternal Magic in Plath's Poetry

Sylvia Plath had extensive knowledge of the European witch-hunts portrayed in early modern plays, mainly in Shakespeare's works that include characters with supernatural abilities like witches and magicians, expressing a gendered understanding of magical powers, and reference to the witch trials. In particular, *Macbeth* borrows elements of the North Berwick witch trials of 1590 during which the accused witches allegedly caused a tempest in the sea trying to sink the ship of King James I of Scotland, VI of England. Plath drew on Shakespeare's witches in *Macbeth* and the powerful Prospero from *The Tempest* to reflect on her ambiguous relationship with her mother and father and the haunting presence of maternal and overbearing control of paternal powers. During her final year at Smith College, Plath was excited about taking a 'superlative course in [s]hakespeare' (*L1* 753). At Cambridge, she studied Elizabethan and Jacobean tragedies and often discussed Shakespeare with Hughes, who quoted lines by heart to her from his plays: 'Ted reads me Shakespeare aloud while I prepare meals so I won't waste any time' (*L1* 1236). Plath studied *Macbeth* for the Tragedy Paper at Cambridge, which was 'a compulsory component of the third-year curriculum in which students think about the historically and generically various forms of "tragedy" and "the tragic"' (The Faculty of English). Plath's exam paper included questions on the plays of Euripides, Shakespeare, and Marlowe, such as: 'Illustrate from any two Elizabethan revenge plays the dramatic and poetic opportunities which this kind of play afforded' ('English Tripos'). More than six decades later, the Tragedy Paper has remained a form of assessment at the University of Cambridge.

In her unpublished poetry collection titled *Two Lovers and a Beachcomber* submitted for her Cambridge Tripos exam, Plath included the poems 'The Lady and the Earthenware Head' and 'All the Dead Dears', which represent the sinister maternal hag figures similar to

Macbeth. In another poem I discuss in this chapter, 'The Disquieting Muses', written in 1958, Plath explicitly named the influence of *Macbeth*'s Weird Sisters on the poem. The Shakespearean allusion expresses an association between literary witches and maternal malice, which comes from the ominous presence of hags as a maternal curse. While Plath reread *Macbeth* during her Cambridge years (*J* 204), she wrote a creative birthday poem for her mother in April 1954, based on the lines spoken by the witches: 'Double, double toil and trouble / fire burn and champagne bubble / I'm stirring up a witches brew / That will, I hope, bring luck to you / HAPPY BIRTHDAY' (*L1* 734). The lines reference the cauldron scene where they meet with Hecate. In her copy of *Macbeth*, Plath annotated lines from the Witches' song; her underlining is reproduced here: 'Double, double, toil and trouble' and 'Finger of birth-strangled babe / Ditch-deliver I thick a drab, / Make the gruel thick and slab' (*SP Complete Shakespeare* 1201). Her attention to the cauldron where the witches allude to infanticide foreshadows her association of the witches with maternal malice. Plath's rewriting of the well-known lines in the birthday wish likewise prefigures her poems like 'The Disquieting Muses' in which the witches and the mother are bonded in the domestic activity of baking. Plath was aware of the significance of the cauldron scene in *Macbeth*, which she alluded to in her works. A reference to the scene also appears in her short story 'The Lucky Stone' (1961) about an experience of wandering around in the haunting and bleak moors of Yorkshire where the narrator notices a walker standing 'before something that looked rather like a witch's tripod' (*Prose* 440). The line demonstrates Plath's association of the weird witches with the uncanny and haunting landscapes in England. I return to this in discussing the short story and the poem 'All the Dead Dears'. While Plath composed her writings inspired by *Macbeth*'s witches in England, this chapter also elaborates on the reception of the play in post-war America and discusses the poetic parallels between the poems of Plath and her contemporaries who sought inspiration from the tragedy and its witches.

As opposed to *Macbeth*, which Plath read during her high school and university education, she had an early admiration for *The Tempest* for its personal and literary significance and inspiration in the works of modernist poets. In addition, Christina Britzolakis notes that the play 'has become an allegorical text not merely for Plath but also her critics' (50–51). At the age of fifteen, Plath co-wrote 'The Island: A Radio Play' with her friend Mary Ventura. It seeks inspiration from *The Tempest* in the portrayal of a haunting magic island that 'increased its magnetic power of attraction' for the protagonist Helen, who is looking for her drowned husband (*Prose* 41). In doing so, Plath follows the example of the modernist writers whom she came to study: Wallace Stevens in 'The Planet on the Table' and T. S. Eliot's *Ariel Poems* and *The Waste Land* reimagined *The Tempest* in their poetry (Axelrod 66). Plath's early literary hero was W. H. Auden, whose long poem, 'The Sea and the Mirror: A Commentary on Shakespeare's *The Tempest*', she admired: he is 'talking in a gravelly incisive tone about how Caliban is the natural bestial projection, Ariel the creative imaginative' (*J* 180). Ariel, Prospero, and Caliban appear directly as references or indirectly as inspirations in Plath's poetry and prose.

In addition to the literary heritages of the play, Plath associated *The Tempest* with her childhood spent on the coasts of the Atlantic Ocean. She commemorated her experience spent on the coast in the essay from 1962 'Landscape of Childhood', which I discuss further in detail. Elaine Showalter highlights that at the beginning of the twentieth century, there was an emphasis on the Americanisation of *The Tempest*, where the magic island represented the United States: the critic Edward Everett Hale argued that Miranda was a 'Massachusetts girl' (29). Massachusetts, the state where Plath grew up, was the first place of successful settlement with the arrival of the Mayflower in the seventeenth century, which prompts the postcolonial reading of the play; Prospero embodies the domineering coloniser and Caliban the colonised slave. In Chapter 7, I further elaborate on the postcolonial reading of *The Tempest* and its influence on Plath's portrayal of the bees as dark and diabolical creatures. In Plath's writings about her father figure, such as the short stories 'Among the Bumblebees', 'Charlie Pollard and The Beekeepers', and the poems 'The Beekeeper's Daughter' and 'The Bee Meeting', Prospero's magic and her father's beekeeping are comparable. They both signify the scholarly knowledge of the patriarch who appears as an ambiguous figure. The early modern portrayal of sinister witches and the intellectual magician offered Plath ways to express ambivalent feelings towards her parents. I read Plath's creative responses, both poems and short stories, in dialogue with post-war artistic reflections on Shakespeare's plays, including American theatre adaptations and works of poets whose allusions to *Macbeth* parallel Plath's writings. Shakespeare's plays, such as *Macbeth* and *The Tempest*, had a significant role in post-war culture through which artists responded to societal and personal issues, including gender inequalities, colonialism, and memories of childhood.

3.1 Maternal Curse and Troubling Presence of Witches

Though Shakespeare was influenced by the historical events and political context of the early modern period, the Weird Sisters are not only the product of the witch-hunt but represent a 'mass of diverse stories, inscrutable in another sense' (Purkiss 207). Shakespeare was also inspired by other contemporary texts, such as Raphael Holinshed's *Chronicles*, whose portrayal of the Weird Sisters has been linked to Scandinavian mythology, particularly the Norns and their power to influence people's destiny (Gibson and Esra, *Shakespeare's Demonology* 196). Scholars likewise considered that the Weird Sisters' prophetic knowledge and ability to vanish make them more than just witches (W. C. Curry 396). The classical counterparts of the witches include Circe, Medea, and Hecate. The latter is the leader of the trio in *Macbeth*, who reappears in other Shakespeare plays and is also the chief witch in the Jacobean play *The Witch* by Thomas Middleton. *Macbeth*'s witches share similarities to female trios from mythology, such as the Fates and the Gorgons, which Plath also highlighted in her radio reading of 'The Disquieting Muses', which I consider in my reading of the poem.

In the United States, Margaret Webster, known for her stage directions of Shakespeare's plays, directed the Broadway production of *Macbeth* in 1941. She wanted 'darkness and black magic' and focused on the spectral presence of the witches who only materialised when Macbeth appeared on stage (Smith 165–66). In the production, the Weird Sisters represented evil whose gender is ambiguous. In the second half of the twentieth century, feminist criticism brought attention to the gender power dynamic: Janet Adelman, writing in 1987, argued that the '[m]aternal power in *Macbeth* is not embodied in the figure of a particular mother [. . .] it is instead diffused throughout the play, evoked primarily by the figures of the witches and Lady Macbeth' (90). Plath lived before the gender of the Weird Sisters was at the centre of critical interpretations. However, even in the 1930s, some critics acknowledged the female gender of the witches: they 'are not solely Elizabethan hags any more than they are Norse wyrds, classical Circes, fates, goddesses, or prophetesses. They are a quintessence of all of these' (Tonge 236). In Plath's copy of *Macbeth*, she underlined in the introduction to the play that the Weird Sisters originate from mythological sources and function as instruments of darkness with divinatory powers (*SP Complete Shakespeare* 1181). Plath's poems likewise point towards an understanding of the trio as sinister beings whose similarity to other female supernatural figures genders them as women and associates their powers with maternal malice. In her poetry, deities, hags, fates, and spiritual beings are merged with amorphous sinister female figures, maternal ancestors, and a paralysing hag-head.

In her BBC radio reading of the poem 'The Disquieting Muses' from 1961, Plath explicitly names *Macbeth*'s sinister female trio as an inspiration for the haunting dummies:

> All through the poem I have in mind the enigmatic figures in this painting – three terrible faceless dressmaker's dummies in classical gowns, seated, seated and standing in a weird, clear light [. . .] The dummies suggest a twentieth-century version of other sinister trios of women – Three Fates, witches in *Macbeth*, De Quincey's sisters of madness. ('The Disquieting Muses' audio)

Plath's emphasis on the shapelessness of the dummies is reminiscent of the metaphysical appearance of the Weird Sisters in *Macbeth*. Her identification of the female figures with other 'sinister trios' aligns with the interpretation that questions whether the Weird Sisters are witches or, rather, an embodiment of metaphysical evil and goddess-like creatures who influence the Macbeth's and her poetic speaker's destiny. In her introduction to her poem, Plath likens the dummies to Thomas De Quincey's female trios in the essay 'Levana and Our Ladies of Sorrow', published in his collection *Suspiria de Profundis* (1845). Plath's copy of De Quincey's collected writings is kept at the Lilly Library, Indiana University. His essay describes the death of one of his sisters during his childhood and personifies grief in the three haunting and sinister sisters whom he names the Ladies of Sorrow. Plath also read De Quincey's influential criticism of *Macbeth* titled 'On the Knocking at the Gate in *Macbeth*' (1886), which discusses the shift to darkness in the play when the murder takes place. Plath referenced the essay in the marginalia of *Macbeth* (*SP Complete Shakespeare* 1192).[1] She also cited the essay in her undergraduate thesis 'The Magic Mirror: The Study of Double in Two of Dostoevsky's Novels', to analyse 'Ivan's Devil' from *The Brothers Karamazov*:

> Like Ivan, we have been bewitched by the apparition of the Devil. Ivan's nightmare is an 'awful parenthesis' in which 'the world of devils is suddenly revealed', for the objective realism of the normal world has given way to the terrible, subjective realism of hallucination. (*Magic Mirror* 43)

[1] Plath made another marginalia note to De Quincey's essay in her copy of T. S. Eliot's *The Waste Land*.

In the passage from her thesis, Plath makes a parallel between the devil's apparition in Dostoevsky's novel and the metaphysical appearance of *Macbeth*'s witches. In her poem, she associates the dummies with female supernatural trios from literature and mythology who are foremost the speaker's companions as gendered beings with malicious supernatural powers.

Plath likens the dummies in 'The Disquieting Muses' to *Macbeth*'s portrayal of witches. The weird figures are described as shapeless dolls whose physical appearance is strange and deformed: 'Mouthless, eyeless, with stitched bald head' (*CP* 75). They resemble the three witches Banquo describes as bearded and deformed:

> By each at once her choppy finger laying
> Upon her skinny lips; you should be women,
> And yet your beards forbid me to interpret
> That you are so. (1.3.41–44)

Plath further alludes to the cauldron scene from *Macbeth* by referencing the mother's mixing the witches as ingredients into the homely baking: 'Mother, whose witches always, always / Got baked into gingerbread' (*CP* 75). The gingerbread house, well-known from the Grimms' tale 'Hansel and Gretel', is combined with witches, which suggests the mixing of the familiar and the uncanny.[2] Gibson argues that in *Macbeth*, 'mixing familiar and unfamiliar, especially in imagining foraging, cooking and consuming, the sisters define the uncanny' (*Rediscovering Renaissance Witchcraft* 33). In a later stanza, the speaker evokes a hurricane during which the disquieting muses enter the house, parallelling the entrance of the witches in the play who create a tempest. In *Macbeth*, metaphorical and literal darkness is frequently associated with the ominous presence of the witches and Hecate. Likewise, in Plath's poem, the speaker is haunted by the three weird women, who cast a shadow over the sky: 'In the shadow cast by my dismal-headed / Godmothers, and you cried and cried: / And the shadow stretched, the lights went out' (*CP* 75). 'The Disquieting Muses' draws on the portrayal of night-time caused by the shadow of female figures, which 'never brightens or goes down' (*CP* 76). The line recalls Macbeth's words to the Weird Sisters: 'How now, you secret, black, and midnight hags!' (4.1.46). The internal rhyme between 'black' and 'hags' accentuates the Weird Sisters' malicious presence. Similar to *Macbeth*, in 'The Disquieting

[2] For more on the topic see my article, 'Sylvia Plath's Reimagination of the Grimms' Fairy Tales in Postwar American Culture', *Feminist Modernist Studies* 5.1 (2022): 36–53.

Muses', there is no escape from the infectious and haunting hag-like figures.

In both the poem and *Macbeth*, the female figures bring bad luck, which is a recurring pattern in the three Plath poems about the evil maternal presence. Plath subverts traditionally loving associations with motherhood, where instead of care, the maternal figures carry misfortune. The beginning of 'The Disquieting Muses' alludes to the fairy tale 'Briar Rose' in which the evil fairy curses the girl, yet Plath moves away from the imagery of the fairy tale. Traditionally, cursing uses blasphemous expressions where ill-wishing manifests in actual harm. Plath also evokes the idea that the maternal line is blamed for the poetic persona's misfortune in 'Daddy'. In the poem, the speaker attributes 'weird luck' to her ancestress (*CP* 223), suggesting an association between her maternal line and misfortune, which I refer to as a maternal curse. In Chapter 5, I look in detail at the magical powers attributed to the performed poetic language, particularly allusions to exorcism in Plath's poetry. In her *WCD*, Plath annotated the definitions of a curse and being cursed:

1. A prayer on invocation for harm or injury to come upon one an imprecation oath.
2. That which is used cursed or accursed. 3. Evil that comes as if in response to imprecation, or retribution 4. That cause of great harm or misfortune; torment. ('curse')

   [. . .]

3. To bring great evil upon; to afflict to harass or torment. ('cursed')

The definitions indicate that Plath foremost understood cursing as a linguistic form of harming someone; and it was associated with evil magical powers. While this dictionary entry does not mention witches or other supernatural figures, in Plath's poems curses are foremost linked to female figures. She likewise references the divinatory power of the Weird Sisters who resemble prophetic goddesses, such as the Fates in Greek and Norns in Scandinavian mythology. In 'The Disquieting Muses', the inescapable presence of the weird dummies suggests they influence the speaker's destiny: 'And nod and nod at foot and head'; 'Nodding by night around my bed'; 'They stand their vigil in gowns of stone' (*CP* 75–76). The poem echoes The First Witch's prophecy to Macbeth: 'Sleep shall neither night nor day' (1.3.18). The witch warns Macbeth of the guilt, malice, and fear he will experience and the omnipresent company the witches will keep him. In the poem, the speaker not only holds the mother accountable for bringing the curse on her but also blames her for not getting rid of the weird women.

Clark quotes Aurelia Plath who said in an interview that Plath's emotionally charged enunciation of the line 'Mother, mother' at the BBC radio reading of 'The Disquieting Muses' particularly hurt her (*Red Comet* 519). Although Plath kept her tone detached from the poetic speaker, her mother felt the blame. There is a similar repetition of calling out mother in Plath's early prose piece titled 'Sarah', written in 1948, a composite sketch about her childhood: '"Mother! Mother!" she shouted jubilantly as she raced from room to room, searching. The figure of a woman detached itself from the shadows in the hall and glided towards the child' (*Prose* 32). In this early short story, Plath associates calling out to the mother with shadowy darkness, suggesting the ambiguities of her presence. Towards the end of her narrative, Sarah's mother informs her daughter that her father cut his leg during wood chopping – reimagining Otto Plath's medical surgery – which results in her mother needing her daughter: '"You just can't leave me now, Sary," whined the older woman. And Sarah was never to forget her mother's accusing eyes' (*Prose* 33). Plath's early writing gives an account of her experience of her maternal relationship as suffocating and overbearing, almost like the supernatural power and haunting presence of the witches, which she further developed in 'The Disquieting Muses'.

While the speaker detaches the dummies from the mother, they replace her as 'traveling companions', implying that their presence is inescapable; thus, they also influence the speaker's fate. 'The Disquieting Muses' expresses the influence of the witches in Plath's portrayal of weird dummies who appear along with the mother. The mother figure in the poem recalls Lady Macbeth's ambivalent attitude towards motherhood as she expresses her care for her child and, at the same time, she fantasises about killing the baby. Plath's poem seeks inspiration from supernatural female figures from different literary and mythological sources to represent her ambiguous feelings about her mother by merging witches, the Weird Sisters, and the imagery of fairy tales. She builds on the prophetic power of the Weird Sisters and their spiritual form, making the dummies haunting and inescapable. 'The Disquieting Muses' prefigures the curse or misfortune associated with the maternal line, which often haunts Plath's poetic speakers.

Plath's two other poems 'All the Dead Dears' and 'The Lady and the Earthenware Head' show a more subtle influence of *Macbeth*'s witches than 'The Disquieting Muses'. The poems portray spectral female figures whose powers lie in their inescapable and ominous presence. While the former poem depicts maternal hags, who haunt the speaker, 'The Lady and the Earthenware Head' describes a sinister hag-head whose paralysing vision evokes Medusa and the prophetic 'vision' of the witches. 'All the Dead Dears' starts with a small note after the title, informing the reader that the poem was inspired by a '*coffin of the fourth century A. D. containing the skeleton of a woman, mouse and shrew*' exhibited at the Museum of Archaeology and Anthropology in Cambridge (*CP* 70). Di Beddow further suggests the poem's origin in the topography of the city: 'The coffin was found in 1952 when a housing estate was being built in the north of Cambridge [. . .] In 2012, the museum was reopened after refurbishment and the skeleton was put back on display' (56). Plath wrote the three poems I described about the haunting female figures in Cambridge where she also revisited *Macbeth*, suggesting a connection between the place and the play that inspired her writing.

In addition to reimaging the archaeological remains as the haunting maternal hag figures, 'All the Dead Dears' blends the familiar (as the familial) and the unfamiliar to create an uncanny and eerie effect. The poem includes six sestinas with a shorter second line (except in the fourth stanza) and a varied rhyme scheme. As the title anticipates, the poem is filled with long vowels, which have eerie and lingering power, reinforcing the spectral presence of the dead. Plath uses the repetition of *k*, *g*, and *t* sounds to create a threatening acoustic effect. In the first stanza, the speaker describes the remains of the bodies as watchful witnesses of the living. She calls the skeleton of a woman a 'lady': a similar identification to the weird dummies in 'The Disquieting Muses'. The speaker reimagines the relics as her maternal ancestors whom she perceives as haunting hags. They bring bad luck to the speaker, similar to *Macbeth*'s Weird Sisters, and have sinister and prophetic powers. From the third stanza, the descriptive narrative turns to the speaker's inner life; she compares the skeleton to her maternal ancestor. She projects her inner fears onto the relic, yet the poetic voice remains distant. For the speaker, the ancient female body and the two other objects personify her hag-like maternal ancestors:

> These barnacle dead!
> This lady here's no kin
> Of mine, yet kin she is: she'll suck
> Blood and whistle my marrow clean
> To prove it. As I think now of her head,
> From the mercury-backed glass
> Mother, grandmother, greatgrandmother
> Reach hag hands to haul me in, (*CP* 70–71).

The maternal hags, like the dummies in 'The Disquieting Muses' and *Macbeth*'s Weird Sisters, have an ominous power over the speaker's fate. The internal rhymes reinforce the inescapable bond between the speaker and the maternal ancestors, such as 'barnacle dead' / 'her head' / 'Reach hag'. The alliteration of the *h* sound in the poem ('hag hands to haul me in') further implies the haunting presence of the female figures. Like the witches from *Macbeth*, they manifest in metaphysical form and embody maternal malice. Plath's poem also recalls the appearance of Banquo's ghost who haunts Macbeth. He addresses the ghost: 'Thy bones are marrowless, thy blood is cold; / Thou hast no speculation in those eyes' (3.4.94–95). Both Macbeth and Plath's speaker in 'All the Dead Dears' associate marrow and blood with the dead who come back and haunt the living.

In the poem, the maternal ancestors appear as a female trio: 'Mother, grandmother, greatgrandmother', suggesting that they are an antithesis of the Holy Trinity, like the Weird Sisters and other sinister female trios. An earlier version of the poem was part of her *Two Lovers and a Beachcomber* unpublished collection, a copy of which is kept in the Al Alvarez Papers in the British Library, where Plath only names the first two maternal figures, leaving out the eldest of the maternal hags. The alteration to the three generations of maternal ancestors in the final version of the poem highlights Plath's awareness of the symbolic power of the three and allusion to literary and mythological female trios that also served as poetic inspiration for 'The Disquieting Muses'. Plath's reference to her ancestors as 'These barnacle dead!', the only exclamation point in the poem, further suggests the overpowering and blood-sucking maternal presence. The metaphor of the barnacle reappears in her 1962 poem 'Medusa', which narrates her ambiguous feelings about her mother. Here, the barnacle signifies the controlling maternal bond: 'Old barnacled umbilicus, Atlantic cable' (*CP* 225). The metaphor is particularly compelling since barnacles have both female and male sexual organs; they are sexually ambiguous. Their sexual ambiguity makes them similar to the witches from *Macbeth* whose gender is questioned by Banquo. The witches represent borderlands between male and female, earthly and supernatural, and evil and good (Purkiss 211). Plath's reimagination of the ancient relics as maternal hags, spectral ladies, and barnacle corresponds to the ambiguous and haunting characteristics of the Weird Sisters.

The maternal ancestors drift in the borders of the physical and the spectral realm. In the fifth stanza, the speaker highlights their ghost-like presence who return to her: 'All the long gone darlings: they / Get back, though soon' (*CP* 71). The shift from 'hags' to 'darlings' highlights the speaker's uncertainty towards her maternal kin. It likewise alludes to Macduff's cry from *Macbeth* 'All my pretty ones?' (4.3.218), addressing the murder of his family. I discuss the influence of the line in Sexton's poetry collection in a later section on post-war poets. In 'All the Dead Dears', Plath does not depict the maternal ancestors explicitly as evil; however, the speaker's ambiguous description shows an uneasiness in their kinship. She portrays the feeling of being cursed, which she links to the maternal ancestors who appear in hag-like shapes.

'All the Dead Dears' is also the title of a short story, the only double-title among Plath's writings. Plath wrote the short story a year earlier in the autumn of 1956, which was influenced by anecdotes of dead ancestors in the Hughes family and set in the eerie Yorkshire landscape. Plath frequently makes a connection between the English countryside, such as 'The Lucky Stone' and the haunting setting of *Macbeth* and its witches. There are some linguistic resemblances to the poem 'All the Dead Dears' and the short story in which Dora, Plath's alter ego, asks about the ghostly relatives:

> 'Not ghosts, exactly Dora,' Neillie Meehan said quietly, modest and reserved as always about her strange gift, 'but *presences* [. . .]'
>
> [. . .]
>
> For a minute she stood in the doorway, gazing after those two figures vanished in the dark, feeling a cold more deadly than any knife strike to the marrow of her bones. (*Prose* 311)

Plath's short story and poem express a shared view of the haunting presence of ancestors associated with eerie landscapes and objects. While the short story distances Plath from the narrative, in the poem, she repurposes ideas and themes to reflect on her own family, particularly her maternal line. In the poems 'All the Dead Dears' and 'The Disquieting Muses', Plath's imagery demonstrates a similar interpretation of *Macbeth*'s witches who appear as shapeless metaphysical female figures. Plath draws on their spiritual form and association with prophetic powers, which make them more than just witches, emphasising their mythological origin.

In Plath's 'The Lady and the Earthenware Head', written in 1957, she associates the hag figure with sinister supernatural power who haunts the speaker. The earthenware head in the poem is based on an actual clay head sculpted by Mary Derr, Plath's peer at Smith College, representing Plath herself (Golden, *Annotating Modernism* 34). Beddow notes that Plath brought the head with her to Cambridge and 'was tempted with giving it a grave in the river, but she rejected this because she felt that it would call to her from "watery aspic," like the sirens in the Lorelei legend' (56). Like 'All the Dead Dears', 'The Lady and the Earthenware Head' was inspired by an archaeological relic that Plath reimagined as an object possessing supernatural powers. They both project the haunting and inescapable presence of ghostly objects to the landscape of Cambridge. In her journals, she noted that her poem draws on 'the compelling mystic aura of a sacred object, a terrible and holy token of identity sucking into itself magnet wise the farflung words which link & fuse to make up my own queer & grotesque world' (*J* 332). Plath's description associates the evil and inescapable powers with the head whose presence haunts her poetic imagination. Ted Hughes wrote a poem with a similar title 'The Earthenware Head' in *Birthday Letters* in which he relies on the head's association with malicious supernatural powers: 'You did not want to fear, if it had gone, / What witchcraft might ponder it' (*BL* 58). Katherine Robinson notes that 'The Lady and the Earthenware Head' 'eschews the word "double," but Hughes's poem does not. It makes explicit, too, the fears fueling Plath's poem' (174). While Hughes's poetic response associates the earthenware head with his memory of Plath, the item remains a haunting and magical object of the poetic imagination, just like the maternal hag figures for Plath.

In 'The Lady and the Earthenware Head', Plath uses Shakespearean allusions in portraying the 'antique hag-head' (*CP* 70). It is inescapable and sinister with an overpowering presence similar to the witches. Plath treats the earthenware head as a sinister hag figure, suggesting that she considers it a representation of the haunting maternal presence, similar to the dummies and the skeleton lady. Her poem likewise evokes the mythological figure of Medusa and her petrifying power in the representation of the head's evil look. By drawing attention to the head's sinister vision, Plath implies its prophetic ability, which recalls the Weird Sisters' 'fatal vision' (2.1.35). The poem also alludes to the witches' brewing scene in *Macbeth*, in which the first apparition is an armed Head who has an eerie presence and prophetic powers, similar to Plath's earthenware head. At the end of the play, Macduff also calls Macbeth's head 'Th'usurper's cursed head' (5.9.22). It is a dramatic evocation of Medusa's slain head (Garber 135). In her copy of *Macbeth*, Plath underlined the line referring to Macbeth's head (*SP Complete Shakespeare* 1212). Marjorie Garber's analysis of the links between *Macbeth* and Medusa demonstrates the merger of literary and mythological witches that Plath draws on in her portrayal of the sinister hag-head.

Similar to 'All the Dead Dears,' 'The Lady and the Earthenware Head' is characterised by varied line length and expressive punctuation. The 'head' both literally and figuratively haunts the poem. It is mentioned five times, changing from a model, a captivating object, to a replica, and finally to an 'antique hag-head' (*CP* 69–70). The descriptions suggest a gradual development from a mundane object to a head with evil supernatural powers. By naming it a 'hag-head', Plath creates an association between the object and witch figures, particularly maternal hags whom she also referenced in 'All the Dead Dears'. She employs mythological (Medusa, Norns, Fates) and literary (*Macbeth*'s Weird Sisters) female figures to express the head's controlling and ominous presence. The poem brings attention to the eye of the head, whose vision is eerie, which anticipates its inescapable presence that brings bad luck. The speaker describes the owner's fantasy of getting rid of the head. She calls the piece an 'effigy', 'coarse copy', and 'mimic' head, resembling an object employed in sympathetic magic in which resemblance or contact to the person or thing one wants to perform magic on is key. Similar to 'The Disquieting Muses' and 'All the Dead Dears', the head comes alive in the speaker's imagination, which argues that it possesses sinister powers associated with female supernatural figures. Further, in 'All the Dead Dears', Plath's speaker brings attention to the skeleton's head: 'As I think now of her head, From the mercury-backed glass' (*CP* 70). The head triggers the speaker's association of the ancient relic with the maternal hags, which shows the connection to 'The Lady and the Earthenware Head'. The head represents a malicious maternal presence influenced by the literary and mythological figures of Medusa, prophetic goddesses, the Weird Sisters, and other hag figures.

Plath transcribed a draft of the poem to her mother in a letter sent in February 1957. During the early stage of her career, Plath regularly sent poems to her mother, as a critic, a role Hughes would play later in her career (Hammer, 'Plath's Lives' 70–71). Her mother's authority over her writing – which Plath later protested in her journals – suggests a similar inescapable connection that the speaker feels towards the clay head. In the draft, the third stanza is more expressive of the head's association with witchcraft:

> In old wives' tales of bond
> Knitting to each original its coarse copy
> (Woe if enemies, in wrath,
> Take to sticking pins through wax!) – felt loath
> To junk it. Scared, unhappy. (*L2* 67)

In this stanza, there are multiple and varied references to witchcraft, such as the wax image, 'dented caricature', alluding to its haggish look, and 'old wives' tales', recalling folkloric maternal figures, who create the 'coarse copy' to perform *maleficium.* The allusion to sympathetic magic – sticking the needles through the wax figure – accentuates the supernatural power of the head. Plath's imagery of the wax figure foreshadows the 'wax image' in 'Witch Burning' and the deployment of the photograph in 'Daddy', which I return to in Chapter 5. The draft further expresses the inescapable presence of the earthenware head, which embodies haunting and malicious powers and is explicitly associated with witches. Plath toned down the references to historical beliefs about witchcraft in the final version of the poem, which implies an erasure of the association between maternal figures and the haggish head. Instead, she focuses on the object as an individual entity that haunts the speaker and brings misfortune. Such alteration or deletion is common in her writing process during which she erased significant evidence of her knowledge of witchcraft beliefs and engagement with the supernatural.

In the final stanza of the poem, the speaker names the head an 'antique hag-head' and explicitly attributes Medusa-like qualities to it:

> Despite her wrung hands, her tears, her praying: Vanish!
> [. . .]
> An antique hag-head, too tough for knife to finish,
> Refusing to diminish
> By one jot its basilisk-look of love. (CP 70)

The internal rhymes of 'basilisk', 'finish', 'vanish', and 'diminish' reinforce the head's inescapable vision. The only exclamation mark in 'The Lady and the Earthenware Head' is the shriek, which reads as a performative line, alluding to the power of spoken words, such as wanting to exorcise the evil spirits from the head. The sentence resembles the ending of 'Medusa': 'Off, off, eely tentacle!' (*CP* 226).[3] In both poems, Plath recalls the incapacitating vision of the Gorgon ('basilisk-look of love'), which paralyses the speaker. The speaker's command also echoes Macbeth's lines from the play: 'With such prophetic greeting? Speak, I charge you. / *Witches vanish* / [. . .] Into the air, and what seemed corporal' (1.376–79). Here, Macbeth demands to know the Weird Sisters' prophecy, but they vanish into the air, which shows their spiritual being. Plath's poem evokes a similar effect of the head: while it is made of dense material

[3] The drafts of 'Medusa ' initially included several exclamation marks, which later Plath crossed out.

(earthenware), she wants the head to diminish, which reminds us of *Macbeth*'s witches. In the play, Banquo suggests that the Weird Sisters possibly originate from the earth: 'The earth hath bubbles, as the water has, / And these are of them. Whither are they vanished?' (1.3.77–78). Even though they come out of earth, they are able to just vanish. 'The Lady and the Earthenware Head' understands the head as an embodiment of spiritual evil that seeks inspiration from *Macbeth*'s witches, maternal hags, and mythological figures, whose paralysing vision, ability to foresee and influence the speaker's destiny, and inescapable presence haunt the poetic persona.

Plath's 'The Disquieting Muses', 'All the Dead Dears', and 'The Lady and the Earthenware Head' demonstrate the influence of *Macbeth*'s Weird Sisters and other supernatural female figures who manifest as shapeless dummies, hag-like maternal ancestors, and an ominous hag-head. While the former shows the direct influence of the Shakespearean witches to portray ambiguous attitudes towards the mother, in 'All the Dead Dears', Plath references the three supernatural female figures by identifying the maternal ancestors with the haunting power of hag figures. In 'The Lady and the Earthenware Head', which Plath wrote first among the three poems, the relic materialises as a powerful hag-head whose sinister and paralysing vision and ominous presence build on elements from mythological and literary female supernatural figures.

Parallel to Plath, other post-war American poets, such as Anne Sexton and John Ashbery, were also influenced by *Macbeth*'s Weird Sisters, demonstrating the profound impact of the witches' curse on the imagination of poets as defining characters of ill-fate and embodiment of inescapable darkness. *Macbeth* was also adapted several times, both in theatre and on screen, in post-war America: Margaret Webster's aforementioned influential production shows that the metaphysical darkness the witches embodied was foregrounded in adaptations. There were several television and film adaptations produced, such as the 1948 film *Macbeth* directed by Orson Welles. Even in 1949, Coca-Cola launched a magazine advertisement featuring the *Complete Works of William Shakespeare* with a slogan that drew parallels between the quality of the drink and the canonical author. Thus, the reception of the play in post-war American culture was mixed, bridging popular culture and high-brow art. The witches from *Macbeth* were regarded as significant characters of Shakespeare's stories who represented inner turmoil, darkness, misfortune, and the haunting past.

Similar to 'The Disquieting Muses', Ashbery's three-part poem 'The Picture of Little J. A. in a Prospect of Flowers, from Some Trees' (1956) evokes *Macbeth*'s witches in reminiscing about his childhood. While Ashbery was part of the 'New York School' of post-war poets (Epstein 3), and Plath is identified with the Boston circle, their poems share similarities in theme and influence. In his poem, the witches also represent the haunting past:

> Darkness falls like a wet sponge
> And Dick gives Genevieve a swift punch
> In the pajamas. 'Aroint thee, witch.'
> Her tongue from previous ecstasy
> Releases thoughts like little hats. (12)

The stanza directly quotes from Act 1 Scene 3 where the First Witch says: 'A sailor's wife had chestnuts in her lap / And munched, and munched, and munched. "Give me," quoth I. / "Aroint thee, witch," the rump-fed runnion cries"' (1.3.3–5). In the quotation, the witch claims that she was rejected for alms. During the witch-hunt period, refusing beggars often led to witch accusations due to fear of being cursed by them (Macfarlane xiv; 76). Ashbery's poem alludes to this scene to warn against the loss of childhood, which he calls 'a white world' in which 'as dirty handmaidens / To some transparent witch' dreams of goodness but 'That beggar to whom you gave no cent / Striped the night with his strange descant' (13). The lines suggest that bad deeds have consequences like a curse, which he employs to make sense of the dullness and darkness of life. Paralleling Plath's employment of the maternal curse, his allusion to the witches' curse implies the inescapability of memories: 'Yet I cannot escape the picture / Of my small self in that bank' (13). Ashbery opposes dark adulthood that 'falls like a wet sponge' with the goodness of childhood as 'mere memory', which recalls the contrasting imagery of Plath's 'The Disquieting Muses'. His poem employs the static imagery of flowers and picturesque childhood 'to freeze experience' (Epstein 242). Helen Vendler notes that Ashbery's poetic abstraction was influenced by painters, like Fairfield Porter's domestic idealism and Giorgio de Chirico's surrealism ('Ashbery's Aesthetic' 81–82), suggesting another resemblance to Plath's 'The Disquieting Muses', influenced by de Chirico's painting bearing the same title. Both Plath and Ashbery rely on an understanding of the witches as metaphysical and abstract embodiments of darkness.

While Plath was university educated like Ashbery, and thus encountered Shakespeare's play in her education, Anne Sexton did not have any formal education, yet *Macbeth* likewise influenced her. Sexton's poetry book *All My Pretty Ones*, published in 1962, borrows the line from *Macbeth*. Sexton recounted the choice of title as almost accidental: a friend paraphrased Shakespeare after learning about the death of Sexton's parents, who then went to look for the quote in *Macbeth* and 'knew the source of her title' (Golden, *Annotating Modernism* 135). Plath owned a copy of Sexton's poetry book, which is kept in the SCSC . The title poem narrates Sexton's experience of her parents' death: 'This is the yellow scrapbook that you began / the year I was born; as crackling now and wrinkly / as tobacco leaves: clippings where Hoover outran / the Democrats' (50). The poem contextualises her memories of her father in the politics of post-war America. 'All My Pretty Ones' reimagines the prophetic lines in the past, alluding to the diaries' of her father about his 'hurly-burly years' (51). She alludes to the Second Witch's lines from the beginning of the play in which the Weird Sisters discuss Macbeth's fate 'When the hurly-burly's done, / When the battle's lost, and won' (1.1.3–4). Sexton seeks inspiration from *Macbeth* to reflect on grief. It offers a different angle to Plath's and Ashbery's poems by referencing Macduff's speech.

The post-war poets share poetic allusions to *Macbeth*, reflecting on childhood memories, parental relationships, and death. Plath's portrayal of sinister maternal figures was influenced by the witches who have an inescapable spiritual presence and control the speaker's fate. They are a poetic embodiment of the haunting maternal curse.

3.2 Paternal Knowledge and Magical Power

Plath's first theatre experience was *The Tempest* in 1945, which she saw in Boston; Aurelia Plath insisted that her children read the play before going to the theatre (Wagner-Martin 37). The performance was a try-out of Margaret Webster's production in the Colonial Theatre, Boston, which was later performed on Broadway (Barranger 158). Like her production of *Macbeth*, staging *The Tempest* was also influential in communicating contemporary understanding of Shakespeare's play in post-war America. Webster's staging was the first performance of the play where Caliban was performed by an African American actor, Canada Lee, who 'wore a scaly costume and grotesque mask, [and] moved with an animal-like crouch' (Vaughan 402). This points towards the increased postcolonial reading of the play. *The Tempest* continued to play a significant role in Plath's life: at Cambridge, she participated for a short while in a drama club where she played Miranda in a reading of *The Tempest* (*L1* 997). In her poems, she regularly positions her speaker as the daughter figure of the Prospero-like father, which she contrasts with the maternal inescapability embodied in monstrous and weird supernatural female figures. The comparison between Plath and Miranda is reinforced in Ted Hughes's poem 'Setebos' published in *Birthday Letters*: 'Who could play Miranda? / Only you. Ferdinand – only me' (*BL* 132). Controversially, in his poem, Prospero is embodied by Aurelia Plath who was 'flying her magic in / To stage the Masque, and bless the marriage' (*BL* 132). Hughes suggests Aurelia's maternal control over her daughter. 'Setebos' echoes 'work by Plath, this again figures Shakespeare, in what is probably the most peculiar way even in Hughes's work' (N. Corcoran 233). For Plath, Prospero represents the educated and powerful father figure who uses his scholarly knowledge – magic – as control. Her portrayal of her father Otto Plath, biology professor-beekeeper, is similar to the figure of the early modern magician. *The Tempest* shaped Plath's association of paternal knowledge with male magical power and mythological sea deities present in, for example, 'Full Fathom Five'.

In *The Tempest*, Prospero tells the audience that he was a scholar of the 'liberal arts' before his exile (1.273). His strong connection to his books suggests that he learnt his magic from books that are 'crucial to his rule over the island' (Mowat 1). Caliban recognises that Prospero depends on his magic books for his power and wants to take them. The postcolonial reading of *The Tempest* positions Prospero as the embodiment of patriarchal imperial power who restricts access to knowledge to maintain his dominant position. In Plath's writings, the Prosperoean father figure's inaccessible knowledge is a recurring theme. In Act 5, Scene 1 of the play, Prospero renounces his magic and says he will drown his book, which recalls the act of a seventeenth-century magus, who could abandon his craft due to the changing hostile environment and association of magic with diabolism (Peters 176). Prospero's power is often compared to 'white magic', which is protective 'in the sense of preventing some misfortune from occurring or warding off some evil spirit or witch' (Levack, *The Witch-Hunt* 6). Frank Kermode's influential introduction for the Arden edition published in 1954 named Prospero a theurgist; he argues that his magic compares to 'the disciplined exercise of virtuous knowledge' (xlvii). By the mid-twentieth century, Prospero's magic was understood as white or Neo-Platonic (Gibson, *Rediscovering Renaissance Witchcraft* 33). Plath draws on this interpretation and portrays the father as an intellectual figure who uses his knowledge to control, similar to magical power. She associates Prospero with Otto Plath based on her childhood memories, in which the father emerges as an idealised and dominant but often ambiguous figure. Prospero's magic compares to her father's beekeeping; they both signify scholarly knowledge and paternal control, to which others, like his daughter, do not have access.

Otto Plath was a biology professor at Boston University. His book *Bumblebees and Their Ways* (1934) was considered ground-breaking; some of his colleagues even called him by the German name *Bienen-König*, meaning 'bee king' (Clark, *Red Comet* 18). The term demonstrates Otto Plath's respected place within the field. In his book, Plath elaborates on his scientific journey, which started when he was a child. He discusses several of his experiences with bees, some of which became themes in his daughter's bee poems, such as observing the habitat of the queen bee, the process of re-queening in the bumblebee colony, being stung by the bees, and transferring them into wooden boxes (O. Plath 1; 13; 72; 97). Otto Plath's self-presentation as a scientist, an observer of the bees, and a beekeeper suggests his hierarchical relationship with the bees. Although Sylvia Plath respected her father's profession, later in her life, this became increasingly associated with patriarchal authoritarianism (Clark, *Red Comet* 19). Though Otto's interest in the bumblebees was genuine, his book often describes experimentations on bumblebees: 'During these past few years I have sometimes had more than fifty colonies under observation, most of which were kept on boards on shady side of a partly covered, abandoned cellar' (112). Here, the entomologist illustrates his dominance and control over the bees. In her writings, Sylvia Plath parallels her father's beekeeping and Prospero's magic based on their shared association with the scholarly knowledge of the father, dominance, and control.

Plath's 'Among the Bumblebees' (1953) centres on Alice Denway's (Plath's alter ego) relationship with her father. The short story introduces the idolised fatherly relationship; Alice worships her father 'because he was so powerful, and everybody did what he commanded' (*Prose* 191). The father's dominant presence and highly regarded knowledge recall Prospero and his use of magic. Even Ariel calls Prospero 'my commander' (4.1.167). Throughout the short story, the father is portrayed as 'a giant of a man' and 'a king, high on a throne, he would call out the names in his thundering voice', evoking Otto Plath's bee king title (*Prose* 191; 193). The girl perceives the father as fearless; he conquers a thunderstorm: 'above the resonant resounding baritone of her father's voice, the thunder rumbled harmless as a tame lion' (*Prose* 195). Plath's description of the father's ability to command the tempest recalls Prospero's powers. Alice's father is not only powerful because of his perceived ability to control and conquer the weather, but he also exerts control over the bees: '[w]ith a laugh, her father would spread his fingers wide, and the bee would fly out, free, up into the air and away' (*Prose* 195). Though Plath describes the scene from the innocence of the child's perspective, it is a cautionary description of patriarchal power, control, and lack of autonomy of other beings. In the short story, Plath compares the father's control of the bee to Prospero's control of Ariel. The parallel is particularly compelling since Ariel compares himself to bees: 'Where the bee sucks, there suck I; / [...] Merrily, merrily shall I live now' (5.1.88; 93). In 'Among the Bumblebees', the father dies, which causes Alice's disillusionment in his power and dominant position, just like Prospero became vulnerable at the end of the play by renouncing his magic book – his knowledge. Plath resolves her ambivalence towards her father figure by narrating the story from the child's perspective; thus, the Prosperoean father remains an idolised patriarch with his scholarly knowledge and commanding presence.

Another short story where Plath links the control of bees to her father is 'Charlie Pollard and The Beekeepers', in which she portrays her experience of beekeeping in Devon in the summer of 1962. Here, the narrator evokes the father's beekeeping against the bees, therefore seeking protection from paternal knowledge. Plath's recurring association suggests that she likened her father's beekeeping to Prosperoean magic, which is paradoxically a source of protection and control. The narrator, like Plath, is unprepared for the encounter: 'Then I saw, on the grass, and in hands, everybody was holding a bee-hat, some with netting of nylon, most with box screening, some with khaki round hats, I felt barer & barer' (*J* 656–57). She describes her feelings of both physical and intellectual vulnerability. To protect herself against the stinging bees, the narrator relies on the father's knowledge of beekeeping: 'I became aware I was in a bone-stiff trance, intolerably tense, and shifted round to where I could see better. "Spirit of my dead father, protect me!" I arrogantly prayed' (*J* 658). The father's evocation and invocation through prayer is a plea for spiritual safeguarding. The paternal knowledge of beekeeping functions as a supernatural power similar to the early modern learned magician that aids the narrator against malice and harm. Despite Plath's criticism of Christianity, she regarded the language of Christian prayers as powerful (*L2* 669). Plath's speaker attributes her plea to a protective function, which corresponds to the power of Catholic prayers against evil supernatural powers (Levack, *The Witch-Hunt* 118). The adjective 'arrogantly' that describes her prayer echoes the phrase in 'Among the Bumblebees' where the girl depicts the father's hierarchical relationship with the bees as arrogant. In the two short stories, Plath portrays beekeeping as a knowledge associated with the father and his dominance, akin to Prospero's magic.

Besides the short stories, some of Plath's poems also portray the father figure as similar to a magician. The first poem of the bee sequence, 'The Bee Meeting', retells the day with the beekeepers in the Devon village in which the poetic persona likens the father's knowledge of beekeeping to protective magic. In Chapter 7, I discuss in detail the poem's engagement with ideas of witchcraft beliefs. In the poem, Plath repeats the narrative of feeling unprotected against the stinging of the bees. The speaker only finds strength by evoking the father, whom she calls a magician: 'I am the magician's girl who does not flinch' (*CP* 212). In both the poem and the short story about the beekeeping experience, Plath's alter egos seek help from the father, whose scholarly knowledge functions as a protective charm against the bees. 'The Bee Meeting' is characterised by the heavy presence of white colour, which is associated with protective materials, such as a 'white straw Italian hat' (*CP* 211). The speaker attributes paternal origin to the knowledge of beekeeping, which she perceives as protective magic. Her vulnerability stems from the father who was not able to pass down his knowledge of beekeeping to his daughter. She is powerless and incapable of beekeeping; therefore, she cannot continue her father's legacy. The speaker's uneasy relationship with the bees suggests ambiguity towards the paternal knowledge of beekeeping, which both controls the bees and offers protection against them.

The daughter's lack of knowledge of the father's beekeeping is also the theme of the 1959 poem 'The Beekeeper's Daughter'. This poem is less critical of the father's control of bees; rather, the descriptions of the father figure resemble Otto Plath's 'the bee king' title as the idolised 'maestro of the bees' (*CP* 118). As in 'The Bee Meeting', in 'The Beekeeper's Daughter,' the speaker expresses her longing for the father's knowledge of beekeeping. Plath's labelling of the father as a 'maestro' and then a 'magician' gives him a Prospero-like character: he is a commander, king, and a magician who can control the symphony of the bees. 'The Beekeeper's Daughter' engages with the question of father-daughter inheritance and who has access to knowledge, in which the beekeeping stands for the father's legacy, similar to Prospero's white magic. The speaker does not control but instead fears the bees: 'My heart under your foot, sister of a stone' (*CP* 118). It indicates the unsuccessful inheritance of the father's knowledge, mimicking Miranda's lack of access to Prospero's magic. The poem directly references Otto Plath's *Bumblebees and Their Ways*, suggesting a paternal origin to Plath's poetic language. The line from the poem 'Trumpet-throats open to the beaks of birds' (*CP* 118) alludes to Otto's observation of the trumpet sound of the bumblebee. He describes it as 'the voice of a Wagnerian hammer, or the discharge electric sparks, finally like the slow roll of a drum' becomes higher pitched, then gradually stops (O. Plath 82). Otto Plath highlights that '[t]he ultimate object of the bumblebee colony is not the production of workers, but of queen and males' (25). Likewise, 'The Beekeeper's Daughter' portrays the fertility ritual of the bees, which is described as a dynasty making. 'The Beekeeper's Daughter' and 'The Bee Meeting' depict the father as physically and intellectually unreachable to the daughter. Plath references Prospero's character to depict the father as a patriarchal scholar with archaic knowledge, which the daughter perceives as his supernatural power. In her writings about the bees, beekeeping functions as a tool of control, anticipating the authoritarian father figure in 'Daddy'.

For Plath, *The Tempest* also signified her 'childhood landscape — the sea' (*L2* 928). Writing in her journal in 1958, she named the play, particularly its seascape, 'a central metaphor for my childhood, my poems and the artist's subconscious, to the father image - relating to my own father, the buried male muse & god-creator' (*J* 381). In her writings that evoke the sea imagery of *The Tempest*, the father emerges as a dominant and inaccessible figure. In the essay 'Landscape of Childhood' published previously as 'Ocean 1212-W', which Plath wrote for a radio programme for the BBC, she links her childhood seascape to her father: 'And this is how it stiffens, the vision of that seaside childhood. My father died, we moved inland' (*Prose* 622). Plath merges the childhood nostalgia of the shores of the Atlantic with the inaccessible father figure. Helle notes that in the photographic memories of Plath's childhood, the 'predominance of women, especially of small groups of women' associates the seascape with a 'convivial female world' (201–2). Yet, for Plath, the New England seascape is an embodiment of the masculine world of *The Tempest* and its father-magician. In her poetic imagination, the paternal 'myth' is created by the absence of vision, which makes the landscape of her childhood seascape 'hypercathected' (Twiddy 106). Elisabeth Bronfen notes that Plath 'repeatedly invokes the lost father as a metonymy for this lost scene of childhood bliss, with both standing in for the state of happiness whose value resides precisely in its irrecuperability' (76). In poems like 'Full Fathom Five' and 'On the Decline of Oracles', *The Tempest* functions as a literary medium through which the absent father is enlarged into the Prospero-like figure. Plath wrote both poems when she returned to Massachusetts, demonstrating the strong associations between *The Tempest* and the early colony.

Plath wrote 'Full Fathom Five' in 1958 and at the time considered it one of her best and most moving poems: in a journal entry written on

4 July 1958, she noted that the subject of her poem was 'my father-sea-god muse' (*J* 399). She initially decided to title her first poetry book, *Full Fathom Five*, before changing it to *The Colossus* the following year (*J* 381). Plath's depiction of her father in her journal alludes to a larger-than-life figure. Like Prospero, the 'sea-god', recalling both Poseidon and Neptune, also has magical powers that control the water. The title of Plath's poem is sourced from Ariel's song from *The Tempest*, in which the spirit sings to Ferdinand about his supposedly shipwrecked and drowned father. For Britzolakis, the poem mourns the archaic father-creator, suggesting that creativity is located in this grieving process and portrays the Freudian 'prehistoric' father (48–50). Peter J. Lowe attributes the poem to a 'darker tone' in which the dead father is 'not transformed, but rather buried (or sunk), only to resurface and unsettle the living' (29). The poem relies on patterns to recreate the sound of the sea, which has a haunting effect. In the first stanza, the dead father, like the waves of the sea, resurfaces into the speaker's consciousness: 'Old man, you surface seldom / Then you come in with the tide's coming' (*CP* 92). The alliteration of the *s* sound mimics the crashing waves on the shore. In 'Full Fathom Five', the father is portrayed as archaic and god-like, implying his power and omnipresent knowledge. He has 'white hair, white beard,' and he is 'The old myth of origins,' yet 'Unimaginable' (*CP* 92). The recurring white colour associated with the father, also present in 'The Bee Meeting,' suggests a pattern in Plath's poetic imagination. Whiteness evokes the magician's dominant, nevertheless protective power, highlighting the ambiguities in Plath's representation of the father as a patriarchal figure with god-like powers.

In the speaker's imagination, the father's haunting absence is like the changing of the tides, linking the Atlantic Ocean to the play. In *The Tempest*, the ebb and flow of the sea are linked to magic: in Act Five, Scene 1, Prospero references Sycorax's ability to control the tides and instructs Ariel to pursue the ebbing sea god Neptune, a metaphor for the water. Plath references the 'sea-change' from Ariel's song, suggesting that the language of mourning of the father is sourced from *The Tempest*. The poem further links the lost father figure to Prospero by alluding to his dominion: 'I walk dry on your kingdom's border' (*CP* 93). The speaker is exiled to the father's isolated kingdom, which references Prospero's banishment to an island. In the play, the island is Miranda's home where she grew up isolated and exiled. 'Full Fathom Five' makes it clear that the father's memory and dominion only exist in the speaker's psyche: 'Your shelled bed I remember / Father, this thick air is murderous. / I would breathe water' (*CP* 93). In the last tercet, the echoes in the internal rhyme give a paternal origin to life, which is associated with the sea imagery, implying the interchangeability between the body of water and the father. The 'sea-change' of the water in Plath's poem suggests the father's inaccessibility who merely exists in the psychic seascape. The speaker relies on the visual and aural memory of the sea to recreate the 'old myth of origin'. 'Full Fathom Five' portrays the father as a magician-deity with supernatural powers who can command the water and defy godhood. The allusion to *The Tempest* indicates the influence of Prospero and his powers who embodies the dominant but desired father figure.

'On the Decline of Oracles' (1958) is an ekphrastic poem inspired by Giorgio de Chirico's painting titled 'The Enigma of the Oracles' (*J* 359). This poem locates the father figure in the sea and explicitly references *The Tempest* as background material for its poetic imagery. It comprises four octaves, the same stanza form Plath used in 'The Disquieting Muses', which is also inspired by Giorgio de Chirico's art. Yet 'On the Decline of Oracles' has little connection to the painting; it is de Chirico's notes about his painting that influenced Plath (Zivley 47–48). His painting is a visual response to the Swiss painter Arnold Böcklin's 'Odysseus und Kalypso' (1883), which portrays a seascape (Greene 115). Böcklin's other painting 'The Isle of the Dead' (1880) gives visual access to the images of the sea and the father in Plath's poem (Zivley 48). Böcklin produced several versions of 'The Isle of the Dead'. Plath's journal entry references the third, paler version: '[A]n island, chunks of marble angular pale stone, set in the pale wash of a sea [. . .] A lonely island – some One buried there, or the island of all, invisible essence of air in the dank caverns of cypress boughs' (*J* 322). Plath's attentive description of the uncanny island as a burial site suggests an interpretation of the magical island in *The Tempest* as a location of paternal mourning and power. The rich visual inspirations behind 'On the Decline of Oracles' demonstrate the merger of sea deities, the Prosperoean magician, a haunting island, and the oracle figure in Plath's poetic imagination. They represent dominance, magical power, and scholarly knowledge only accessible to the patriarch figures.

In 'On the Decline of Oracles', the speaker remembers the father by looking at Böcklin's painting: with the echoes sea that '[o]ld Bocklin missed, who held a shell / To hear the sea he could not hear' (*CP* 78). Like in 'Full Fathom Five', the dead father is inaccessible to the speaker, which is represented by the echo of the uncertain sea. Sally Greene argues that in Plath's poems, the sea signifies wholeness, which the death of the father frequently disrupts; the 'speaker must thereafter rely, as Böcklin had, on a re-creation that only memory and the senses can combine to produce' (113). The seaside paintings function as a medium through which the father figure is located in the visual and aural realms of the sea. In *The Tempest*, Prospero associates their arrival to the island with the voice of the sea: 'hear the last of our sea-sorrow / Here in this island we arrived' (1.2.170–71). In both the play and Plath's poem, the aural and visual appearance of the sea signifies the origin of the father-daughter relationship, presenting the Prosperoean father as a protective yet inaccessible figure. He is associated with the high-status mythological figure of the oracle, who has Prospero-like characteristics. Britzolakis highlights that Plath's oracular father figure resembles Prospero, 'who has in his keeping a magical or prophetic power lost to an ignorant age' (62). The poem alludes to Prospero's drowning of his grimoires, expressing that the father and his knowledge are unreachable: 'He willed his books and shell away. / The books burned up, sea took the shell' (*CP* 78). The speaker did not get the father's books and oracular powers since he 'willed' them away; therefore, he guarded his knowledge from the daughter. Parallel to the bee writings, the question of father-daughter inheritance references Miranda's relationship to Prospero in which the magician controls who has access to his knowledge and art of magic. The speaker of Plath's poem finds the only legacy of her father in the 'voice' of the sea: 'But I, I keep the voices he / Set in my ear, and in my eye / The sight of those blue, unseen waves' (*CP* 78). The rhymes between 'I' and 'eye' and 'sea', 'hear', and 'ear' give visual and aural effects to the changing waves. In the second stanza, the rhyming 'waves' and 'away' further reinforce the ghostly seascape. The sea becomes the location of mourning the lost paternal relationship. Just as the voice of the sea remains an echo, the waves are also 'unseen' (*CP* 78). The poem portrays the father as paradoxically both present and absent. His possessions are abandoned – however, desired by the speaker – which resembles Prospero's renunciation of his magic books in *The Tempest.*

Plath's next poem about the powerful father figure is 'The Colossus', written in 1959; the title poem of her first collection. In this breakthrough poem, Plath uses a cinquain structure and mythological references to depict the father as an ancient and inaccessible figure. 'The Colossus' parallels 'On the Decline of Oracles' and 'Full Fathom Five' in alluding to the cypress trees, oracles, whiteness, and the mourning of the father. Clark notes that Plath 'incorporates elements of *The Tempest*, *Robinson Crusoe*, and *Gulliver's Travels*' in her 'angry yet tender paternal elegy' (*Red Comet* 576). In 'The Colossus', the speaker's tone expresses blame and resentment towards him who is not an idolised figure anymore. In 'The Colossus', Plath returns to the oracle figure to position the father as a possessor of archaic knowledge: 'Perhaps you consider yourself an oracle, / Mouthpiece of the dead, or of some god or other' (*CP* 129). The daughter blames the father for his dominance and control of knowledge: no matter how much she 'labored' she is 'none the wiser' (*CP* 129). While 'Full Fathom Five' makes a parallel between the father and the ebbing water, in 'The Colossus', he is compared to a Roman Forum, suggesting his presence in the past and patriarchal rule. While Plath moves from the imagery of the aquatic surface to land, in both cases, there is a physical and visual inaccessibility associated with dominance and hierarchy. 'The Colossus' is a 'metaphorical rejection of all Fathers and their monumental authority. Plath mocks patriarchal tradition, which she cannot or will not master' (Clark, *Red Comet* 576). The poem foreshadows Plath's anger expressed in her later poems like 'Daddy': 'No longer do I listen for the scrape of a keel / On the blank stones of the landing' (*CP* 130). She voices her ambiguous perception of the patriarchal father similar to Prospero, whose supernatural powers and mythical origin make him a colossal figure in the speaker's imagination. Despite his death, his presence remains dominant and his knowledge and legacy are inaccessible. In the poems influenced by *The Tempest*, Plath contemplates her relationship with her father and the ambiguities of paternal inheritance. The father figure is physically unreachable but metaphysically inescapable, which creates a tension that climaxes in 'Daddy'. The Prosperoean father is a source of security in Plath's water poems, yet his archaic, patriarchal, and scholarly knowledge indicates his power and authority. *The Tempest*'s magician functions as a poetic inspiration for Plath to portray the dominant and unreachable father figure. As Prospero does away with his books, Plath drowns the paternal relationship in the sea.

Plath's depiction of the Shakespearean magician and witches suggests a binary and gendered understanding of supernatural characters and their powers that correspond to maternal and paternal figures. Her representation of maternal witches who often carry an evil spiritual presence seeks inspiration from *Macbeth*'s portrayal of the Weird Sisters. She likewise brings the trio into parallel with other weird supernatural female figures, such as the three Fates, the shapeless dummies, and maternal hags, demonstrating her knowledge of literary and mythological women and their magical powers. Her allusions to the Weird Sisters build on their spiritual form, paralysing appearance, and prophetic power that signify the inescapable maternal presence, which her speakers perceive as a curse.

References to *Macbeth* in the works of other post-war poets highlight the significant association of the play and its witches with memory and grief. In contrast to the haunting maternal figures, for Plath, *The Tempest* simultaneously has literary and personal significance, associating it with poetic inspiration, the dead father, and her childhood. She associates Prosperoean father figure with the protective power of white magic, scholarly knowledge, and patriarchal control. These paradoxical ideas can coexist, which shows the ambiguities of the father's power and the various interpretations of white magic. *The Tempest* is not only a metaphor for Plath's childhood seascape, but there is a larger historical parallel and colonial connotation of the magic island and the Massachusetts Bay Colony, to which Webster's production also alluded. In Plath's psychic and poetic realms, the haunting shores of the Atlantic become one with the loss of paternal knowledge and power. Although Plath employs less expressive supernatural imagery regarding the father, his scholarly knowledge of beekeeping, control and protection, and connection to the sea make him a larger-than-life figure who resembles the white magician. Plath's depictions of Shakespearean witches and the magician give an account of her ambiguous feelings towards her parental relationships and her complex understanding of the intersections between gender, magic, and power.

CHAPTER 4

Doctor Faustus and Demonology in Post-War America

Sylvia Plath's understanding of the binaries between white and black magic originates from early modern plays, such as Shakespeare's *The Tempest* and Marlowe's *Doctor Faustus.* Faustus and Prospero are the two most well-known magicians from Elizabethan stage writing, and Shakespeare likely used some of Marlowe's themes in his plays (Sawyer 42). In some respects, Doctor Faustus and Prospero are opposites, standing for the diabolical and the benevolent magician, yet they share many similarities in their art of magic; for example, they value the knowledge that comes from their magic book. The magicians also differ in their attitudes towards magic: Faustus desires magic for power, while Prospero is more concerned with using magic for 'moral' purposes (Logan 200–201; 208). During the nineteenth century, the Faust legend was adapted in Goethe's two-part tragic play *Faust* (1808, 1832), giving a romantic interpretation to the necromancer-scientist who sold his soul to the Devil for knowledge and access to magical powers. References to the Faustian plays are prominent in Plath's juvenilia, in which she alludes to the sexualised demon (succubus) when exploring the dark sides of romantic relationships.

In addition to Plath's direct engagement with the literary representation of demons and devils, she was familiar with the concepts of demonology, diabolism, and the Faustian bargain used in popular psychoanalytic and political discourses. In Freud's writings, references to diabolism describe the oppressive father, which influenced Plath and her contemporaries, such as John Berryman and Anne Sexton, in their depiction of ambiguous paternal figures. Berryman's style shaped confessional poets like Robert Lowell and Sexton. Golden notes that 'Berryman's and Plath's academic careers intersected during the summer of 1954 at Harvard University', while Berryman was teaching and Plath was studying there, though they did not meet (*Annotating Modernism* 91). Berryman's breakthrough poetry book *77 Dream Songs* (1964) won the 1965 Pulitzer Prize for Poetry; it centres on his poetic alter ego and narrates alienation, depression, and his father's suicide, which he follows up in *Love & Fame* (1970). I discuss in this chapter Berryman's poems in relation to the psychoanalytical understanding of demonic possession. I also pay attention to some of Sexton's posthumously published poems, which likewise reimagine demonic possession as a gendered and domineering interpersonal bond. I read these poems in conversation with Plath's works, such as 'Daddy'.

In her mature writings, Plath's allusions to diabolism and demons demonstrate her knowledge of the diabolical rhetoric used in post-war politics. Poets like Karl Shapiro, Allen Ginsberg, John Berryman, and Edith Sitwell equally employed the Faust legend and the vocabulary of black magic to identify the Third Reich with the Devil's work and reflect on the immoral and sinister politics, which then Plath mirrored in her poetry. Ginsberg even argued that the political apocalypse of the Cold War is like black magic, which can only be conquered with white magic (Hungerford 41). Thus, Plath's employment of diabolical imagery that critiques authoritarian Nazi politics, which has often been at the forefront of criticising her depiction of the Holocaust, is not an isolated phenomenon: she builds on poetic traditions and political discourses of the era. While Plath's poetry, personal writing, and sections of *The Bell Jar* are the focus of this chapter, I also look at the broader discourses of post-war politics in which poetics on diabolism and the rhetoric of the Faustian bargain emerge. Reading Plath's prose and poetry in conversation with mid-century poets who utilised such powerful and emotive supernatural expressions shows the wide-ranging influence of *Doctor Faustus* and demonology in the post-war era and the Atomic Age.

Whereas Marlowe's *Doctor Faustus* portrays early modern beliefs about the diabolical magician and the Devil, inspired by the German Faust legend, Goethe's *Faust* is a vital literary work in European literature, representing diabolism and engaging with the question of redemption. Although Marlowe's and Goethe's plays present different adaptations of the legend, they both were influential for Plath. She read *Faust* in November 1955 and *Doctor Faustus* in March 1956, writing to her friend that she was 'mourning Faustus trying to leap up to his god' (*L1* 1013; 1130). Plath took the module 'German 12 Intermediate' at Smith College, where she studied Goethe (Steinberg, 'Smith College 1954–1955'). Aurelia Plath, who often read canonical literature to her children, also wrote part of her thesis on *Faust* at Boston University (Christodoulides 247). In spring 1958, Hughes was teaching *Faust* at the University of Massachusetts, Amherst, in his Great Books course where he likely used Plath's copy of Goethe's play since they already shared a copy of *Crime and*

Punishment, which they both annotated (Golden, *Annotating Modernism* 178–79; 190). Plath further gained insight into the Faust legend, demonology, and conjuration, which are central themes in both plays, by studying them at the University of Cambridge, particularly for her Tragedy Paper, discussed in Chapter 3. Marlowe's play portrays early modern beliefs on black magic performed by Faustus and Mephistopheles. In *Doctor Faustus*, the demon's name is spelt as Mephostophilis, however, I refer to him with the commonly accepted spelling of the character. Faustus first conjures the demon with an incantation from his magic book: 'Faustus, begin thine incantations, / And try if devils will obey thy hest' (A 3.5–6). He draws a circle in which Mephistopheles appears, first in the shape of a friar, and then Faustus makes a pact with him. The pair perform necromancy, the dark magic of communicating with the dead or raising their spirit, during which Mephistopheles summons Helen of Troy who appears as a succubus, a female erotic demon (Kiessling 206). In Scene 12, the kiss between Faustus and Helen suggests a sexual encounter with the demon, which was considered a sin among Catholics (Levack, *The Devil Within* 164). Plath's encounter with *Doctor Faustus* was formative in her understanding of the Faust legend, early modern demonology, and the ways in which devils and demons were referenced in politics and culture of the post-war era.

Plath's copies of *Doctor Faustus* and *Faust* are kept in university archives and they are filled with her annotations, demonstrating her well-equipped knowledge of the plays and her interest in the themes of the Faust legend. While no scholarly work has previously explored Plath's annotations in these books, Diane Ackerman's poem 'On Looking into Sylvia Plath's Copy of Goethe's Faust' (1998), alluding to Plath's 'On Looking into the Eyes of a Demon Lover' poem, suggests a prominent literary connection between Plath and *Faust*. The poem reflects on the haunting presence of the archives, exploring Plath's annotations of the book: 'Your underlined 'jugglery of flame' / with ink sinewy and black as an ocelot'; 'keen for Faust's appetite, not Helen's beauty' (Ackerman 175). Ackerman finishes the poem with a psychoanalytical interpretation of demonology: 'But you were your own demonology, / balancing terror's knife on one finger, / until you numbed, and the edge fell free' (175). The poem emphasises the links between Plath and *Faust*, in which Plath gets her redemption. Plath's copy of *Faust* held at Penn State University was displayed as part of their 'The Secret Lives of Girls and Women' exhibition in 2019. Photos of the exhibition show that Plath heavily underlined the book and annotated parts of the conversation between Wagner and Faust from Scene II.

Next to Wagner's lines 'How otherwise the mental raptures bear us, / From page to page, from book to book!', Plath added the notes 'rejects life for book' (*SP Faust* 39), alluding to her interest in the opposition between life and knowledge-seeking in the Faust legend. On the same page, Plath annotated Faust's speech starting with the line 'Two souls, alas! reside within my breast' and added "half dust, half deity" in double quotation marks on the right margin of the page (*SP Faust* 39). Plath's copy of Marlowe's plays, including *Doctor Faustus*, is held at Smith and includes the inscription: 'Sylvia Plath, Cambridge 1956', suggesting that it was the copy she used to study for her Tragedy paper at Cambridge. Her marginalia and annotations show that she read several of the plays, including the Introduction from which she underlined the line 'Marlowe's play was probably the first dramatisation of the Faust legend' (*SP Marlowe* xxxvil). Plath's annotations of *Doctor Faustus* unpick the themes of the play, focusing on magic as knowledge, Mephistopheles's appearance, and Faustus's renouncing of magic, the demon-Helen's kiss, redemption, and damnation. The themes underlined in Plath's copies of these plays reappear in her poetry.

Plath's annotations in her *WCD* likewise reinforce her ongoing interest in demonic figures. She underlined the first two definitions in the entry of Beelzebub, a demon, that define him as '1. The prince of demons; the Devil. 2. A leading devil' ('Beelzebub'). Although Plath read Milton's *Paradise Lost*, she did not annotate the third definition that alludes to the fallen angel from the text. Under the entry of devil, highlighted in Chapter 1, there are three definitions that Plath carefully underlined: '1. In Jewish and Christian theology, the personal supreme spirit of evil and unrighteousness. 2. A lesser evil or malignant spirit; a demon 3. A malignantly wicked person; a human fiend.' ('devil') The dictionary entries reference both the theological and metaphorical devils that appear in Plath's poetry. Further, they blur the boundaries between the capital Devil and the lower case devils as demons, which is mirrored in Plath's poems, particularly on the diabolical personality of the romantic partner.

4.1 Demon Lovers

Plath's juvenilia show her engagement with themes from *Faustus* and *Faust*, portraying the romantic partner as a demonic and devilish persona. Plath wrote the poem 'Circus in Three Rings' in 1954, and revised it in 1955, which was published in the same year in *The Atlantic* (Steinberg, 'Circus in Three Rings'). 'Circus in Three Rings' is written in three sestets and is characterised by the formalism and heightened vocabulary of Plath's early poems, influenced by Edith Sitwell's poetic style (Bryant, 'Queen Bees' 200). In a later part of this chapter, I return to Sitwell's poetry that draws on *Doctor Faustus*. Plath's poem explores the vulnerability and uncertainty that come with love, which she compares to the various challenges of circus performances. The poem links the fiery love with hell by referencing the 'jeopardy flames' in her hair and the lover as her 'demon of doom' (*CP* 321–22). In the last stanza, Plath likens her lover to a devil, alluding to the fiend from the Faust legend: 'Mocking as Mephistopheles, / eclipsed by magician's disguise, / my demon of doom tilts on a trapeze' (*CP* 322). Plath's explicit naming of the devil expresses her attentive reading of *Faust*, in which the demon appears as a witty and persuasive character who is able to influence others. The alliterations of 'Mocking as Mephistopheles' and 'demon of doom' suggest a strong bond between Mephistopheles and the lover. The poem implies that the romantic partner, like the devil, is cunning and mischievous, and the speaker has made a bad deal with him. Ferretter argues that 'Circus in Three Rings', like many of Plath's early love poems, focuses 'on the traumatic, excessive and violent emotions her speakers feel in love' (62). In the poem, the speaker does not compare herself to Faustus/Faust, yet she alludes to the pact with the devil, which she regrets. Plath evokes the sexual encounter with a demon, expressing that the speaker's romantic relationship is doomed to fail because they belong to different worlds.

Another early poem that borrows elements from the sexual-romantic encounter with a demon is 'On Looking into the Eyes of a Demon Lover', written in 1955. The poem, as mentioned, inspired Ackerman's 'On Looking into Sylvia Plath's Copy of Goethe's Faust'. The title of Plath's poem references the lines from Coleridge's 'Kubla Khan' (1816): 'As e'er beneath a waning moon was haunted / By woman wailing for her demon-lover' (297). Plath also seeks inspiration from Elizabeth Bowen's short story 'The Demon Lover' (1945), published in *Ivy Gripped the Steps and Other Stories* (1948). Plath interviewed Bowen for her *Mademoiselle* Guest Editorship and read the book in preparation for her interview (*L1* 629). 'The Demon Lover' is a short story with gothic and supernatural elements in which a married woman visits the property where she and her previous husband once lived before he went to fight in World War I. Mrs Drover is haunted by the memories of her first marriage despite not remembering the face of her late husband. She leaves the property in a taxi, whereupon, looking into the eyes of the driver, it is suggested that she is faced with her former husband who kidnaps and kills her: 'Through the aperture driver and passenger, not six inches between them, remained for an eternity eye to eye' (Bowen 87). Plath's 'On Looking into the Eyes of a Demon Lover' alludes to the eye-to-eye contact between the lovers.

The poem comprises six quatrains with a somewhat irregular alternate rhyme scheme. Similar to several of Plath's juvenilia, she borrows elements from the world of fairy tales (Burton 162). 'On Looking into the Eyes of a Demon Lover' suggests that the lover's eyes pose a danger to any woman who is bewitched by his charm. His eyes are a burning weapon that

> turn back to injure
> the thrusting hand
> and inflame to danger
> the scarlet wound. (*CP* 325)

Plath contrasts each 'lovely lady' with the 'thrusting hand' of the lover who causes 'the scarlet wound'. He is portrayed as a devilish and dangerous person who inflicts pain. Plath returns to the imagery of fire, linking the burning passion of the demon lover to hellish pain. In the last two stanzas, the focus shifts from the demonic lover who inflicts pain to the speaker whose beauty and virtue are contrasted with his character. She recognises that instead of 'the body / of a toad' and 'witch's face', she is a 'radiant Venus' (*CP* 325). The speaker navigates her identity between the contrasting ideals of womanhood: the ugly witch and the feminine Venus. She critiques the male perception of beauty and power, which limits the poetic persona who has already been wounded by the demon lover. Here, Plath also alludes to Goethe's *Faust*, in which Helena is not portrayed as a demon, but she signifies eternal beauty, similar to Venus (Curran 174). Goethe's play is a romantic reimagination of the demon-Helen in *Doctor Faustus* in which she represents the sin of diabolism and desire (Stockholder 213). 'On Looking into the Eyes of a Demon Lover' reverses the gender roles and likens the male lover to a seductive demon. Plath associates the lover with the fiery underworld and compares him to the real demon, who is cunning, evil, and bewitching, similar to Mephistopheles in both *Doctor Faustus* and *Faust*.

Plath's poem shares similarities with Isabella Gardner's 'On Looking in the Looking Glass'.[1] In Harriet Rosenstein's research papers on the interview with Peter and Jane Davidson about Plath's Smith years, Rosenstein

[1] The poem was also published as 'The Looking Glass' in *The Sewanee Review* in 1959, the same issue Plath published 'Point Shirley' and 'Departure of the Ghost'.

notes that Plath's adored poets at the time were Elizabeth Bishop, Isabella Gardner, and Dylan Thomas; she '[p]articularly liked Gard[e]ner's intricate syntaxes' (Davison, Peter and Jane, 1972–75). Gardner was a cousin of Robert Lowell and the great-niece of the Boston-based art collector Isabella Stewart Gardner. Plath mentions the poetry of Gardner in her journals; she even dined with her in 1958 (*J* 322; 360; 469). In Gardner's poem, the speaker searches for her image; she perceives her identity as divided into a youthful and ageing self, which is reflected in the mirror image as a spirit:

> I light to the glint
> of your daemon, that Familiar whom you stint
> so prodigally. Shunting, shan't –
> ing wincing fabricant
> I see the maker that you want
> and aren't. (450)

In the lines, the speaker calls her other self a 'daemon' and a 'Familiar', alluding to the spiritual companion of witches. Gardner uses enjambment and acoustic effects to create playfulness in her poem (shan't —/ ing; chanting), suggesting the magic of the mirror. She employs the object to imagine a meeting with the two selves: 'And now just now I closed your eyes / your infant ancient naked eyes' (451). Similar to Plath's poem, Gardner draws a connection between the eye and the mirror, which shows the true self of a person – whether they are evil or innocent in their spirit.

In Plath's unfinished short story 'The Matisse Chapel', inspired by her trip to France with Richard Sassoon in 1956, the love interest is similarly 'described as diabolical' (Ferretter 66). Drawing on the same gazing romantic relationship as 'Circus in Three Rings' and 'On Looking into the Eyes of a Demon Lover,' Plath depicts her 'mad lover' in her journals as a 'denying devil' (*J* 204). While 'The Matisse Chapel' does not have an explicitly supernatural vocabulary, Ferretter argues that in her short story, 'Plath creates imaginative works based on the same relationship' in which her protagonist is 'able to fight back the demonic lover' (66). In 'The Matisse Chapel', the character based on Sassoon is described as 'writing blasphemous poetry', and in their fights, he tells Sally, Plath's alter ego, that she has no love in her (*Prose* 740–41). The fragmented story ends with some reconciliation; however, Sally sees her lover now with 'cruel clarity' (*Prose* 741). Although she can resist her demonic lover, her portrayal of the relationship sources the language from demonology and diabolism. The characterisation of romantic partners as demons positions men as sexual predators who seduce innocent women. 'Circus in Three Rings' explicitly mentions the devil from *Faust* and thereby directly references the devilish character of the lover. 'On Looking into the Eyes of a Demon Lover' draws on Bowen's short story to portray the violent and demonic lover and also alludes to early modern beliefs about sexual encounters with demons – the male incubus and female succubus – that were thought to seduce men and women and commit demoniality, as portrayed in the Faust legend. Plath's comparison of romantic partners to evil supernatural figures in her juvenilia warns against the sexual danger and harm the men pose to young women, engaging with the complex gendered power dynamics of post-war American dating culture in which women were often vulnerable and exposed to unwanted sexual advances. The portrayal of the demonic lovers reveals that the language of the supernatural is associated with sexuality. The literary representations of demons portrayed in, for example, *Doctor Faustus* and *Faust*, offered Plath a vocabulary to explore the ambiguities of heartache, vulnerability, anger, and betrayal in romantic relationships.

4.2 Demonic Possessions

In the early modern period, demonic possession was understood as the act by which an evil spirit possessed someone's body. Historians today interpret demonic possession as a theatrical performance in which the different parties, the demoniac, the priest, and the relatives, act according to a 'script' (Levack, *The Devil Within* 139). Using theatre as a metaphor for demonic possession not only provides a new interpretation but likewise highlights the varied relationship between superstitions, magic, and performance. Stephen Greenblatt argues that ritualistic performance of exorcism both by Catholic and Puritan priests was made for the spectators; it was a 'cunning manipulation of popular superstitions' (100). In the early modern period, magic and theatre were often undifferentiated, particularly by extreme Puritan antitheatrical pamphleteers who saw the stage as diabolic, which fueled emotions and encouraged the audience to copy the black magicians (Deats 16). *Doctor Faustus* staged the dark magic and demons: during the performances of the play, many actors quit because they believed that there were actual devils conjured on stage (Purkiss 182). While Marlowe's play does not portray demonic possession, it illustrates the blurred line between concepts of magic, conjuration, and performance (Sofer 2). The study of demonology in, for example, Kramer's *Malleus Maleficarum* considered the theological aspects of demons and made connections between demons and witchcraft (Behringer 408–9). Thus, being possessed could be considered a sign of being a witch, and exorcism by clergy was needed to cleanse the soul from evil spirits. In Chapter 5, I return to the subject of ritualistic exorcism, examining the linguistic and performative allusions to ritual magic in some of Plath's poems.

The possession of the body and mind by evil spirits, and their subsequent exorcism evolved to a metaphorical understanding of demons and the state of being possessed. In particular, modern psychiatry has interpreted demonic possession as physical and psychological disorders or illnesses (Levack, *The Devil Within* 113; 127). In Freud's essay, 'A Seventeenth-Century Demonological Neurosis' (1923), he analysed the case of the self-proclaimed possessed person Christoph Haizmann who argued he had made a pact with the Devil who appeared in front of him. Freud references Faustus's pact with Mephistopheles to interpret Haizmann's case: 'Since he rejected magical arts, money and pleasures when they were offered him by the Devil [. . .] it becomes really imperative to know what the painter in fact wanted from the Devil when he signed a bond with him' (80). Freud continues by arguing that the Devil – seen by Haizmann – is a symbolic father figure: 'to apply this idea of the Devil as a father substitute to cultural history, we may also be able to see the witch-trials of the Middle Ages in a new light' (87). His interpretation of the paternal Devil focuses on mourning and melancholia shaped by the loss of the ambivalent father. Such an understanding of demonic possession was influential among post-war poets like Plath.

Plath was well-versed in the psychoanalytic and anthropological studies of demonic possession: she used Freud's case study essay for her undergraduate thesis (Axelrod 224). For her university work, she read Dostoevsky's *The Possessed* (1872), also translated as *Demons*, which employs the concept of demonic possession in a metaphorical sense in nineteenth-century Russian society (*L1* 716). In her journals, Plath drew on the language of popular psychoanalysis to address her 'inner demon', most notably in the 'Letter to a demon' from October 1957: 'The demon would humiliate me: throw me on my knees before the college president, my department chairman, everyone, crying: look at me, miserable, I can't do it. Talking about my fears to others feeds it' (*J* 619). In the entry, the concept of demonic possession functions to separate a part of her from her identity, which she perceived as dark and destructive. In 1958, Plath revisited the subject of demonic possession by reading the anthropological study *Possession: Demoniacal & Other: Among Primitive Races in Antiquity, the Middle Ages, and Modern Time* (1930) by T. K. Oesterreich. Oesterreich uses an umbrella term to cover different phenomena across cultures and religions from Christian demonic possession to African shamanism. According to Plath, the cases were 'extremely diverting – but also inspiring – metaphors for states of human experience as well as the experience itself' (*J* 415). Her description gives an account of the way in which the various interpretations of demonic possessions inspired her creative writing. Plath's engagement with the concept of demonic possession was, therefore, twofold: she understood it as a culturally and religiously diverse phenomenon, relating it to human experiences, and employed the concept of the demon to discuss her fears and anxieties by using the language of psychoanalysis.

Plath also read and saw plays that portray demonic possessions, which highlight her continued interest in the subject. The dramatic adaptations of demonic possessions further reinforce the understanding of possessions as a scripted play, a performance. In January 1955, she saw the play *The Dybbuk* by S. Ansky in New York, a 'tale of the possession of a young girl's body by the spirit of her lover' ('The Dybbuk') who died before his time and had no other home in eternity' (*L1* 864). The dybbuk is a demon in Judaism that 'demonstrates the cultural specificity of demonic possession' (Levack, *The Devil Within* 168). The play exemplifies the traditional beliefs about the dybbuk by portraying the protagonist Leah as speaking in a male voice in her possessed state. In *The Bell Jar*, Plath references her experience of seeing *The Dybbuk* and likens Hilda's malicious words to demonic possession:

> The night before I'd seen a play where the heroine was possessed by a dybbuk, and when the dybbuk spoke from her mouth its voice sounded so cavernous and deep you couldn't tell whether it was a man or a woman. Well, Hilda's voice sounded just like the voice of that dybbuk.
>
> [. . .]
>
> So I said, 'Isn't it awful about the Rosenbergs?' [. . .] Fascinated, I stared at the blind cave behind her face until the two lips met and moved and the dybbuk spoke out of its hiding place, 'I'm so glad they're going to die.' (*TBJ* 95–96)

Though Plath saw *The Dybbuk* a year and a half after her *Mademoiselle* internship, she inserts the experience in the novel to imply Hilda's unpleasant and hateful character. While Esther's attitude towards the Rosenbergs shows her empathy, the comparison to the dybbuk 'instantly erases Hilda's humanity' (Cardon 57). Hilda's voice is described as mannish, which suggests that it is not she who is speaking but the voice of tyranny, embodying the rhetoric of McCarthyism. Ferretter argues that 'the dybbuk in Plath's lexicon stands for a woman who has allowed herself to become something less than Plath believed a woman ought to be' (103). The reference to the dybbuk links the Rosenberg couple's Jewish ethnicity to the demon from Judaism that 'possesses' Hilda, positioning her loathing of the Rosenbergs within the antisemitism and anti-communism of the post-war period. Plath's allusion to the dybbuk shows her knowledge of the theology of demonic possession and demonstrates a third way she interpreted the concept: one in which devilish control and the alienated self embody the politics of division of the McCarthy era. In 1961, Plath saw the play *The Devils*, written by John Whiting based on Aldous Huxley's non-fiction novel *The Devils of Loudun* (1952) about a demonic possession and exorcism in seventeenth-century France (*L2* 582). Plath's encounter with the play on demonic possession during the time she wrote *The Bell Jar* suggests that she was reminded of her previous theatre experience of *The Dybbuk*. The literary representations of being possessed bear the influence on her writings in depicting the oppressive powers of authority figures.

Parallel to Plath, in the works of American poets from the confessional school the theme of demonic possession emerges about the father figure: post-war American father elegies often include 'curses, condemnations, and exorcisms' and 'denouncing, mocking, ravaging and exposing their parents in stunning acts of confrontation' (Ramazani 221–22). Anne Sexton's poem 'Divorce, Thy Name is Woman', published in the posthumous collection *45 Mercy Street* (1976), compares divorcing from a spouse to the separation from her father who is positioned as the Jewish demon: 'I am divorcing daddy – Dybbuk! Dybbuk! / I have been doing it daily all my life' (545). Here, the exclamation mark after the twice-repeated 'Dybbuk' suggests that the speaker is performing an exorcism of the spirit. Another poem from the same collection, '"Daddy" Warbucks', which references the fictional character Sir Oliver 'Daddy' Warbucks from the comic *Little Orphan Annie*, also interrogates the father-daughter relationship through materiality and mortality: 'Just me and my "Daddy" / and his tempestuous bucks / [. . .] But I died yesterday, / "Daddy," I died' (544). In the lines, the speaker refers to her close relationship with her father; however, instead of experiencing his absence, she alludes to her own death, implying that his spirit has possessed her. Gill notes that Sexton's late poems such as '"Daddy" Warbucks' draw a connection between patriarchal and sexual power and material wealth: the poem critiques the culture of affluence in post-war America and concludes that the charge of male power 'is female subordination, silence, and denial' (*Anne Sexton* 75). Sexton's poems were likewise influenced by Plath's 'Daddy' in which she associates the lover and the father figure who both 'possess' the speaker (Ramazani 1154). Chapter 5 presents a detailed analysis of 'Daddy' concerning ritual magic; here, I draw attention to Plath's merger of the two demonic men, the lover and the father: 'If I've killed one man, I've killed two—' (*CP* 224). The speaker understands banishing the men from her life as killing them, expressing that their physical presence was overpowering and domineering on her psyche. Although Plath explicitly names the lover a vampire in the poem, the recurring diabolical imagery, allusions to exorcism, and the referenced Jewish identity of the speaker in 'Daddy' suggest that he is a demon and not a blood-sucking figure. Sexton's and Plath's poems employ demonic possession to write about symbiotic and often unhealthy relationships towards fathers and lovers in which their speakers feel powerless, as if they are being possessed by the men. The dybbuk's ability to make the possessed speak with a man's voice further implies a power imbalance in which the women struggle to separate their identity and voice from the men in their lives.

Similar to Plath's 'Daddy', in John Berryman's 'Of Suicide', the speaker feels overpowered by the spirit of his dead father. Berryman's confessional style poem summons the father in the first line – the only mention in the poem – which suggests that he blames the father for his own failures: 'Reflexions on suicide, & on my father, possess me. / I drink too much. My wife threatens separation' (*Love & Fame* 69). The speaker recalls the dead father and drinking problems to reflect on generational trauma and addiction. The short sentences and use of casual punctuation marks imply that this poem is an intimate reflection. 'Of Suicide' parallels Sexton's and Plath's poems in their references to possession to untangle their complex relationship with their father figure. Plath's reading of psychoanalytical writings on demonic possessions and encounters with plays like *The Dybbuk*, *The Devils*, and *Doctor Faustus* demonstrate her broad understanding of early modern concepts of diabolism and its interpretation in the mid-twentieth century. Excerpted from *The Bell Jar*, 'Daddy' and Sexton's poems further express a political aspect of demonic possessions, suggesting a hierarchical, and often gendered, power dynamic between the possessed and the possessor.

As opposed to American post-war poets who were writing forceful father elegies inspired by concepts such as demonic possession and diabolism, in the works of English poets, such as Ted Hughes's 'First, Mills' and Tony Harrison's 'School of Eloquence', the father appears as a victim of poverty and class, which the poets tried to escape. Harrison and Hughes share a preoccupation with the heritages of British social and class issues as they both come from a working-class background and grew up in the North of England. Harrison's 'School of Eloquence' sequence from 1978 references *Doctor Faustus*, in particular, the Faustian pact that he made to progress his life (Roberts 78). In the poem 'Aqua Mortis', Harrison pre-emptively mourns the father figure and 'contextualises the poet's mourning with the future anterior' (Rowland 172): 'Alchemists keep skulls, and you have one / that stretches your skin taut and moulds your face, // [. . .] My study is your skull. *I'll burn my books*' (Harrison 137). In the last line of the poem, Harrison directly quotes Faustus from the play: 'Come not, Lucifer; / I'll burn my books!—Ah, Mephostophilis!' (A 19.190). The speaker of 'Aqua Mortis' is similar to Faustus who 'now desperately craves the paternal love from which his learning has estranged him' (Spencer 85). The allusion positions the father figure as the devilish demon to whom the speaker is pleading. In Hughes's 'First, Mills' also published in the late 1970s, the loss of the father is associated with the drained land (Bate 396). Hughes makes notes of the 'whitened' hair and face of the dead and the 'childhood of earth' (*THCP* 462–63). Although not referencing any supernatural occurrence, Hughes suggests a form of spiritual connection between the paternal bond and the land that is now foreign and barren to him, like the exhausted, empty, and traumatised body of the dispossessed. Like Plath, Harrison and Hughes rely on literary examples of possessive bonds to portray the father as ambiguous whose domineering presence haunts the poetic personae.

The works of British and American poets from the second half of the twentieth century show the deep penetration of the concepts of demonic possession, the dybbuk, and the influence of Marlowe's play in post-war literature, culture, and politics. The themes of early modern demonic possession also resurfaced in psychoanalytical and literary discourses that interrogate complex family dynamics, particularly concerning the father figure. Freud's study of demonic possession provides an effective interpretation of poems from Plath, Sexton, and Berryman in which the speaker unleashes against the demonic figure whose spiritual presence possesses them. Plath's and Sexton's allusions to the Jewish dybbuk in their writings further demonstrate that the poets' knowledge of demonic possession was nuanced, and their references have a political dimension. Plath's poetic representation of the relationship between the demon-father and the speaker seeks inspiration from the concept of demonic possessions and *Doctor Faustus* in which the magician is subjected to the devil's powers.

4.3 The Politics of the Faustian Bargain

The Faust legend and its dramatic adaptations, interrogating morality, redemption, and the relationship between science and magic offered a metaphor for political and public debates, similar to the Salem witch trials in American politics. In the nineteenth century, Goethe's *Faust* was an emerging influential text in American literature: in 1836, Henry Wadsworth Longfellow gave annual lectures at Harvard on *Faust*, in which his focus was on Faust's humanity and Goethe's moral teaching in the joy of life (Chamberlin 71–72). Longfellow wrote his lectures in an age of renewed religious conflict in which extreme Puritanism was in contradiction with Goethe's moral philosophy (Durrani, '19th-century' 405). Some of Nathaniel Hawthorne's short stories, written between 1842–49, present 'different characterizations of a Faustian hero' (Stein 87). 'The Birthmark' was published in *Hawthorne's Short Stories* (1955), a collection that Plath owned. She likewise taught the short story at Smith in 1957. In 'Birthmark', Aylmer – the Faust-inspired character – is a scientist who works in a 'laboratory' but has strong spiritual interests. Aylmer is obsessed with his lover Georgiana's birthmark on her cheek, which he attempts to remove with an 'elixir of immortality' ('The Birthmark' 184). However, as soon as her birthmark disappears, she dies. Aylmer, like Faustus, loses his lover because of his self-interests and belief that the pursuit of knowledge – scientific or magical – is always beneficial and progressive. Aylmer's depiction reveals that he is a scientist without a moral compass. In Plath's copy of Hawthorne's short stories, she underlined in the Introduction that 'The Birthmark was an "allegorical little drama," and in the table of contents, she noted: 'perfection in earthly form' (*SP Hawthorne's Short Stories* 18). She also heavily annotated parts of 'The Birthmark' and made annotations, for example, noting several times that Aylmer is 'God-like' and even wrote 'Faustian' on the top of the page where the protagonist is portrayed as a scientist-magician (*SP Hawthorne's Short Stories* 155). Plath organically made a connection between the morally corrupt Aylmer and Faustus who sells his soul to advance scientific knowledge.

Marlowe's *Doctor Faustus* and Goethe's *Faust* also offered valuable metaphors for understanding the complex relationship between politics and science in the Atomic Age. The Faust legend 'does present the scientist's pursuit of knowledge as the means by which Mephistopheles believes he can lead Faust away from his already confused service of the Lord' (Halpin 366). Even for atomic scientists, research in nuclear power symbolised the

Faustian pact that many physicists made. In Freeman Dyson's *Disturbing the Universe* (1979), the theoretical physicist portrayed himself and colleagues, like Oppenheimer, as redeemable Faustian characters who only wanted to advance scientific knowledge: 'The remarkable thing about the Faust legend is that everybody to some extent still believes in it. When you say that some piece of technology is a Faustian bargain, everybody knows what you mean' (9). He identifies the diabolism of the early modern period with the Atomic Age in which Mephistopheles has a metaphysical not material presence, representing the evils and demands of contemporary society. The parallels between Faustus and theoretical physicists like Oppenheimer are particularly apparent in later adaptations, such as Peter Sellars's opera *Doctor Atomic* (2005). Poets of the post-war era reflected on the political landscape at the time and linked nuclear warfare to the legend of Faust. However, the popular media's reporting on theatre and film adaptations of *Faust* and *Doctor Faustus* made no association between the Atomic Age and the politics of the Faustian bargain. An article from 1950 published in *The Christian Science Monitor* discussed the 1949 film *Faust and the Devil* originally titled *La leggenda di Faust*, directed by the Italian director Carmine Gallone, and praised the additional scenes included in the film, set in the underworld and alluding to Dante's *Inferno* (Rogers 4). The *New York Times* reported on several adaptations of both plays: in 1949, the New York–based broadcasting house WNYC aired the BBC Playhouse series, including Marlowe's *Doctor Faustus* and in 1950, they noted that Yale University staged a production of *Faust* to mark Goethe's bicentenary birth anniversary (*New York Times* 24; Haven 1). While mass media focused on the artistic merit of the adaptations and broadcasts of *Faust* and *Doctor Faustus* and avoided relating it to contemporary politics, poets saw the Faust legend materialised through the scientific and political evils that were unleashed by World War II and the Cold War.

Karl Shapiro was part of the generation of poets before Plath, which included W. H. Auden whom she widely read. In his poetry, Shapiro drew on his experience as a soldier during World War II and his Jewish heritage to reflect on the social and political turmoil. Plath encountered Shapiro when he was the editor of *Poetry* magazine during the 1950s. In his poem 'The Progress of Faust', Shapiro reimagines Faustus's life during World War II and directly references *Doctor Faustus*, linking the early modern black magician to the Atomic Age. First published in 1946, the poem portrays Faustus as a victim, portraying him 'not as a symbol or originator of Fascism, but his legacy to the world is far from beneficial' (Durrani, 'Faust in the Nuclear Age' 477). The poem introduces Faustus's history to the reader: 'He was born in Deutschland, as you would suspect, / And graduated in magic from Cracow / In Fifteen Five' (Shapiro 28). Shapiro portrays Faustus as a student, academic, and global citizen who 'toured the Continent for a hundred years' (28). Here, Faustus is an ordinary man who is present in every period, focusing on his redeemable character. Faustus 'published penny poems about his sins', until he was 'expelled / From the Third Reich in Nineteen Thirty-nine' (Shapiro 28). In World War II, Faustus becomes an outlaw, seeking shelter in a desert in the United States. However, when the war ends, a new horror emerges, embodied by the atomic bomb, which implies that despite wanting to redeem himself, damnation reaches him in the form of nuclear warfare. 'The Progress of Faust' interrogates the concepts of morality and sin within the political context of post-war America by portraying the black magician as a victim of authoritarian politics. Shapiro references Faustus's German heritage and Polish education, implying the Jewish ethnicity of the magician who had to leave his homeland during the rise of the Third Reich. Yet, instead of finding a new homeland in the United States, the development of the nuclear bomb emerges as the seductive force of Mephistopheles.

In addition to Berryman's father elegy that associated demonic possession with the overbearing dead father figure, some of his poems reflect on the political horrors with the language of diabolism. He associates events of World War II with Christian evil in the second poem of the sequence, 'Eleven Addresses to the Lord': 'at this instant of time, all evil men, / Belsen, Omaha Beach, // incomprehensible to man your ways. / May be the Devil after all exists' (*Love & Fame* 87). The speaker asks God to address his disbelief in humanity: the 'evil men', representing fascist authoritarianism, are like the Devil who caused death and suffering for many. In another poem, 'The Wholly Fail' from 1950, Berryman warns us of the 'Faustian mind that is drawn to experiments whose outcomes are uncertain' (Brunner 199): 'Sir Partofall, our Best, O the Physicist is / (Wizards of Oak Ridge and Los Alamos) / [. . .] O lucky Doctor. Let us hang our faith / – To master the power of the grave, much; more' ('The Wholly Fail' 191). The scientist-magician finds power and knowledge that is 'Useful although uncertain' ('The Wholly Fail' 191), which positions the Faustian figure in the anxiety-ridden age of the Cold War. Berryman's speaker is a physicist, a wizard, and a doctor at the same time, referencing Doctor Faustus's character. Similar to Berryman, in Plath's late poetry, the doctor figure frequently appears as a powerful man and gatekeeper of scientific knowledge: in 'The Surgeon at 2 a.m.', the surgeon joins bodies, recalling the clinical experimentations on people's bodies during World

War II. As discussed in Chapter 2, in 'Lady Lazarus', Plath merges various patriarchal figures from the doctor, the torturer, and the executioner, who are the enemies of the witchlike speaker. Plath's portrayal of the doctor builds on the moral ambiguity associated with scientists who seek knowledge for the greater good. In her political poems, Plath follows the tradition of employing dark and diabolical imagery to represent the contemporary evils in society. She participates in a dialogue with post-war poets in her portrayal of the diabolical Nazi figure in 'Daddy:' 'Not God but a swastika / So black no sky could squeak through' (*CP* 223). The lines allude to black magic and the Mephistophelian devil, which post-war poets related to contemporary political horrors as the Faustian bargain of their generation.

Plath's poem 'Man in Black' from 1959 likewise links World War II with symbolic darkness. Plath repeats the expression 'man in black' in two other poems: in 'Daddy', the diabolical Nazi father is the 'man in black with a Meinkampf look' and in 'The Bee Meeting', the speaker asks, 'Which is the rector now, is it that man in black?' (*CP* 211; 224). The shared imagery highlights Plath's critique of the intertwined and tyrannical powers of politics, science, and religion. In Ted Hughes's poetic response 'Black Coat', he alludes to Plath's powerful and emotive portrayal of the garment, replacing 'all his own memories' of the event walking on the beach (Robinson 175). Plath's 'Man in Black' consists of seven stanzas that follow the simple tercet form. The poem follows the man in black on the seashore, transitioning from the natural landscape to the industrial prison in Massachusetts: 'Barb-wired headland of / The Deer Island prison' (*CP* 119). Plath references the prison, usually used for short-term sentencing, which also appears in *The Bell Jar*. Esther wonders what crime she would need to commit to get into the prison:

> 'No, how do you get *locked* in?'
> 'Oh,' the guard laughed, 'you steal a car, you rob a store.'
> 'You got any murderers in there?'
> 'No. Murderers go to a big state place.' (*TBJ* 144–45)

For Plath, sin and violence are represented by institutional imprisonment and the politics of the post-war era and the Cold War. The violent imagery of the prison gate also reappears in 'Daddy' ('It stuck in a barb wire snare' [*CP* 223]), and 'Little Fugue' ('A yew hedge of orders, / Gothic and barbarous, pure German' [*CP* 188]), further associating immoral and sinister politics with darkness. In 'Man in Black', the speaker addresses the dark man with the personal pronoun 'you', similar to 'Daddy'.

He walks across the pale 'Stones, strode out in your dead / Black coat, black shoes, and your / Black hair till there you stood' (*CP* 119). Plath rhymes 'dead' and 'black' to create destructive imagery, shifting the focus from the blackness of the place to the person. Her use of the colour references the barren landscape and positions a man in black as a source of ambiguity and sin. 'Man in Black' is evocative of the parallels between black magic and the Third Reich that poets like Karl Shapiro emphasised and Plath explored further in 'Daddy'.

The diabolical blackness associated with the horrors of World War II is also a theme of Edith Sitwell's poem 'Still Falls the Rain' (1940), subtitled 'The Raids, 1940. Night and Dawn'. Writing from a British perspective, Sitwell directly quotes *Doctor Faustus* to echo the looming presence of the war during the London Blitz in her war poem. Plath wrote essays on Sitwell's poetic craft in 1951 and 1953 at Smith College and returned to her poems when she was teaching at her alma mater (Bryant, 'Beelines' 200). It is unclear when Plath encountered 'Still Falls the Rain', but she knew of it, which is characterised by the presence of darkness. The refrain of 'Still falls the Rain' appears at the start of six stanzas out of the seven. The poem has a strong religious iconography of the suffering Christ and Lazarus who are representatives of the war victims:

> Still falls the Rain
> At the feet of the Starved Man hung upon the Cross,
> Christ that each day, each night, nails there, have mercy on us –
> On Dives and Lazarus:
> Under the Rain, the sore and the gold are as one. (Sitwell 265)

The stanza juxtaposes the diabolical sinister figures of the war and suffering Christ and humanity. In the fifth stanza, Sitwell quotes a line from Faustus, 'O Ile leape up to my God: who pulles me doune' (266). In *Doctor Faustus*, the line appears in the play when the magician is begging for redemption 'The devil will come, and Faustus must be damn'd. / O, I'll leap up to my God! Who pulls me down?' (A 13.144–45). In Sitwell's poem, Faustus's line is uttered 'by a character who refuses to be saved. Easy consolations, even of the religious kind, are apparently no longer appropriate in modern war poetry' (Emig 548). Plath underlined Marlowe's lines in her copy of his plays and noted on the margin, 'cf [cross-reference] Sitwell', demonstrating that she was aware of the allusion in Sitwell's poem (*SP Marlowe* 227). The reference to Marlowe's play in 'Still Falls the Rain' suggests that there is no godly redemption from the evils of the war, the contemporary form of diabolism.

Another post-war American poet, Randall Jarrell, employs the Faust legend in his poem 'A Conversation with the Devil' (1951). Although Jarell is less frequently brought into parallel with Plath, his poetry and criticism were impactful in mid-century American literature, which Plath also recognised (Clark, *Red Comet* 215). In 'A Conversation with the Devil', Jarrell makes a parallel between the Devil's temptation and American capitalism and consumerism (Beardsworth 160). In the long poem, the speaker is a poet who converses with the Devil about his disappointment with post-war American culture, particularly of being a poet with 'too few' readers in a consumerist society. When offered to him, however, the poet does not take the Faustian bargain:

> Our real terms were different
> And signed and sealed for good, neither in blood
> Nor ink but in my life: *Neither to live*
> *Nor ask for life* – that wasn't a bad bargain
> For a poor devil of a poet, was it? (3)

The speaker calls himself 'a poor devil of a poet', suggesting that he is a morally grey person similar to Faust. He argues that the bargain was signed 'neither in blood / Nor ink but in my life', which alludes to Faustus's signing his contract with Mephistopheles. Adam Beardsworth notes that while the Devil 'attempted to seduce individuals by employing the strategies of advertising, he is now overpowered by the seductions of postwar capitalism' (161). The poem recalls the Faustian bargain as a critical commentary on post-war affluence; in particular, he interrogates the question of sin in a secularised consumerist society. In 'A Conversation with the Devil', the speaker-poet does not require Mephistopheles's temptation anymore as 'Free will appealed so much to him', yet he has 'no choice' (Jarrell 6). The poem concludes that the Mephistophelian malice is part of the culture of post-war American consumerism and politics. Reading Plath's poems in conversation with Shapiro, Berryman, and Sitwell demonstrates that her use of diabolical imagery builds on the way in which poets – many of whom she adored – engaged with the themes of morality and sin portrayed in *Doctor Faustus*.

American poets of the post-war era employed the Faust legend and Faustian bargain and their literary representation in Marlowe's and Goethe's plays in a variety of ways. Their poems interrogate what morality, evil, sin, and redemption mean in contemporary culture and society, especially relating these terms to World War II and the Atomic Age and drawing on nineteenth-century discourses and interpretations. Faustus's character shifted from a black magician to a redeemable scientist whose pursuit of knowledge led to irreversible consequences, unleashing the evils in society that led to World War II and nuclear warfare. Plath engages with literary representations and political discourses of the Faust legend and draws on the complex and layered interpretations of demonology and demonic possessions. While her juvenilia express the direct influence of Marlowe's and Goethe's plays, her mature poems demonstrate a more nuanced understanding and interest in how contemporary discourses from psychoanalysis to politics sought inspiration from *Doctor Faustus*. The Freudian understanding of demons as a representation of the dark inner self helped Plath to address her fears and anxieties in her journals. Modern psychoanalytical interpretations of demonic possession that expose family power dynamics prompted poets like Plath, Sexton, and Berryman to reflect on their relationship with their fathers. Supernatural concepts, such as diabolism and the Faustian bargain, had an important rhetorical and metaphorical function to express and understand the complexities of human behaviour, morality, and evil, particularly about World War II and its aftermath. The early modern concepts portrayed in *Doctor Faustus* offered a vocabulary for poets like Plath to interrogate modern political horrors. By referencing diabolism, the highest form of sin in Christian belief, the poets reworked the concept of evil and linked it to contemporary political affairs.

CHAPTER 5

Ritual Magic and Plath's Poetic Spellcasting

Sylvia Plath was familiar with the historical and literary understandings of ritual magic, which she drew on in her poetry to describe magical intended outcomes, such as exorcism or spiritual purification. She was likewise inspired by the supernatural powers attributed to language in prayers, invocations, and the spellwork in performances of witchcraft. Additionally, the rhythmical repetitive language, ritualised acts, and symbolic use of mundane objects, such as a photograph and a deck of cards, to assist the performance contribute to ideas of ritual magic in Plath's poetic spellcasting.

In July 2021, Frieda Hughes put numerous items up for sale at the Sotheby's auction, 'Your Own Sylvia', including Plath's writings and belongings. One of the most anticipated items on sale was Plath's Tarot de Marseille deck: it even initiated crowdfunding on social media, with many wanting to own one of the seventy-eight cards. The Tarot pack was the highest-grossing item sold for £151,200 to an anonymous buyer. Numerous articles tried to understand why such a haunted item – which Plath received for her twenty-fourth birthday from Ted Hughes – would be the most expensive piece to be sold (Sheehan; Crowther, 'What cost, Sylvia Plath?'). The auctioned Tarot cards, often identified with the pack portrayed in 'Daddy', exposed the ongoing interest from scholars and members of the general public to collectors in Plath's affiliations with ritualistic performances of magic, such as the divinatory use of Tarot cards.[1] This chapter reflects on the way mundane objects can possess supernatural qualities and become tools to aid ritualistic performances with magical intentions. In the case of Plath, the 'magic of handling original Plath documents' reinforces the supernatural attribution of everyday objects (Crowther and Steinberg, *These Ghostly Archives* 27). The historical and literary sources on and beliefs about ritual magic offer a reading of Plath's ritualistic poetic language, particularly in the drafts of

[1] Though as I discuss later, the cards in 'Daddy' reference to Tarock, suggesting a different card deck.

her poems, and prompt debates about supernatural labels and associations of her expressive poems.

A basic definition of ritual magic is a ceremony in which ritualistic acts and ritualistic language reinforce each other. To realise its intended outcome, a ritual builds a connection with the supernatural world. Studies of Western esotericism and magic have long tried to untangle the complexities of ritual magic. Eliza Marian Butler, who worked as a literary scholar of German at Newnham College, Cambridge and retired four years before Plath started her studies there, notes in her 1949 book that ritual magic is 'aimed principally at control of the spirit world' (3). Her description interprets the concept of ritual magic as the control of the supernatural, exemplified by Prospero's command of Ariel to create a tempest during which he uses ritualistic acts with incantatory speech (Butler 17). In another early modern play I discussed in Chapter 4, Marlowe's *Doctor Faustus*, the black magician conjures Mephistopheles with an incantation from his magic book. The focus on the figure of the magus interprets ritual magic as a formal ceremony performed by the (male) practitioner. Plath was familiar with the early modern portrayal of ritual magic as a ceremonious formal performance. In her *WCD*, Plath underlined definitions of 'ceremony'. The entry highlights symbolic and formal performances or acts: '1. A formal act, or series of acts often symbolical, prescribed by law, custom, or authority, in matters of religion, of state etc. 2. A conventional act of civility or etiquette. 3. A mere outward form' ('ceremony'). Plath's annotations demonstrate that she considered the formal and symbolic characteristics of ceremonies a key feature, which defines her understanding of the relationship between ritual, language, and magic. In the same dictionary, though lacking any annotations, a ritual is defined as 'the form of conducting worship; religious ceremonial' ('ritual'). The entry contains associations with the magical and supernatural realms, mainly within religious practices.

Ritual magic can also be informal, spontaneous, and performed by diverse individuals. In the late nineteenth and early twentieth centuries, new spiritualist movements, such as the Hermetic Order of the Golden Dawn, prompted a renewed interest in ritual magic. Francis King proposes that the revival of ritual magic has been linked to 'the early lives and beliefs of such apparently diverse characters as W. B. Yeats, Aleister Crowley, and Charles Williams' (9). Plath was particularly drawn to Yeatsian occultist practices and rituals: her journals and letters give evidence of her use of informal ritual magic, such as bibliomancy, which is the practice of fortune-telling by interpreting an arbitrarily selected passage from a book, often the Bible. In November 1962, Plath used W. B. Yeats's book as a fortune-telling device, prompting her to rent the poet's flat in London: "I opened a book of his plays in front of Susan as a joke for a 'Message' & read 'Get wine & food to give you strength & courage & I will get the house ready'" (*L2* 905). Her wording shows the attribution of magical powers to the informal performance of the ritual. Plath's copy of Yeats's *Collected Plays* is kept at Smith and includes her annotation in the mentioned selected passage from *The Unicorn from the Stars*: "Nov. 13, 1962 the prophecy–true?" (qtd. Van Duyne 53). In December 1962, Hughes retold the narrative to his sister in a letter, alluding to witchcraft: 'Sylvia has finally, by a series of extraordinary flukes-which she calls her witchcraft-acquired the top two floors of the house in which Yeats lived as a child-Fitzroy Road' (*THL* 210). The framing of Plath's bibliomancy and domestic magical rituals as an act of witchcraft was not uncommon at the time. Among the Harriet Rosenstein research papers, several interviewees, for example, Jillian Becker and Suzette Macedo, emphasised a similar narrative. During the early years of their marriage, Plath and Hughes experimented with different occultist practices, which they used as poetic inspiration. For Plath, such acts were associated with the literary heritages of the occult, expressing a magical-poetic connection between the Yeats couple and her own marriage (*L1* 1327). Plath's performances of informal ritual magic were confined to domestic spaces; they were prompts for poetry writing. E. M. Butler highlights that ritual magic has creative powers: it is the aesthetic element of the ceremony that captivates people, such as the use of different objects, and instruments, and performing poetry or prayer (4). The creative-aesthetic dimension of ritual magic offers a reading of Plath's poems in which mundane objects are turned into magic aids, such as a photograph, a letter, cards, and a pair of boots.

Plath was also familiar with anthropological books, such as Sir James George Frazer's *The Golden Bough* (1890) and Robert Graves's *The White Goddess* (1948), describing performances of ritual magic. The first volume of Frazer's book elaborates on ritualistic offerings and sacrifices to gods and goddesses, while his definition of sympathetic magic can be considered a type of ritual magic, which I discuss further in this chapter. Among the annotations in Plath's copy of the book, she underlined sentences in the chapter on Sympathetic Magic and marked the section on ritualistic exorcism in the chapter on Tabooed Acts: '[T]o conclude a peace with the Turks had reached their destination, they were received by shamans, who subjected them to ceremonial purification for the purpose of exorcising all harmful influences' (*SP The Golden Bough* 226). The citation focuses on fire used in exorcising rituals, which becomes a defining theme of Plath's 'Burning the Letters'. Robert Graves likewise mentions rituals in which incantations played a role, such as an Irish poetic rite in which fingertips and mnemonics were used; he calls the fingers the 'oracular agents' of the poet (*The White Goddess* 198). Hughes and Plath sought inspiration from Graves's book, expanding their literary understanding of ritual magic with anthropological and linguistic approaches. Plath's knowledge of ritual magic came from diverse sources, from early modern plays to mundane domestic performances, to which she often attributed magical powers. In her poetry, she transforms the spontaneous and personal practices to ritualistic magical performances.

In ritual magic, incantations and repetitions define the uttered language, creating the ritualistic effect. The language of rituals emphasises 'concrete iterative structures that index register, genre, and intent. Speakers' reflexivity and self-awareness regarding ritual language as register or genre often take the salient form of paired utterances, also called couplets' (Tavárez 519). Within the genre of poetry, techniques such as repetition and alliteration are used as linguistic and rhetorical devices. They help to 'release' the power generated by the magical charm (Weston 179). Repetition functions as a mnemonic device, which highlights the significance of the performativity of poetry. W. H. Auden, Plath's beloved poet of her youth, defined poetry in his Introduction to *The Poet's Tongue* (1935) as a 'memorable speech' (v). Here, he also attributes an almost supernatural character to emotionally moving poetry: '[T]he stimulus is the audible spoken word and cadence, to which in all its power of suggestion and incantation we must surrender, as we do when talking to an intimate friend' (Auden v). Auden's words show an influence on Plath's approach to poetry, particularly on the power of performative language. In a public lecture in 1978, Ted Hughes highlighted the relationship between poetry and magic: 'Poetry is traditionally supposed to be magical'; he argued that magic 'is one way of making things happen the way you want them to happen' ('The Critical Forum' Series). Hughes reflected on the spell-like effect of poetry writing in a letter in 1992 to Anne-Lorraine Bujon: 'I was aware in a gleeful sort of way that I was making a spell: I was conjuring into being an order of words, a density and (for me) essential simplicity of vocabulary that was inseparable from the substance of my life' (*THL* 630). Hughes's understanding of poetry as an act that possesses magical power shares similarities with the way Plath engaged with poetry writing as a ceremonious release of power through words. Plath's 'Daddy' and 'Burning the Letters' are examples where the performative utterances and repetitions create a spell-like effect: the former presents the intended outcome of exorcising the father's demonic spirit, and in the latter, the speaker performs a cleansing ritual and banishes the spiritual presence of the letters. While they have a similar supernatural intention, their poetic style and approach to ritual magic are different.

When composing her *Ariel* poems, Plath highlighted the significance of the performative aspects of poetry in a BBC interview in 1962: '[T]hey are written for the ear, not the eye: they are poems written out loud' (*AR* 195). Plath also asserted to Al Alvarez that her poems, such as 'Daddy', have to 'be read out loud' (Alvarez 31). Audio archives of Plath's reading of her poems inform us about her changing attitude towards the performativity of her poems. For example, she altered the highly formal voice she read *The Colossus* poems with, reading poems, such as 'Lady Lazarus' and 'Daddy', in a way that does not only sound like a performance but conveys the energy, passion, and power of spoken words. Kate Moses notes that in reading her poems out loud, Plath's voice adjusted 'to her breath, her delivery, her nuanced emotions riding the surface of her poems as well as her carefully measured statements – her performance, in other words' (90). Performativity is not only a mode of reading, but it also defines the poems. Tim Kendall argues that in Plath's late poetry, the poetic language is 'something ritualised, rhetorical and incantatory, conscious of its status of performance' (149). This chapter examines in detail the kinds of traditions Plath builds on that attribute magical power to language. The changes and erasures she made throughout the drafts of 'Daddy' and 'Burning the Letters' demonstrate her engagement with the concept of ritual magic and performance of poetic spellcasting.

5.1 The Ritual of Exorcism in 'Daddy'

'Daddy' narrates the overcoming of the paternal relationship in which ritualistic speech and acts aid the speaker. The alterations Plath made throughout the drafts demonstrate that the speaker expresses her ambiguous attitude towards the father by uttering the German words that disempower his spirit. 'Daddy' is a performance of exorcism for which the speaker employs quasi-magical German words and magical performances, such as the image-making of sympathetic magic. In her *WCD*, Plath underlined the definition of exorcise which is defined as '[t]o expel or drive off (an evil spirit) by adjuration, esp. by use of a holy name; to deliver (a person, place, etc.) from an evil spirit' ('exorcise'). Plath's annotation put an emphasis on the performance and not the religious connotation of exorcism, highlighting the way in which she engaged with this magical practice in her poem. The supernatural allusions and exorcism present in 'Daddy' have been the subject of scholarly criticism, such as Guinevara A. Nance and Judith P. Jones's use of Frazer's concept of sympathetic magic, noting that the poem performs an exorcism of the father (125). Stanley Plumly also argues that Plath's employment of Nazi imagery is linked to diabolism (16). Plath adds a political dimension to the supernatural imagery, thereby contributing to the tensions: the father moves from a 'bag full of God' to 'every German' and 'Panzer-man', 'Not God but a swastika', 'devil', 'man in black with a Meinkampf look', and finally, he is only a 'bastard' (*CP* 224–25). Thus, the German language uttered in the poem simultaneously has a political and magical dimension: the speaker subverts the expressions associated with Nazism to dispel and disempower the father.

In 'Daddy', the speaker both wants to resurrect (necromancy) and banish (exorcism) the father's spirit. E. M. Butler observes the blurred lines between exorcism and conjuration by relying on early modern sources. She summarises Reginald Scot's recording of a ritual in *The Discovery of Witchcraft* (1584), who mocked witchcraft beliefs:

> It goes into fearful detail about the last hours of the doomed man, during which the sorcerer binds himself to pray for the soul of the condemned criminal all the days of his life; and the latter engages to return from the other world and do all the necromancer's bidding on pain of everlasting damnation [...] The urgency of the language, the relentless pressure brought to bear on the victim whose last hours are spent listening over and over again, twenty-four times at least, whilst the other reads the bond, repeating inexorably: 'Remember thine oath and promise', all contribute to producing a ghastly impression. (Butler 239–40)

This description resembles the ritual magic performed in 'Daddy': the speaker admits to summoning the father's spirit, who is a dark and diabolical figure, while repeating her incantation. The definition of necromancy by the historian Frank Klaassen offers a reading of Plath's narration of the ritual magic performance in 'Daddy': necromancy 'concerns itself principally with conjuring demons, though sometimes also angels [...] It employs repurposed liturgical fragments and structures, a variety of consecrated objects and lengthy ritual invocations reflecting the standard rhetoric of prayer and exorcism' (201). The ambiguous perception of the father, a worshipped figure and a devil, shows the complexities of the ritual magic in 'Daddy'. The poetic persona first resurrects the father's spirit to reconcile the paternal relationship and employs the rhetoric of exorcism to break free from the binding bond by disempowering him with the politically charged language used as spellwork.

The speaker calls on the different identities of the father (daddy, bastard, Nazi, and the devil), which she uses as curses. In Plath's copy of Frazer's *The Golden Bough*, she added the marginalia on the top of the sections on Tabooed Words that reads: "names can never hurt me" (284). Her remark is in quotation marks, suggesting that it is an utterance or taken from a text. Plath heavily underlined the section that aligns with the way she employs the father's name in 'Daddy': 'The custom of abstaining from all mention of the names of the dead [. . .] was a fear of evoking the ghost' (*SP The Golden Bough* 293). Here, Frazer suggests the power of naming the dead, in particular when discussing a taboo or invoking the dead. The frequent and various names of the father in the poem mean that the speaker is not afraid of summoning the father's ghost. The title word 'Daddy' is usually uttered by a loving child; however, in the poem, Plath reverses the speaker's attitude towards the paternal bond with the names: the father is not a source of intimacy and protection anymore but of possessive power, threat, and violence. Further, the word 'daddy' always appears in the lines expressing the wish to break free from the relationship, reinforcing the magical intent.

'Daddy' presents a strong gendered and political power imbalance, which contributes to the tensions. The speaker confronts the father whose association with German confined her to a state of repetition that recalls ritualistic utterances. She claims that the German language is 'stuck in a barb wire snare. / Ich, ich, ich, ich' (*CP* 223). Langdon Hammer originates the imagery from Plath's German book: 'The "snare" is an image generated by the visual effect of the Gothic script in Plath's German grammar, where German and English are printed in different fonts' ('Plath's German' 256). Similar to the repetition of 'daddy', the echo of 'ich' is a ritualistic speech. The personal pronoun expresses ambivalence since it both helps the speaker to gain autonomy and traps her in a repetitive state of selfhood. Plath employs the second person singular 'Du', which is the informal 'you'. The German pronoun cannot be translated into English; she misplaces the father by uttering: 'I thought every German was you' (*CP* 223). The speaker's unsuccessful attempt to locate the father in the English language evokes Rudolf Steiner's linguistic theory, which claims that high German language (*Hochdeutsch*) – the language of Goethe and Hegel – is abstract and has a spiritual implication for 'the German soul': it is impenetrable by other languages, such as English, making it untranslatable (45). The inaccessibility of the German language is implied in the poem; the speaker hears and utters it, yet she cannot reach it. According to Steiner, when you hear a foreign language, you 'have to use your power of abstraction, the pure power of conceptualising' (49). The speaker cannot understand the German words, which makes the process of translation and transformation impossible. The dynamic energy of 'Daddy' comes from the tension that the lack of comprehension produces. The poem employs the German language like spellwork in which the magical powers of language are sourced from the seemingly nonsensical foreign meaning, which I discuss further in this chapter.

The violent German expressions associated with the Nazi figure, who is an Aryan, Panzer-man and has a 'Meinkampf' look, aim to disempower the father's spirit. These are particularly prominent in Plath's draft: in the undated holograph, the second page is filled with crossed-out lines, smudges, and alterations, implying her dynamic writing. She employs heavily loaded expressions in the holograph, including the explicit mention of Hitler. Plath contrasts the violent imagery with the intimate possessive pronoun of 'you', which she toned down in the later versions of the poem. Violence and intimacy are even more intertwined by the father figure's affection for Nazism. In the draft, Plath slightly misspells the German word *Durchmarsch*, which means march or walkthrough. In her *WCD*, Plath underlined the definition of Luftwaffe, a term she then used in the poem: 'The air force of the Third Reich' ('Luftwaffe'). She likewise annotated the definition of the swastika, which foremost refers to the 'svasti welfare' ('swastika'). The double meaning of the word highlights the conflict between violence and intimacy in the poem that comes from the father's lack of 'parental role as caregiver' (Keniston 46). By placing the violent German expressions next to the childlike language like 'daddy', Plath further draws attention to the powers of the paternal and patriarchal German language. In the drafts, Plath's handwritten dashes are sharp like a knife cut: they function as extra-textual violence towards the addressed father and reinforce the role of punctuation as an expression of the ambivalent paternal relationship. Dashes in, for example, Emily Dickinson's poems can signal a 'dialogic interchange' (Wylder 212). The two other dashes in 'Daddy' appear after lines mentioning the murder or death of the father, for example: 'If I've killed one man, I've killed two—' (*CP* 224). Plath's em dashes contribute to the performative reading and reinforce the intimate yet violent relationship between the speaker and the addressed father's spirit.

Besides the violent political force of the German expressions in the poem, the language reflects Plath's family heritage. For her parents,

German represented privacy, the public scrutiny and negative perception during World War I and II, and professional achievements: it was a 'language not only of domestic intimacy, but of cultural authority, the language of the higher scholarship and the modern university' (Hammer, 'Plath's German' 246). German signifies one of the peaks of European culture: the language of Thomas Mann, Goethe, Kafka, the Grimms' fairy tales, and Freud. Clark argues that in 'Daddy', the metaphor of the Holocaust is 'a fantasy of purgation and purity: only by aligning her speaker with the enemy of the Germans could she reject her own Germanness, which, in the wake of the Holocaust, seemed like a curse' (*Red Comet* 6). The understanding of German as a curse on Plath and her poetic speaker further implies the magical powers attributed to the language in the poem. E. M. Butler likewise identifies German language and literature with one of the main traditions of ritual magic 'from puerility and squalor into poetry, fairy-tales and romance' (251). Plath had a lifelong struggle to learn the language of her ancestors; her calendar in Smith shows that she took regular German classes during the spring and summer of 1962 and developed an extensive vocabulary to learn it. Her handwritten notes of German words are also written on the Smith pink memo paper. In the poem, Plath codes the German expressions as foreign and quasi-magical utterances, through which she expresses the ambivalence of the paternal bond. It is equally violent ('Panzerman', 'Luftwaffe'), intimate ('Du'), and seemingly nonsensical ('gobbledygoo'). The latter resembles magical phrases and spells in which the meaning – and attributed magical power – comes from a foreign word (Vernel 141). Historical examples demonstrate the role of foreign languages in spellwork: in ancient Greece, philosophers considered Greek the language of contemplation and foreign languages the expressions of rituals and magic: 'They operated on the premise that Greek and foreign languages have their own special characteristics on either side' (Struck 402). A well-known example of the foreign origin of magic words is 'abracadabra', whose etymology is either Hebrew, Greek, or Aramaic (Waterman). During the medieval period, in English legal documents, the term 'anathema maranatha' was a curse, in which the second word with Aramaic origin functions as a 'quasi-magical incantatory expression' (Danet and Bogoch 152).[2] Amy Hungerford notes that in Allen Ginsberg's poetry, he uses Sanskrit as a sacred language

[2] The term 'Anathema Maranatha' appears in the King James Version of the Bible, for example, in 1 Corinthians 16:22 in the New Testament, in which the first word means accused and the second refers to the arrival of Lord.

similar to Latin, the language of chanting and magic, which, like Plath's gobbledygoo 'appear[s] to be gibberish' (31). The cultural beliefs about and literary allusions to the foreign origin of magic words interpret the incantatory German language of 'Daddy' as a spellwork that can neither be fully acquired nor forgotten. The speaker remains haunted by language associated with the supernatural and the paternal spirit.

Whereas the speaker associates German identity with the father, her maternal line is linked to Jewish identity: 'With my gipsy ancestress and my weird luck / And my Taroc pack and my Taroc pack / I may be a bit of a Jew' (*CP* 223). The speaker's 'weird luck' echoes the maternal curse from 'The Disquieting Muses' and recalls the three hag-like maternal ancestors in 'All the Dead Dears', which I discussed in Chapter 3. In the holograph of 'Daddy', Plath refers to the maternal ancestors explicitly and names her maternal grandmother. Plath annotated the definition of 'gypsy' in *WCD*, which expresses her interest in nomadism, not the ethnicity of the identity: 'One of a <u>wandering</u> Caucasian race coming originally from India' ('gypsy').[3] Hughes alludes to Plath's association of the 'gypsy' woman and cursing in his poem 'The Gypsy', implying that the curse of the French woman whom they met in Paris foreshadowed the death of Plath: 'Among the tables and vanished, leaving her words / [. . .] Bigger, darker, founded far deeper // [. . .] But you / Went on writing postcards' (*BL* 117). In the poem, '[i]t is Hughes who fears her curse', not Plath (Wagner 128). The association that both Hughes and Plath engage with harnesses harmful stereotypes by conflating nomadism, ethnic identities, and the tradition and practice of fortune-telling. These, however, were frequently used at the time and are still employed in contemporary political discourses. In the Preface of *The Painted Caravan: A Penetration Into the Secrets of Tarot* (1954), which Plath bought in 1956, Basil Ivan Rákóczi argues that the 'esoteric key' to the doors of Symbols is controlled by the 'Master Gypsy' who 'is generally a woman in spite of her title' (8). Rákóczi's book includes an inscription, mentioning T. S. Eliot's long poem: 'At the end of the book you find on the left the Hanged Man of Gipsy Initiation Rites and on the right, the Drowned Phoenician Sailor, a card under the sign of Ward described by T. S. Eliot in "The Waste Land"' (6). Plath engages with some of these racial and racist stereotypes, though she does not refer to the fortune-telling card associated with Roma and Jewish people, which I discuss later in detail. In the holograph, Plath

[3] The term 'gypsy ' comes from the word Egyptian as Roma people were believed to come from Egypt, while they originate from India. It is a term controversial at best and deemed offensive by many.

ordered the lines differently, and they tie together misfortune and the Jewish identity, alluding to the Holocaust. In the final version of 'Daddy', she significantly alters the meaning by bringing forward the repeated 'Taroc pack', which links the cards to the speaker's maternal ancestors and misfortune.

The conflict between violence and intimacy in 'Daddy' is further reinforced since both Jews, Roma, and Sinti people were persecuted by the Nazi regime, contrasting the speaker's maternal and paternal heritages. Monica Black argues that '[t]he idea that Jews had magical power surfaces in a variety of German cultural artefacts, before and during the Nazi period' (219). Additionally, in the early modern period, the prosecutions of witches often coexisted with prosecutions of Jews. Jewish religious terminologies, such as the sabbath, shabbat, or synagogue, were appropriated to describe the gathering of witches, demonstrating the perception of Judaism as 'anti-Christianity, indeed as a form of Devil-worship' (Cohn 145). Plath's poem reflects the prejudices and adds a political and gendered dimension to this link by opposing the father's Nazi identity with maternal Jewish heritage. Plath sailed several times across the Atlantic and had a European immigrant background with possibly Jewish heritages from Austria and Hungary (Clark, *Red Comet* 773). Thus, the merger of identities and blend of personal and national histories suggest her uncertainty about her ancestry. Her reference to the Tyrol, a region between Austria, Germany, and Italy, highlights the ambiguities of ancestry. For Plath, visiting the place of her maternal ancestors was a significant quest, which she never got to do. In her non-fiction piece 'The Ideal Summer,' written in 1953 for the *Mademoiselle* College Board Contest, Plath dreams about visiting 'Geneva, and then Vienna and the Tyrol where our grandparents were born. Here we should stay in the ancestral inn that our relatives still run, and we shall spend days in them, skiing in the mountains' (*Prose* 524). Plath's handwritten draft of 'Daddy' explicitly highlights the tension between the Aryan Nazi father figure and the idealised landscape of Vienna and Tyrol. The maternal ancestry becomes central to exorcising the father's spirit from the speaker's psyche.

In the poem, the 'Taroc pack' refers to a family inheritance. Julia Gordon-Bramer differentiates between Tarot and Tarock; the former is the fortune-telling pack, and the latter is a European card game that originated in Italy, naming Plath's version of the cards 'Bavarian' (235). Plath received a pack of Tarot cards from Hughes for her birthday in 1956, and as mentioned, it was auctioned in 2021. She inherited the other pack of cards from her maternal Austrian ancestors. In 'Daddy', Plath attributes a symbolic meaning to her only possession, employing it for protection and not for its divinatory powers. In her letters, Plath distinguished between the two packs of cards: when she acquired W. B. Yeats's London flat, she wrote to Harriet Cooke that she started reading her 'Tarot cards earnestly now' (*L2* 924). An entry from December 1959 references Tarock as a game: '[T]aught Ted's sister and Hilda's daughter [. . .] how to play Tarock, and we play a great deal' (*L2* 378). Not long after finishing 'Daddy', she noted using the same pack as a fortune-telling device: 'I look forward to the directions of the Tarock pack'; and as a game: '[B]ringing the Tarock cards [to Winifred Davies] as she is having friends' (*L2* 888; 905). In *Letters Home*, Aurelia Plath specifies that the family cards are 'the Viennese version of the Italian game' (*LH* 360). It was a family gift from Plath's maternal grandmother who came from Austria, which likely got lost and was never part of any archives. In the Harriet Rosenstein research papers, several interviewees, including Suzette Macedo, mention a 'great-aunt, a Viennese aunt who had left her these cards' (Macedo, Suzette and Helder). The deck has many local variations within Europe, including its specific cultural settings and heritages, like clothing, landscape, and nineteenth-century fashion and various occupations. A common element of the pack is that they have four suits and depict moments from rural life, monarchs, and a fool. William M. Johnston notes that Tarock was also Freud's favourite Saturday evening activity and the only leisure activity that transcended all classes in Austria (241).[4] Plath's reference to the deck associated with her maternal heritage has cultural and historical connotations, which she employs as a protective power against the authoritarian father. The 'Taroc pack' in the poem recalls the creative-aesthetic element of ritual magic in which mundane items are transformed into magical aids during the performance. Plath does not refer to the fortune-telling cards but seeks maternal guardianship, which de-problematizes the stereotyping of ethnic identities.

The ritualistic act in the poem is performed in the eleventh stanza in the lines, 'You stand at the blackboard, daddy, / I made a model of you' (*CP* 224). 'Daddy' is not the first poem in which Plath suggests effigy making – a type of sympathetic magic – as a magical performance; as we have seen, some earlier poems, such as 'Witch Burning' and 'The Lady and the Earthenware Head', allude to this magical performance associated with witches. 'Daddy' employs the family photograph to reconcile the

[4] Freud's pack consists of fifty-four cards and is produced by the Viennese card brand Piatnik. It is on display in the Sigmund Freud Museum in Vienna.

relationship. Helle highlights that the photograph, kept in SCSC, symbolises the tensions between personal and political: it reflects on the 'associations between this figure and the father/führer already present in German folklore and Nazi propaganda' and the character of the 'German professional' recognised by German-American immigrants (41–42). The photograph mediates the violence and intimacy of the ambiguous paternal relationship through which she summons the father's spirit. He is both the devil and the victimised effigy, which reinforces the ambiguity of the bond.

Plath's reference in the poem to torture devices, such as the rack, intensifies the tension between violence and intimacy, alluding to the fact that the violent Nazi father had used these. Plath annotated the definition of the rack in her *WCD*: 'An engine of torture consisting of a large frame having rollers at each end to which the limbs were fastened and between which the body was stretched' ('rack'). In the early modern period, the rack was also used as a torture device on witches: it was believed that the witch's 'integral, diabolic personality might be stripped away by the application of pain to uncover the truth' (Roper, *Oedipus and the Devil* 204). Plath repeatedly merges the authoritarian father/torturer/executioner in her October 1962 poems, evoking historical periods, such as the witch-hunt and World War II, during which torture was used. The speaker finishes the ritualistic performance with the speech act, 'I do, I do' (*CP* 224). The repetition does away with the father and creates a ritualistic effect, enhancing the performance. The tension is resolved by confirming that the 'voices just can't worm through' (*CP* 224). The absence of the father's voice confirms that his German language has vanished, banishing the language of violence with the use of ritual magic.

In an undated typescript, Plath ended the poem with a handwritten stanza in which the speaker summons the village community to do away with the father: 'They are dancing ~~shoe, boot, shoes~~ and stamping on you' (TS 'Daddy', undated). Here, the crossed-out boot is evoked as an object, which was previously the father's 'boot in the face', a metonym alluding to Nazism. Suzanne Macedo claimed that the boot in 'Daddy' refers to an actual object, remembering that there was a discarded pair of boots in Plath's North Tawton cottage ('Macedo, parts three and four'). Similar to the pack of cards and the photograph, the boot is deployed as a tool, representing both intimacy and violence. The crowd's violence resembles stoning, used as capital punishment, which suggests that the father has, indeed, committed a crime. The line 'They always knew it was you' suggests his long-suspicious character, which justifies his removal from the community. The father's exclusion from the group evokes the ritual of excommunication. Harriet Rosenstein remarked that Aurelia Plath told her that the villagers' violence in 'Daddy' was a reference to Ted Hughes whom the small North Tawton community allegedly disliked ('Lucie-Smith, interview recording'). The ritualised banishment of outsider figures in the poem also recalls 'The Bee Meeting' in which the villagers perform an initiation ceremony. Here, the speaker experiences alienation from the others and seeks protection from the father's spirit. Although they present different narratives of rituals, both poems portray a collective ritualised performance in which there are clear boundaries between who is outside and who is a trusted member of the community. In the final version of 'Daddy', Plath reduces the mob mentality and violence of the ritual, which is instead presented as a celebratory event.

'Daddy' utilises ritualistic language, such as repetitions, rhymes, and echoes and engages with the characteristics of the language of magic by uttering the German expressions to which Plath adds a political meaning reinforcing the tensions presented in the poem. She employs the creative-aesthetic elements of ritual magic, which appeal to practitioners: the speaker uses mundane objects either to disempower and exorcise the father's spirit with the photograph and boot or to protect her heritage with the pack of cards. 'Daddy' achieves its goal with the last utterance, and the speaker breaks free from the possessive paternal bond. Though the final version of the poem erases or alters some of the ritualistic and expressive content, Plath builds on historical and literary traditions of ritual magic to portray the poetic exorcism.

5.2 Dispelling Spirits in 'Burning the Letters'

'Burning the Letters' shares some characteristics with 'Daddy' in presenting ritual magic to narrate the banishing of spirits. However, here the speaker performs the act of burning to dispel the harmful spiritual presence of the letters and uses repetitive sentences, which enhance the ritualistic effects. Behind the narrative of 'Burning the Letters', an autobiographical story unfolds. The anecdotes about and descriptions of the event are loaded with witchcraft and ritual magic, exaggerating certain elements of the bonfire-making where Plath burnt some of Hughes's letters and poems, the manuscript of her second novel, and letters from her mother. Clarissa Roche, an acquaintance of Plath, told Rosenstein in a voyeuristic style that Plath selected the date of this ritual corresponding to the full moon, and in the middle of a circle in the garden, she read from a book 'magic words' resembling 'abracadabra' and 'mumble jumble', as a joke ('Roche, part three'). Ted Hughes also claimed that Plath 'had been practising "witchcraft"' during the autumn of 1962; however, her neighbour David Compton stated that the bonfire-making was a spontaneous act of Plath cleaning her home (*Red Comet* 739). The varied accounts parallel the ambiguous perception and unclear boundaries between mundane domestic practices and ritualistic burning with magical aims. In addition, in post-war Britain, burning household waste, or 'separation and incineration', was common until the 1960s and a favoured way to dispose of rubbish (Stokes, Köster and Sambrook 84). Items, such as food waste, old papers, and sanitary towels, were likewise often burned in the garden (Castelow). There is no textual evidence that Plath disposed of household waste by burning, therefore, the destruction of personal items in a bonfire holds significance. The practice of burning items simultaneously articulates a spontaneous and domestic practice and a ritualised performance of magic. Plath's poem allows the mundane and the magical to be equally present, while interrogating the boundaries between household items and letters containing spirits.

'Burning the Letters' partakes in epistolary discourses defined by physical and spiritual presence and absence. Typically, there is a time delay between writing and receiving and reading letters: an epistle 'lends itself to the temporal ambiguity whereby past is taken for present' (Altman 132). The textual *I* and *you* do not exist in the same space and time, suggesting that the writer and recipient are spiritually present (as handwriting) and absent (as the addressed). Emily Dickinson noted the hauntology of letter writing in a letter to T. W. Higginson in 1869: 'A Letter always feels to me like immortality because it is the mind alone without corporeal friend' (196). 'Burning the Letters' addresses the immortality of the epistolary subjects in the last line: 'What immortality is. That it is immortal' (*CP* 205). Jonathan Ellis argues that Plath's poem 'represents the culmination of Plath's view of letter writing as a quasi-magical form in which the author and the recipient of the letter are somehow literally present' ('On Sylvia Plath's Letters' 24). Despite wanting to destroy them, the speaker summons and interacts with the writer and recipient of the letters, performing a ritualised act where she attributes magical powers to the letters. The metonym of treating the letters as the spirits of the people who wrote them implies the presence of the supernatural in the ritual of burning. Plath's poem, like the letters themselves, 'reverses time and miraculously brings the dead back to life' (Ellis, 'Last Letters' 244). By doing so, the speaker aims to transform them from objects containing spirits to mere ashes, symbolising both committing a harmful act against the people and performing a cleansing ritual on them.

Reading 'Burning the Letters' in parallel with literary and epistolary discourses contextualises the ritualistic burning of letters and their magical powers. Margaretta Jolly argues that '[d]estroying a personal letter is especially associated with love or family gone wrong, just as the preservation of personal letters is typically a woman's task'; however, she adds, recent psychotherapy and New Age spiritualist movements also 'advise cathartic epistolary bonfires or even writing letters expressly for a ritual destruction' (25–26). 'Burning the Letters' shares the characteristics of the traditionally feminine domestic task of preserving and destroying letters and the therapeutic benefits of burning them. The letters function as vessels of the spirit, thus, burning them symbolically severs ties between the people and destroys their spiritual presence. Plath draws on literary texts on epistolary discourses, such as *Jane Eyre*, in which Jane discovers that her letters to Mr Rochester did not get delivered since Bertha Mason started a fire, which burned down Thornfield: 'No wonder that letters addressed to people here had never received an answer: as well despatch epistles to a vault in a church aisle' (414). The annihilation of the manor house ends the destructive relationship between Rochester and his wife and symbolises the rekindling of passion between Jane and him. Brontë's novel further implies that Rochester's ghostly voice that Jane hears is the spectral presence of unanswered letters.

The therapeutic effect of burning letters also appears in contemporary culture: today, handwritten letters are much less common, therefore, they hold an additional personal significance, often associated with a noteworthy event, grief, trauma, or heartache. A recent example of the therapeutic burning of letters is Taylor Swift's lyrics in the song 'evermore' (2021), in which the speaker writes epistles to the burning flames. In the song, Swift references her mental anguish and uses letter writing and burning as self-reflection and a ritualised cleansing from the past. Her healing becomes possible with the simple transformation of words – from 'would' to 'wouldn't' – which attributes purifying powers to the reflective letter writing. The poem by the American contemporary poet Daniel Hall likewise emphasises the belief that the letters embody the spirit of a person: 'Believers in the afterlife perform / this purifying rite' (46). The poem 'Love-Letter-Burning' from 2013 acknowledges that for the archivist's eye, such an act is pure destruction; however – similar to Plath's 'Burning the Letters' – the 'sacrificial fire' purifies from the once beloved. Burning epistles is a metaphor for purification and it can only achieve its goal of cathartic cleansing if one believes in the spiritual afterlives of letters.

'Burning the Letters' deploys the purifying and protective function attributed to fire rituals. Plath draws on magical practices of burning spirits presented in *The Golden Bough* on the fire's cleansing effect (Gill, 'Your story. My story' 78–79). Frazer writes that

> ceremonial fires have no necessary reference to the sun but are simply purificatory in intention, being designed to burn up and destroy all harmful influences, whether these are conceived in a personal form as witches, demons, and monsters, or in an impersonal form as a sort of pervading taint or corruption of the air. (744)

The reference to witches and demons further contextualises the burning imagery in Plath's October 1962 poems, such as 'Lady Lazarus', 'Fever 103°', and the draft of 'Ariel', in which her poetic personae inhabit, consume, and aid themselves with fire. Among her earlier poems, 'Witch Burning' expresses Plath's attribution of cleansing powers to the fiery burning. A similar narrative unfolds in 'Burning the Letters', in which fire functions as a magical agent to purify the speaker's surroundings from the spirits. The speaker interacts with the spirits of the epistles who are partaking in the ritualistic burning. Kendall highlights that many of Plath's October poems are addressed to a specific person or persons (161). Brain also notes that these poems 'have epistolary qualities, and owe much to her apprenticeship as a letter writer' ('Sylvia Plath and You' 89). 'Burning the Letters' centres on the speaker's interaction with the letters; however, the earlier versions of the poem are explicit about the magical attributes of the burning ritual, which later Plath changed to more disguised or metaphorical allusions. The drafts highlight a strong presence of ritualistic elements with the attribution of magical powers to the poetic language. The developments in 'Burning the Letters' show Plath's interest in ritual magic by transforming the domestic practice of getting rid of household rubbish into a spontaneous magical performance.

There are seven drafts of 'Burning the Letters', which are filled with crossed-out lines, words written over the top of one another, and rearranged stanza order. The first draft is a heavily edited holograph, which is the most indicative of magical allusions. The second draft is a similarly untidy part-typescript and part-holograph. These first two undated versions do not have a clear structure, which reveals a lively and dynamic writing process; however, the repeated crossed-out lines and marginalia make the reading challenging. Plath's writing becomes cleaner in the fourth draft, yet the typescripts suggest that she had difficulties with reconciling some parts of the narrative. While the earlier versions are written in one block, only in the fifth draft, an undated typescript, does Plath arrange the text into stanzas. The seventh draft is dated 12 October 1962 and features two drawings, an owl and a cat on the right side of the paper. This version is the closest to the final poem. The drafts expose that Plath struggled with the outline of the last stanza and until the third draft, and the poem contained several passages that enhance the magical attributes of ritualistic burning.

'Burning the Letters' comprises four stanzas, in which the first introduces the initial stage of the performance, the creation of the bonfire. The speaker justifies the burning of the letters by blaming them for the knowledge they possess: 'What did they know that I didn't?' (*CP* 204). In the first holograph, the poem starts with the first-person possessive pronoun, which proposes an intimate relationship between the speaker and the fire; it is something that she summons. The phrase also refers to her burning passion, suggesting either her love or her revenge. The fire is both destructive and excites the speaker's imagination: 'This fire may lick and fawn, but it is merciless' (*CP* 204). The poetic persona directs fire not at the self but at others. In this draft, the speaker utters her reason for burning the letters: 'And here is your handwriting, ~~paper after paper~~ the spry hooks, they lie' (MS 'Burning the Letters', undated). The crossed-out repetition of 'paper after paper' creates a ritualistic effect, suggesting a dynamic reading. By the fourth version of the poem, Plath erased both the personal significance of the letters and the motive for burning them. She only alludes to her loneliness. The shift from 'your handwriting' to 'the writing' distances the speaker from the epistles. Plath's early drafts present the burning of the letters as an intimate dialogue between the addressed person and the speaker, alluding to sympathetic magic, which marks the epistolary discourse.

Plath initially referenced not only the burning of the epistles but also other personal belongings. On the second page of the first holograph, the following line reinforces the magical attributes of the burning ritual: 'So I burnt the letters and the dust puffs and the old hair' (MS 'Burning the Letters', undated). The mixture of the domestic (hair, dust) with the professional (writings) demonstrates that the fire was not only made to burn the letters but the speaker also has to cleanse the home from the negative spiritual presence, which recalls Frazer's study of the purifying and protective effect of fire rituals. The items are significant objects that embody the addressee: by burning such personal belongings, she gets rid of the spiritual presence of the lover. Plath continued the draft by starting the next three lines with the same expression of 'At least', then followed it up with allusions to cleaning, which suggests the purifying characteristic of the burning. In the later versions, Plath erased the powerful three-time repetition and the lines alluding to an intimate burning ritual. In the second draft, she crossed out the burned items with a more personal significance and added them as marginalia, implying that the epistles and the burning are incomplete. Although Plath kept the cleaning effect of the burning, the erasure of repetitions diminishes the ritualistic effect of the lines. Van Dyne reads Plath's deletion as a substitution with 'the repetitive whine of the trapped and friendless housewife, the oddly defiant smoke signal of the carbon birds' (*Revising Life* 37). In the final version, the lines rather narrate the speaker's anguish: 'And at least it will be a good place now, the attic. / At least I won't be strung just under the surface, / Dumb fish' (*CP* 204). The shorter lines create a dynamic reading, and the internal rhymes contribute to the ritualistic effect. The repeated 'smiles' of the spry hooks are a metaphor for the letters identified with the lover; nevertheless, the speaker is alone. There is a shift in Plath's writing from the intimate 'your handwriting' to the metaphorical 'hooks' and 'smiles'. The final version of the stanza lacks the purifying effect of the burning, which was dominant in the first three drafts. The removal of the intimacy of the epistolary discourse also erases the spiritual attribution of the letter burning.

The earlier versions of the poem demonstrate a personal but ambiguous relationship between the speaker and letters: '~~Spirit~~ word after ~~spirit~~ word ~~gives itself up~~ is lit! / They darken like Joan of Arc, the heart is a cinder' (MS 'Burning the Letters', undated). Plath's alliteration in the draft enhances the ritualistic effect of the repetition. The crossed-out wording of '~~Spirit~~ word after ~~spirit~~ word' further attributes magical power to written words. The exclamation mark highlights the performativity of the line, which resembles an incantation. Once again, the drafts show that Plath erased the magical allusions of the ritual and focused on the destruction of the epistolary writings. Ellis argues that the speaker wants to burn the letters as 'textual remains' embodying an actual person; he compares this textural revival to the bodily resurrection in 'Lady Lazarus' and 'Fever 103°' ('On Sylvia Plath's Letters' 25). Plath's speaker treats the burning letters as people who could 'save themselves'. The likening of the letters to the martyr shows an ambiguous relationship. As highlighted in Chapter 2, Joan of Arc's figure fascinated Plath and influenced some poems like 'Lady Lazarus' and 'Fever 103°'. In 'Burning the Letters', the speaker perceives her act as murder; like Joan of Arc, the spirit of the letter is annihilated. In the third draft, Plath reinstated the lines in the second half of the poem but removed the spiritual power attributed to the epistles. The unstable position of lines with references to martyrdom, witch burning, and spiritual purification expresses that Plath was not clear in her perception of the letters. Her use of martyr imagery identifies the rival with the ambiguous figure of Joan of Arc. Van Dyne argues that the drafts reveal Plath's uncertainty toward the rival girl who is represented as a martyr/witch: 'Plath fails to resolve [. . .] whether she murders or is herself ghoulishly tormented' (*Revising Life* 37). The drafts also suggest that she struggled to reconcile whether the letters are merely objects that she can get rid of or the spiritual embodiment of the individuals who possess her and how much power they have over her. While earlier drafts read the poem as a form of a spell that banishes the spirits of the epistolary person(s), the final poem treats the letters as objects, not as spirits, concluding the elimination of their magical power. Plath's abandonment of the martyr/witch imagery alters the speaker's ambiguous response to the epistles.

One of the most significant changes happened in the second draft: in the middle of the second page, Plath's speaker appears as a murderous persona, alluding to a ritualistic murder similar to 'Daddy'. Here, the speaker references a photograph, representing the person she aims to harm. Plath's draft further gives evidence of the violent sacrificial element of the purification, which mimics the purifying fire rituals described by Frazer: 'Not uncommonly, effigies are burned in these fires, or a pretence is made of burning a living person in them; and there are grounds for believing that anciently human beings were actually burned on these occasions' (706). Plath did not annotate this part of her book but the earlier version of 'Burning the Letters' reveals the explicit performance of ritual magic with the employment of sympathetic magic for spiritual purification. The draft portrays a significantly more violent performance than mere burning epistolary writings. The purifying burning, repetitive language, and the spiritual presence of epistolary persons(s) express the performance of ritual magic. The violence of the ritual is reinforced by Plath's personification of the letters that she burns, attributing supernatural powers to the epistles.

In the final version of 'Burning the Letters', the last stanza portrays the release from the tension. The line 'Pale eyes, patent-leather gutturals!' rules the stanza not only with its commanding *p* sounds but by featuring the only exclamation mark of the poem (*CP* 205). It is the most dynamic part of the poem, which mimics the casting of a spell. In the first holograph, Plath concludes the poem with this line, suggesting a cleansing power to the repetitive sounds. Here, there is no decline from the intense emotions but it ends with a moment of force, which contributes to the magical power attributed to language to dispel the spirits. In the line, 'gutturals' refer to harsh sounds produced in the back of the throat, which is particularly prominent in, for example, the Hebrew language (A. L. Miller 56–57). Gutturals are also one of the first sounds that infants produce, which recalls the childlike 'gobbledygoo' in 'Daddy', implying that the 'gutturals' in 'Burning the Letters' form a quasi-magical language that utilises the power of spellwork. In the final version, Plath ends the poem with a repetition, highlighting continuity: 'What immortality is. That it is immortal' (*CP* 205). The line references the cathartic violence in the stanza, evoking the fox's 'red burst and a cry' that keeps 'Dyeing the air' (*CP* 205). 'Immortality' indicates the cyclical character of repetitions, which accentuates the ritualistic effect of the poem and reinforces the spiritual characteristic of the letter. The echoes and excessive repetitions of sounds, words, and expressions contribute to the dynamic and lively reading of 'Burning the Letters'. The erased passages from the drafts indicate ritual magic: they employ ritualistic language and act with the attribution of supernatural powers to language. Throughout her writing process, Plath reduced and then almost completely eliminated the spiritual presence of the letters. 'Burning the Letters' reinforces the pattern in Plath's poetry whereby she erased the magical elements that are common in the initial versions of her poems and chose more allusive and metaphorical poetic devices. The final version of the poem diminishes the repetitions and alters the sound patterns recurring in her drafts. Plath shifts the focus of the poem from the magical powers of the uttered language that develops the ritual to enhanced poetic techniques.

'Daddy' and 'Burning the Letters' are performances in which ritualistic acts accompany ritualistic utterances. Although the poems have significant differences in their poetic language, rhyme scheme, and structure, they express a magical intent. Whereas 'Daddy' presents the ritual of exorcism and the speaker deploys repetitions to create a ritualistic effect, 'Burning the Letters' offers a subtler portrayal of the ritual magic through the burning of the letters as vessels containing spirits. Both poems have earlier versions where the language and performance of ritual magic are presented directly. During the process of writing 'Daddy', Plath altered the often highly charged language to more allusive phrases and reduced the magical dimension of the politically charged German language. In 'Burning the Letters', she erased the magical powers the letters possess and changed the incantatory language to neater and tighter poetic lines, focusing on purification without implying ritual magic. Plath encountered the concept of ritual magic from early modern plays, occultist practices used as creative inspirations, and anthropological works like *The Golden Bough*. Her experimentation with the magical attribution of informal rites was likewise influential on her poetry. An attentive reading of Plath's drafts reveals her interest in the magical powers of domestic rituals and mundane objects, alluding to the creative-aesthetic element of rituals. 'Daddy' and 'Burning the Letters' articulate ideas, cultural beliefs, and literary traditions in associating magical powers with poetry and the poetic language.

CHAPTER 6

Supernatural Transformations

Plath's poems frequently employ transformation narratives to interrogate women's struggle for autonomy and access to power. She draws on literary, historical, and folkloric sources on witches, mythological figures with transformational powers, and classical myths on the metamorphosis of women through which she critiques gender norms and societal boundaries between human and nonhuman subjects. The term 'supernatural transformation' refers to any physical transformation with a supernatural element, such as the change from human to vegetal form, hybridity, and shapeshifting to an animal form. Narratives about altering the female body challenge or reaffirm women's access to autonomy and power and discuss what is considered normative and where the boundaries are – if any – between humans and nonhumans. While metamorphosis, shapeshifting, and hybridity portray diverse narratives on female power these concepts also share similarities: they depict a physical change, which exemplifies that women's bodies can be modified and transformed. They raise questions about gendered bodily autonomy and retell the narratives previously reserved for the male-dominated literary tradition, for example, the concept of metamorphosis associated with stories from Ovid's *Metamorphoses*. From an early age, Plath employed classical mythology in her poetry, such as in her 1949 poem 'To Ariadne (deserted by Theseus)', anticipating the influence of classical stories on mistreated women with ambiguous power relations in, for example, 'Electra on Azalea Path', 'Virgin in a Tree', and 'Edge.' In her *Ariel* poems, she often narrates a poetic reclamation of the female body and autonomy through the supernatural transformations of her heroines.

This chapter focuses on Plath's poems, such as 'Virgin in a Tree', in which she seeks inspiration from myths and classical sources to retell women's violent metamorphosis. Her writings show her well-informed knowledge of beliefs about witches and shapeshifting creatures, such as 'Goatsucker', and her experimentation with hybridity and fluidity in

'Ariel'. In addition to her poems, I pay attention to her letters, journals, a section of *The Bell Jar*, and her short story 'Day of Success', which show her continuous engagement with the subject. I also read Plath's writings in conversation with the poems of female poets, for example, Anne Sexton, Margaret Atwood, and Adrienne Rich, who employ transformation narratives on women and associate the autonomous poetic personae with animals and mythological creatures. This chapter argues that Plath retells and subverts culturally negative connotations associated with flying women, such as witches, and focuses on female autonomy in foregrounding transformation both as a restrictive and liberatory practice.

Transformations of women in classical mythology are defined by metamorphosis. In Ovid's tales, metamorphosis is 'the magical alteration of physical form from one species to another' (Barkan 19). Leonard Barkan's definition implies that metamorphosis fundamentally has a supernatural component. Ovid's work portrays metamorphosis as a new state of being; it shifts between change and permanency (Sharrock, 'Gender and Transformation' 38). However, this transformation is often a violent process, signifying not only a corporeal but psychological change, particularly after sexual assault. Plath studied Ovid's *Metamorphoses* and Latin at Gamaliel Bradford High School, Wellesley, where Ovid's poetry has remained part of the syllabus until today (Ranger, 'Ovid, Plath, Baskin, Hughes' 14). Holly Ranger argues that Plath was interested in the 'gendered Ovidian imagery and themes to explore the female body in metamorphosis' ('Sylvia Plath and Ovid's Daphne' 219). Plath draws on the Ovidian myths to narrate the powerlessness of women who undergo metamorphosis: 'Virgin in a Tree' portrays the woman's bodily transformation into vegetal forms, implying her lack of agency. Narratives of metamorphosis in Ovid's tales 'are stories of similarity and affinity as much as they are about change and alterity' (Sharrock, 'New Bodies' 1). Thus, looking at different states of beings and how the human and the nonhuman subjects are intertwined is central to reading Plath's poems responding to women's lack of bodily autonomy within a male-dominated society. Though revisionist mythmaking has been an important literary tradition of second-wave feminism highlighted in, for example, Adrienne Rich's 'When We Dead Awaken: Writing as Re-Vision' (1972) and Alicia Ostriker's *Stealing the Language* (1986), Plath lived before such feminist traditions were fully realised. Rather than reading Plath's transformation narratives as a mere feminist practice, I look at her engagement with supernatural transformations presented in literature from classics to the early modern period and folkloric stories about women and power, which shows her well-informed understanding of the subject. Plath's poetry and her personal writings, such as letters and journals, give an account of her extensive knowledge of mythological stories about the gendered aspects of metamorphoses, approaching contemporary issues on female autonomy with the vocabulary and narratives of the supernatural.

In addition to metamorphosis, a supernatural transformation associated with classical literature and myths, shapeshifting also occurs in Plath's poems. Shapeshifting describes a transformation from human to animal form; it is usually associated with magical women across folklore and mythology. In Plath's poetry, shapeshifting appears as a narrative strategy that reflects on women's right to autonomy. Plath researched beliefs about folkloric birds associated with the history of witchcraft and witches, which I discuss further in this chapter. In her poems, like 'Goatsucker', 'Stings', and 'Lady Lazarus', Plath relies on the beliefs about shapeshifting women. These poems present women's access to autonomy through changing their form or discarding the female body. In 'Goatsucker', Plath draws on folkloric beliefs about shapeshifting witches, which has been an under-appreciated influence in the past. I read Plath's poetic narratives on shapeshifting in conversation with Sexton and Atwood who also seek inspiration from the animal world to interrogate women's bodily autonomy.

While Plath's knowledge of folkloric beliefs about witches and mythological creatures influenced the portrayal of her poetic speakers' shapeshifting, in poems like 'Ariel', the exchange of bodies is more fluid, which I consider a merger of the different forms and subjects. In 'Ariel', the non-hierarchical relationship between the rider and the horse counteracts the forces of rigid gender and human boundaries. I look at the manuscripts of the poem to demonstrate the diverse ways in which Plath imagined the relationship between the human and nonhuman subject in the drafts, echoing the narrative strategies of, for example, the bee poems. While Hughes's criticism of 'Ariel' foregrounds its mythological origin, the corresponding poems of Sexton and Rich show the women's poetic traditions Plath engages with by bonding wild animals with women's liberation, suggesting that horse riding is similar to the motion of flying. 'Ariel' presents ideas of hybridity in which Plath reimagines the relationship between the horse and the rider in motion as a fluid transformation. Plath's employments of diverse narratives on supernatural transformations, from mythology to folklore, depict the liberatory or restrictive forces on women's access to power through supernatural means.

6.1 Human to Nonhuman Metamorphosis

In the first book of Ovid's *Metamorphoses*, Daphne and Syrinx flee from the predatory male sexual desire, as a consequence, they are transformed into a tree and a reed. Although in ancient Greece, there was a belief about the 'origin of humankind from trees', stories of metamorphosis into trees are frequently associated with women due to their believed connection to nature (Sharrock, 'New Bodies' 1). In the case of Daphne and Syrinx, the metamorphosis does not save them but signifies women's loss of humanity and vulnerability: their immobility makes them persistent subjects of violence. Ovid's transformations also indicate the 'permanence of the psychological trauma' that the women suffer (Bloch 18). In the myth of 'Apollo and Daphne', the Sun God uses the Daphne-transformed laurel as an accessory, which further objectifies the female body: "Exclaimed: 'Since you can never be my bride, / My tree at least you shall be! Let the laurel / Adorn, henceforth, my hair, my lyre, my quiver'" (1.558–60). Even after the metamorphosis, Apollo still treats 'Daphne-tree as female', not as an arboreal being (Sharrock, 'Gender and Transformation' 39). She is trapped in a gendered arboreal existence that continues the sexual violence. The myth exemplifies the interchangeability of the female body and vegetal life, which is a recurring theme in Plath's poetry. Twentieth-century and contemporary female poets, such as Plath, Sexton, Louise Glück ('Mythic Fragment'), Eavan Boland ('Daphne with her thighs in bark'), and Carol Muske-Dukes ('Daphne, After') revisited Daphne's myth to interrogate power, gender, agency, and womanhood through the concept of metamorphosis. Plath alludes to the myth in 'Virgin in a Tree', where the female body is violated, exploited, or objectified.

Plath wrote 'Virgin in a Tree' in 1958, which retells Daphne's myth to reflect contemporary gender relations and norms. The poem was inspired by Paul Klee's 1903 etching 'Virgin in the Tree', portraying the female body as 'organically one' with the dead tree (Zivley 40). 'Virgin in a Tree' is a dialogical poem in which the speaker takes up the role of the narrator. The poem is written in five-line stanzas with irregular lengths, which are stressing the stiffness of the transformed female body. The speaker introduces the theme in the first lines by mocking the metamorphosis tale. Her satirical voice anticipates that the poem is a parody of the myth, informing the reader about the brutal nature of the subject: 'Approving chased girls who get them to a tree / And put on bark's nun-black' (*CP* 81). The lines describe the one-sided sexual pursuit from which the bark provides shelter to the girl. However, the gendered imagery of the bark rather reinforces entrapment into a vegetal state and implies that female sexual desire is regulated. The virgin's metamorphosis depicts women's lack of autonomy over their bodies.

In the second stanza, references to Daphne's sexual pursuit become more direct: 'Ever since that first Daphne / Switched her incomparable back' (*CP* 81). The enjambment at the beginning of the stanza ('bark's nun-black') references the nun's habit, particularly the black tunic. The imagery associates the virgin's transformed arboreal form with chastity. It is this habit that protects virgins from 'All amorous arrows' (*CP* 81). The lines evoke the scene from the myth in which Cupid shoots an arrow at Apollo, making him long for Daphne; then he fires another one at the girl, so she flees from the love. In the poem, the girl's body is protected and covered, which opposes the active phallic symbol. In her later writings, Plath reverses the position of her heroines who rather become the arrow, shooting any way they desire. In 'Ariel', the speaker is an arrow that freely flies and in *The Bell Jar*, Esther Greenwood reflects on her gender identity through the phallic symbol: 'The last thing I wanted was infinite security and to be the place an arrow shoots off from' (*TBJ* 79). The arrow metaphor, similarly in the poem, contemplates women's access to power.

In her poetic retellings of Ovidian tales, Plath shows an awareness of women's lack of bodily autonomy and critiques the limited choices women face within their sexual expression, let it be an ancient Greek myth or post-war American sexual containment, detailed in Chapter 1. 'Virgin in a Tree' also alludes to Ovid's 'Syrinx and Pan' myth in which Pan is the male pursuer of the nymph who, upon being caught, is transformed into a reed and becomes Pan's musical instrument. Plath portrays the sexual pursuit as a violent act: 'Pine-needle armor protects / Pitys from Pan's assault!' (*CP* 81) The description recalls Plath's earlier poems, such as 'Faun' and 'Pursuit', both written in 1956. In 'Faun' – originally titled 'Metamorphosis' – the lover is compared to Pan who walks home at night: 'Goat-horns. Marked how god rose / And galloped woodward in that guise' (*CP* 35). In 'Pursuit', she describes the sexual chase as more playful, yet it is also initiated by the male who is compared to a panther: 'There is a panther stalks me down: / [. . .] The hunt is on, and sprung the trap' (*CP* 22). 'Virgin in a Tree', 'Pursuit', and 'Faun' share similarities in their portrayal of male sexual desire and a one-sided sexual chase. Ranger argues that Plath's poems suggest the lack of vocabulary she had for expressing female sexual desire as she 'remains trapped in the 1950s discourse on femininity' ('Sylvia Plath and Ovid's Daphne' 237).

In 'Virgin in a Tree', the virgin loses her human characteristics, which recalls the faceless dummies from 'The Disquieting Muses', both portraying amorphous faceless women. Kendall remarks that Plath described herself as 'faceless' in her journals during her Smith years, which became a mode of constructing female identities in her poetry (51; 61): 'Girls, girls everywhere, reading books. Intent faces, flesh pink, white, yellow. And I sit here without identity: faceless. My head aches' (*J* 26). Plath's wording evokes Rhoda from Virginia Woolf's *The Waves* (1932) who similarly describes herself as faceless: 'I have no face. Other people have faces' (23). Rhoda finds consolidation in merging with nature, suggesting an inspiration for Plath's poem on the morphing of human and nonhuman subjects. In 'Virgin in a Tree', the description 'Unfaced, unformed' emphasises the loss of the human identity of the female body. The association of flowers with the woman's breast ('nipple-flowers') foreshadows the imagery of 'Edge'. In Klee's artwork, the woman's 'full, pointed, pendulant breasts' are the only recognisably human anatomical features (Zivley 40). Plath's poem associates the soft flowery femininity with the deceased body ('suckle darkness'), suggesting that the girl loses her autonomy and agency by being only the object of desire. The poem implies an ambiguous attitude towards women's preservation of virginity 'for virginity's sake' (*CP* 82). The speaker calls women's safeguarding of chastity a 'pact' (*CP* 82). Plath uses short words and hard-sounding consonants to highlight the crudeness of the virgin's transformation: 'Lain splayed too long in the tortuous boughs: overripe' (*CP* 82). The words 'ripe' and 'overripe' code virginity with the language usually reserved for edible plants. Ranger notes that in Ovid's tales, '[o]nce the woman has renounced her sexuality, she is dehumanized and described more like a tree than a woman' ('Sylvia Plath and Ovid's Daphne' 235). In her arboreal shape, the female body is even more violated: 'Stiff as twigs, her body, woodenly / Askew, she'll ache and wake' (*CP* 82). The new form neither saves nor ends the girl's life: she continues to be confined in a gendered shape. The end of the poem returns to the loss of humanity of the girl by the 'un-' phrase: 'Untongued, all beauty's bright juice sours. / Tree-twist will ape this gross anatomy' (*CP* 82). The speaker names the transformed female body 'gross', which evokes the grotesque presentation of the female body in Klee's artwork. The medical term 'anatomy' foreshadows Plath's hospital-inspired poems, such as 'Tulips' and 'The Surgeon at 2 a.m.' in which the female body is an object of the male doctors. The ambiguous presentation of the sexual pursuit in the poem concludes that neither chastity nor a one-sided sexual hunt is appropriate, critiquing societal norms on sexual expression. Plath's portrayal of the violent transformation of the female body into the grotesque tree dehumanises the virgin. The girl is stuck in a gendered plant-like form, which is both sexualised and virginal with descriptions like 'nun-black' and 'nipple-flower', expressing her lack of control over her body.

Anne Sexton also retells the classical myth to respond to the issues of gender and power in 'Where I Live In This Honorable House Of The Laurel Tree', published in *To Bedlam and Part Way Back* (1960), two years after Plath's poem was written. Unlike 'Virgin in a Tree', Sexton's poem is spoken from Daphne's perspective; her body has already metamorphosed into a laurel tree, which presents a more personal narrative of sexual abuse, pain, and trauma. The poem is not divided into stanzas but is written as one block of text, which emphasises the stiffness of the transformed Daphne. She is immobile, which is reinforced by the repeated lines at the beginning and the end: 'I live in my wooden legs and O / my green green hands' (Sexton 17). The repetition of the colour green highlights the persona's entrapment in the arboreal form. The assonance of the 'o' sounds creates an elegiac effect, which underpins the speaker's hopelessness. While limp 'legs' and 'hands' allude to a human shape, she compares her transformed self to a tree that remains humanoid: '[B]lood moves still in my bark bound veins' (Sexton 17). For Sexton, the transformation is bloody and violent: it 'helps us to think about aspects and phases of experience (sex, childbirth, old age), in which we conceivably remain ourselves' (Fowler 389). The metamorphosis results in alienation from the female body. Gill argues that in both Sexton's and Plath's versions of the myth, the 'escape becomes a new form of imprisonment', which displaces the female subject into the natural world (*The Cambridge Introduction* 55–56). Sexton's speaker mourns her choices wishing 'I had not run from you, Apollo', however, by the end of the poem, she shifts the blame to the god: 'You gave me honor too soon, Apollo' (17–18). Like Plath's poem, Sexton's speaker suggests that she had no choice between chastity and sexual desire. Both Sexton's Daphne and Plath's virgin are trapped in their arboreal shape and feel abandoned by the world, which reflects the psychological damage of trauma.

Plath returns to women's metamorphosis narratives from classical myths in her *Ariel* poems, negotiating the boundaries between life and death, human and nonhuman. She portrays a more nuanced metamorphosis in 'Edge' in which the female body is violently transformed into a nonhuman form. The poem bears the influence of visual depictions of classical stories and mythologies, such as de Chirico's painting 'Ariadne', portraying Theseus's abandonment of Ariadne (Clark, 'P(l)athography' 367). Plath's revision of Medea's myth likewise emerges indirectly in the poem (Bassnett 20–21). She borrows elements from the Ovidian metamorphosis to narrate the transformation of the female body into a vegetal form. In 'Edge', the active and passive phrases demonstrate an association between the 'perfected' body and vegetal form of existence, which resembles the female corporeal transformation in 'Virgin in a Tree'. The poem links metamorphosis to the loss of sexual reproduction, suggesting women's lack of agency over their bodies. 'Edge' opens with a brutal portrayal of the woman in a remote and bleak atmosphere, evoking the perfection of classical art: 'The woman is perfected. [. . .] / The illusion of a Greek necessity' (*CP* 272). The brokenness of the female body is reinforced by Plath's enjambments, separating the adjectives from nouns, such as 'dead // Body'; 'bare // Feet' (*CP* 272). The harsh and dense line breaks reinforce the lifelessness of the woman. In the handwritten draft of the poem, Plath added and then crossed out two adjectives, indicating her indecision regarding whether the woman was dead or alive. The additional adjective of 'terrible' echoes the queen bee's survival in 'Stings': 'Now she is flying / More terrible than she ever was' (*CP* 215). Despite the potential dynamic rebirth, Plath settled on the line, 'The woman is perfected', which alludes to passive, statuesque, and art-like femininity. She is not perfect but made into perfection without agency (Clark, 'P(l)athography' 366). The poem presents the violent aftermath of the woman's transformation, not the metamorphosis itself.

Plath suggests the ambiguity of the transformation by the woman's 'smile of accomplishment' (*CP* 272), foregrounding an active movement. The smile expresses that the woman is not completely lifeless; however, the noun 'accomplishment' acknowledges that she is at a moment of closure. 'Edge' is filled with active verbs ('flows', 'coiled', 'folded', 'bleed'), which demonstrate a fluid movement of the female body. Vendler also notes the presence of life in Plath's poem:

> If the children resemble Cleopatra's consoling asps, they have assisted in the only possible escape (as Shakespeare's queen saw it) from future shame and humiliation before the public. If the breasts are now empty of milk, they used to be full, as if lactation (representing the hourly physical demands on a mother) could stop only in death. (*Coming of Age as a Poet* 146)

Vendler recognises that the poem originates from an active life and narrates the life struggles of the woman. Furthermore, 'Edge' centres on female bodily transformation, not death. Plath emphasises the fluidity in the smooth movement of the woman's body and her clothing that 'flows' and 'scrolls'. Plath resists the objectification of the woman and draws attention to the details of her body. The poem reveals that the female subject has been in the process of motion, but it has ended: 'We have come so far, it is over' (*CP* 272). The speaker's transformation has finished, resulting in a new form of existence. Unlike many *Ariel* poems that focus on rebirth, 'Edge' presents a metamorphosis from an old into a new shape. Like 'Virgin in a Tree', this neither alive nor dead existence entraps the woman.

From the fifth couplet, there is a change in the perspective; the woman's body is at the centre. We see that she has not been alone, but the narrator references her children, who are described as 'white serpent', and her breasts as 'Pitcher[s] of milk, now empty' (*CP* 272). Plath alludes to Shakespeare's *Anthony and Cleopatra*, in which Cleopatra kills herself by putting a venomous snake onto her breast to bite her (Clark, 'P(l)athography' 367). The poem evokes the scene from the play when Cleopatra likens herself to a marble statue: 'My resolution's placed, and I have nothing / Of a woman in me: now from head to foot / I am marble-constant; now fleeting moon' (5.2.238–40). In Plath's copy of Shakespeare's plays, she annotated the lines starting from 'now' until 'moon', which demonstrates the play's influence on her portrayal of the female body in the poem (*SP Complete Shakespeare* 1285). There is a parallel between Shakespeare's enjambement ('nothing / Of a woman') and Plath's line breaks ('Her dead / Body'), emphasising Cleopatra's role in 'Edge'. In some of Plath's poems, Cleopatra signifies female beauty: in 'Virgin in a Tree', 'Cleo' is mentioned in the company of Eve and Helen of Troy and is contrasted with the 'green virgins' (Ranger, 'Sylvia Plath and Ovid's Daphne' 232). In 'Face Lift', the speaker undergoes a physical transformation and compares herself to Cleopatra: 'They've changed all that. Traveling / Nude as Cleopatra in my well-boiled hospital shift' (*CP* 156). The allusion to Cleopatra's figure in 'Edge' expresses Plath's ambiguous attitude towards male ideas of female beauty: she portrays the woman's transformation from an admired maternal figure to a disfigured nonhuman form.

While the woman escapes the objectification of her body, without agency and autonomy, she is trapped in a flowery form and only has aesthetic value. The verb 'folded' argues that, as difficult as it may be, it was her choice. Constance Scheerer links 'Edge' to 'Tulips', arguing that both poems portray a 'series of marbleized images' in which Plath creates her 'garden' (477). 'Edge' also recalls the rose garden in Yaddo, the artists' community in New York, where she and Hughes were residents in 1959, which is 'known from its magnificent rose gardens, as well as a collection of imported statues' (Connors 82). Merging the memory of the rose garden with classical mythology and the male poetic tradition, Plath creates a vision of the female subject that is visually pleasing but distorted and wounded. She contrasts the stillness of the marble statues with the vegetal flowers, which, even in dying, are in the process of transformation. Like 'Virgin in a Tree', in 'Edge', the floral imagery describes an amorphous existence. In Ovid's tales, '[h]uman and bestial, animate and inanimate, male and female can flow into one another' (Segal 11–12). Plath creates fluid boundaries between the human and vegetal world, mother and murderer, static and flowing, which demonstrate the instability of the female identity. The fluid boundaries of forms and subjects are a theme in 'Ariel', too, which I return to in this chapter. The flower imagery shifts from blooming to the closing of the petals; finally, it '[s]tiffens and odors bleed' (*CP* 273). The word 'Stiffen' resembles the 'Stiff as a twig' phrase from 'Virgin in a Tree', reinforcing the connection between the two poems. 'Face Lift' likewise evokes the imagery of sterile stiffness by alluding to the sore muscles that stiffen after an extended period of work: 'Nude as Cleopatra in my well-boiled hospital shift' (*CP* 156). In 'Edge', Plath contrasts the fluidity of bleeding with the static stiffening, implying that the metamorphosis alternates between different forms. The expression 'odors bleed' evokes the woman's sexual reproduction, such as menstruation or miscarriage, similar to the bleeding Daphne in Sexton's 'Where I Live In This Honorable House Of The Laurel Tree'. In Plath's poems, such as 'Barren Woman', 'Tulips', and 'Edge', flowers are symbols of miscarriage, loss, and illness. Plath juxtaposes the powerful visual and olfactory imagery with the whiteness and bleakness of the statuesque woman in her toga.

The last two couplets change perspective; the focus is now on the moon, who is an uninvited spectator of the scene. The stanzas personify the moon, which is suggested by the female pronoun. In other Plath poems, such as 'Barren Woman' and 'The Moon and the Yew Tree', the presence of the moon symbolises death and loss. The opposition between the moon's blackness and the whiteness of the woman's toga highlights the imagery of the double. In 'Edge', the moon is neither cruel nor sympathetic towards the woman. The speaker implies that the moon regularly witnessed such transformations of women. Tunstall notes that in her *WCD*, Plath underlined the definition of 'drag' associated with 'the indefatigable pull of the moon': in Plath's poems, 'the moon is transformed by "drag" into a vampy femme fatale, giving the scene an atmosphere of stagey noir' ('Vision and Visual Art' 254). The verbs 'crackle and drag' describe a slow and painful movement. The consonants enhance the harshness, which suggests that the transformation is rough and violent. The woman is not dead but exists in another form, which recalls the Ovidian metamorphosis. The poem offers hope for a continuous transformation, proposing that the lifeless vegetal state might not be the woman's final form. The verbs 'wears', 'flows', and 'come' express an active state: the woman is still alive, and she can overcome the aesthetic constraint of perfection and the fatigue of her sexually marked body.

Through the rich references to classical Ovidian tales, Plath examines women's violent metamorphoses and interrogates their access to power and autonomy. 'Edge' and 'Virgin in a Tree' demonstrate the influence of classical literature and mythology in Plath's poetic representation of gender and magic. In these poems, the feminine gendered imagery of the vegetal form accentuates the continuity of women's entrapment. Plath draws on the vocabulary of the Ovidian metamorphosis to respond to gender-based violence and women's limited choices regarding their sexuality. In the classical stories and Plath's poems, metamorphosis expresses a passive and involuntary transformation of women into a nonhuman form, which shows women's lack of agency.

6.2 Shapeshifting Birds and Witches

As opposed to metamorphosis, shapeshifting is a type of voluntary supernatural transformation during which the self's body is changed to animal form. It 'breaches fundamental boundaries, such as those between humans and animals and between the divine and mundane realms' (Young 8). This supernatural transformation is mostly associated with magical women who transgress gender boundaries and norms, mainly witches or similar female supernatural figures. The concept of shapeshifting goes back to classical mythology: in ancient Rome, *striges* were believed to be women transforming into owl-like creatures who lived on human flesh and blood, for which Ovid's *Fasti* is one of the key sources (Cohn 162). I return to the superstitious beliefs about owls and their association with witches later in this section. Classical texts differ on whether *striges* were flying women, transformed by some by supernatural power, or purely birds; they are also described as resembling Harpies, the half-bird half-woman mythological monster (Ogden 10–11). The *striges* are a central source of the folk belief that witches can fly by transforming into birdlike creatures when gathering for their sabbath. During the medieval period, Regino of Prüm's *Canon*

Episcopi, a guide to ecclesiastical laws and morals, introduced the idea of the night flight of witches (Cohn 168): '[S]ome wicked women [. . .] believe and profess themselves, in the hours of night, to ride upon certain beasts with Diana, the goddess of pagans, and an innumerable multitude of women' ('Popular Beliefs' 179). Another parallel between the *strix* and the witch is the idea that they eat infants, which shows the development of popular beliefs in the Western imagination. Cohn argues that 'it was the educated elite who, in the name of Christian doctrine, rejected the night-witch; while the common people continued to believe in her' (166). Narratives of flying witches and shapeshifting creatures continued in early modern literature, such as Ariel's ability to shapeshift in *The Tempest*, and oral storytelling during the witch trials and beyond on shapeshifting figures from folklore. Historically, shapeshifting has been associated with magical women and witches through which they gain freedom, power, and autonomy over their bodies.

For female poets of the twentieth century like Plath and Sexton, narratives of shapeshifting offered ways to explore freedom without the limits of gender norms and expectations. In Plath's poems, female poetic personae transform into an animal form signalling the rebirth of the autonomous self. In 'Lady Lazarus', the speaker compares herself to a cat before she transforms into a phoenix. In the bee poems, the subject of Chapter 7, Plath merges the queen bee with her poetic alter ego. In 'Witch Burning', the speaker likens herself to a moth in the process of her burning transcendence. Parallel to Plath, Sexton's 'Her Kind' references the night flight of the witches, which I read along with 'Goatsucker'. In some of her poems, Margaret Atwood also relies on the bird, particularly owls, to interrogate narratives about witches and shapeshifting women. This section examines the pattern in the poems of Plath and other twentieth-century female poets of equating the autonomous poetic self to birdlike creatures, suggesting the significance of shapeshifting narratives in responding to questions about gender, (magical) power, and female sexuality and autonomy.

Plath wrote 'Goatsucker' in 1959, initially for Esther Baskin's *Creatures of Darkness* (1962), a book on nocturnal animals, however, the poem was not featured in the end in Baskin's book. *Creatures of Darkness* includes one of Hughes's poems and is illustrated by Esther's husband Leonard Baskin. The book has a dark owl illustration on its cover. Plath owned a copy of *Creatures of Darkness*, which is kept in Smith College Special Collections. Her copy is unannotated, though it includes the inscription 'Sylvia Plath, 23 Fitzroy Road, London NW1'.

The book describes the goatsucker or nightjar as a superstitious night creature, similarly to Plath's poem:

> The nightjar, with great gaping mouth, flies through the dusky forest and heath ahunt for insects and moths. His mouth is capacious trap to catch small flitterers in the twilight air. Like an owl's, his head and eyes are large, as he flies noiseless through the umbrage [. . .] The nightjar is also known as the goatsucker: this is because in Italy and Greece he is thought to suck the milk from goats. Aristotle has it that this milk-sucking bird causes the goat to go dry and blind. ('The Nightjar')

Baskin uses the male pronoun referring to the bird, which Plath likewise employs in 'Goatsucker'. The pronoun shows the tendency to use the male subject as the standard signifier; however, it also suggests the ambiguous association of the folkloric bird, particularly with gender, power, and autonomy.

In early 1959, Plath encountered several folkloric beliefs about the bird when she went to research the subject in the Boston Public Library. In her subsequent letter to Esther Baskin, Plath informed her of finishing the poem and detailed her research:

> [T]he Bird's also called the Puckerbird, or Puckeridge after a disease it's supposed to give cows & weanling calves in England, so it's a double threat, in superstition, to cows as well as goats. And it's called the Devil-bird in Ceylon. (*L2* 293)

Plath highlights the predatory character of the bird, which likens the goatsucker to the figure of the *strix*. Her notes show a variety of cultural beliefs from England to Sri Lanka, a British colony until 1972, recalling Adam White's *A Popular History of Birds* (1855), which describes many of the beliefs and characteristics of the goatsucker that Plath's notes and poem convey. In the same letter, Plath quotes from Robert Graves's 'Outlaws,' which draws on the folkloric and mythological origin of the nocturnal birds: 'Old gods, tamed to silence, there / In the wet woods they lurk' (*The Complete Poems* 91). Plath's 'Goatsucker' mimics the description of superstitious birds as misunderstood creatures. In her journals, she wrote the following remarks: 'Superstition- peasants: in all languages'; 'Puck- disease in cattle | mischievous demon' (*J* 594–95). Her notes further depict the oral reciting of folkloric beliefs she alludes to in her poem.

'Goatsucker' is written in sonnet form: the octave focuses more on the superstitions about the goatsucker, while the second six-line stanza takes a closer perspective on the identity of the nocturnal creature. The speaker recalls beliefs by referencing the folkloric stories: 'So fables say the Goatsucker moves, masked from men's sight' (*CP* 111). Plath uses alliteration of the 'w' sound to emphasise the diabolical features of the creature to signal danger: 'Who wakes with darkness and till dawn works hard / Vampiring dry of milk each great goat udder' (*CP* 111). The emphasis on the vampirism of the goatsucker evokes the *strix*, having similar predatory behaviour. Plath compares the wings of the goatsucker to the black cloak of witches, reinforcing the bond between flying creatures and shapeshifting women. The goatsucker appears in the European folkloric imagination, it was believed to have 'the sound of witches hiding in the bushes' (Sharps). A similar belief was present during the Salem witch trials in which Tituba recalled a bird during her confession. Elaine G. Breslaw links the magical attribution of the bird to 'the supernatural ancestor' of the goatsucker among Indigenous communities (547). To date, Tituba's reference to the bird is part of the retelling of the witch trials in the Salem Witch Museum in Massachusetts (Salem Witch Museum). The folkloric and historical accounts reinforce the associations between beliefs about witches and birds.

Plath's portrayal of the 'ruby fire' eyes of the goatsucker and its 'ill-famed' murderous character anticipates the phoenix-like poetic persona in 'Lady Lazarus' with her red hair: 'Out of the ash / I rise with my red hair' (*CP* 247). Plath's imagery also seeks inspiration from 'Kubla Khan': 'And all should cry Beware! Beware! / His flashing eyes, his floating hair' (Coleridge 298; M. Ford). The association of flying creatures with the characteristics of witches creates a parallel between 'Goatsucker' and 'Witch Burning', both comparing the poetic subject to a moth. In 'Goatsucker', Plath describes the bird as a 'luna moth' (*CP* 111), which she first capitalised in the typed draft in a letter to her mother: 'Cockchafers and the wan, green Luna moth' (*L2* 295). At the end of 'Witch Burning', written in November 1959, the speaker compares herself to a moth, desiring autonomy from her confinement. Esther Baskin's book likewise suggests that '[l]una moths are grotesquely large as birds'; she adds that '[q]uivering and agasp in search for light and fire, they end their short lives in it and burn in an auto-da-fé' ('Luna moth'). Baskin's reference to auto-da-fé, the burning of heretics, describing the tragic death of the luna moth demonstrates the rich literary, folkloric, and textual sources Plath encountered. Chapter 2 mentions that the poem 'Fever 103°' initially included the term 'auto-da-fé' to portray the poetic persona's burning as she ascends to heaven, demonstrating Plath's familiarity with medieval and early modern inquisitorial prosecutions. Plath links women's autonomous selves to flying creatures like a moth and goatsucker or the dew that flies in 'Ariel', which demonstrates the variety of sources she seeks inspiration from, including the history of the witch-hunt to folkloric beliefs about witches.

'Goatsucker' shares similarities to Anne Sexton's 'Her Kind', also written in 1959, which 'speaks for women whose passions have not been given prominent literary treatment' (Golden, *Annotating Modernism* 16). While Plath considered transformation narratives early on in her poetry, the creative exchanges between Sexton and Plath prompted both poets to explicitly link shapeshifting to female autonomy. Sexton's 'Her Kind' references beliefs about flying witches, suggesting that the night flight is a liberatory movement:

> I have gone out, a possessed witch,
> haunting the black air, braver at night;
> dreaming evil, I have done my hitch
> over the plain houses, light by light: (15).

There are several parallels between Plath's and Sexton's poems, such as flying being associated with women's freedom, reference to black/ebony air, the seemingly dangerous and misunderstood female personae, and the naked riding in a cart that Plath returns to in 'Ariel'. Sexton's imagery in 'Her Kind', 'where your flames still bite my thigh' (16), also resembles Plath's line in 'Witch Burning': 'My ankles brighten. Brightness ascends my thighs' (*CP* 136). Though Plath's poem was written in the artists' community at Yaddo in 1959, Robert Lowell's writing workshop at Boston University the previous spring prompted Plath's and Sexton's 'two-way exchange of ideas, influences, and writing styles' (Crowther, *Three-Martini* 137).[1] Sexton and Plath seek inspiration from similar sources and narratives: in 'Goatsucker' and 'Her Kind', they both critique the negative associations between autonomous women and the idea that sexually liberated women are dangerous. They employ popular imagery of flying women, such as witches and the *strix*, and evoke Lilith, who is attended by screech owls in the King James Version of the Bible: '[T]he screech owl also shall rest there, and find for herself a place of rest' (Isaiah 34:14). The allusions to flying associated with autonomy, disguise, vampirism, and negative connotations of superstitious creatures demonstrate

[1] Plath drew on Sexton's poem elsewhere, such as in 'Daddy', she borrows the cadence from Sexton's 'My Friend, My Friend' (Cam 432).

that while Plath's poem is about the goatsucker, it draws on various sources about shapeshifting women.

In addition to her poems, in her prose, Plath likewise builds on superstitions and folkloric beliefs that associate misfortune with autonomous women who are perceived as dangerous. The short story 'Day of Success' (1961) about female rivalry includes references to the links between menacing women and ominous birds. Though Plath's alter ego is not identified with the bird, rather she uses the association to foreshadow the menacing rival. The protagonist Ellen receives the news about the promiscuous redhead Denise Kay from the ex-wife of her husband, Nancy Reagan, who she compares to '*a professional magpie, a bird of ill-omen*' (*Prose* 453). Sylwia Gryciuk argues that '[h]aving been struck by a tragedy which drained her life out of deeper meaning, Nancy is now reduced to a disquieting caricature, a phantom whose tidings "lucky women" should apprehend' (17). In the short story, Ellen further highlights Denise Kay's sexual nature and career-focused attitude, reinforcing the threatening character of the redheaded woman. When Ellen and her husband Jacob can afford to move to Cornwall, she overcomes the rivalry and menace by deciding to create a new hairstyle for herself: 'Braids are back in style this season, love – the latest thing for the country wife!' (*Prose* 457). When Plath composed 'Lady Lazarus' the next year, her association of female autonomy with hair became bolder: as noted in Chapter 2, the speaker's red hair in 'Lady Lazarus' is a source of power and autonomy. 'Day of Success' portrays the established association of ill-fated birds with promiscuous women and relies on such negative stereotypes, demonstrating the diverse influence of the cultural and folkloric beliefs about the *strix* and witches on Plath's writing.

Plath's engagement with superstitious birds also includes owls. In Plath's 1958 poem 'Owl', she references the owl as a night creature who comes out when the '[c]locks belled twelve' (*CP* 101). The poem focuses on the night flight of the owl and associates its '[d]ense-feathered, fearfully soft to / Look upon' the dead city 'shaken by owl cry' (*CP* 102). The imagery echoes 'Elm' from April 1962 in which the speaker understands her inner darkness and power as a bird: 'All day I feel its soft, feathery turnings, its malignity' (*CP* 193). Plath's preoccupation with birds, particularly owls, is also demonstrated by her drawing on the top of a seventh draft of 'Burning the Letters', suggesting her association of the nocturnal bird with solitude and autonomy. Baskin's *Creatures of Darkness* highlights that owls 'have inspired myths of diabolic intent and dark superstitions of ill omen. It is an owl's wing that is crowingly potent ingredient the Witches add to their noisome brew in *Macbeth*' ('The Owl'). Plath acquired the book in 1962, which suggests she further sought inspiration from the superstitious birds, such as owls, in constructing her poetic narratives about shapeshifting and autonomous witchlike speakers.

Drawing on the historical and folkloric beliefs about superstitious birds and night creatures, particularly owls, Margaret Atwood continues the poetic tradition of women writers, such as Plath and Sexton, to retell narratives about shapeshifting women. Atwood employs mythological female figures with abilities to transform and fly to interrogate female bodily autonomy and reimagine witch executions. In *Morning in the Burning House* (1995), the poem 'Owl Burning' portrays a magical woman and her shapeshifting powers: 'Of course she practised magic. // [. . .] Held her breath at midnight, uncrossed her fingers, / and owl's feathers sprouted all over her' (Atwood 70). She contributes to the poetic reclamation of the witch figure by referencing the mythical figure of the *strix*. 'Owl Burning' compares the burning of witches to the killing of an owl-woman and reflects on beliefs about shapeshifting women as witches: 'We watched her smoulder and got drunk after // Her heart was the ember' (Atwood 71). Her poetry book includes the poem 'Half-Hanged Mary', which narrates the tragic story of a woman who was unsuccessfully hanged during the Massachusetts witch trials. The poems of Plath, Sexton, and Atwood are interested in narratives about magical and autonomous women who shapeshift into birds. They draw on historical, folkloric, and mythological sources on superstitious birds associating the nocturnal creatures with witches and magical women. Plath's shapeshifting narratives focus on female autonomy and challenge the stable categories of the human and nonhuman subjects.

6.3 Hybridity in 'Ariel'

While shapeshifting signals a complete change from human to animal form, Plath also engages with the possibilities of a fluid transformation. In 'Ariel', the horse riding describes a symbiotic transformation between the human and animal bodies. In the drafts of the poem, Plath imagined a different relationship between the rider and the horse, yet transformation is at the centre of the narrative, which I discuss later in detail. Van Dyne calls the speaker's transformation into Lady Godiva explicitly sexual and erotic, while Clark notes that Plath's juvenilia poem 'Tulips at Dawn' pre-empts the 'metaphorical flight' in 'Ariel': '[t]he speaker shape-shifts, becomes pure motion' (*Revising Life* 122; *Red Comet* 115; 795). There is a supernatural element to the merger of human and nonhuman subjects, which exceeds gender and human boundaries and creates a fluid shape for the speaker's autonomous self. The hybridity of the supernatural transformation is more explicit in Plath's drafts of 'Ariel'. The manuscripts are written on pink Smith College memo paper and they include an undated holograph, numbered 1, followed by pages numbered 3 and 4; consequently, there is possibly a missing page 2. In the initial draft, the stanzas are dense and long, yet Plath's handwriting is clear and neat. The pages numbered 3 and 4 have significantly more corrections. Number 3 is dated 27 October 1962 and is a revised version of the draft numbered 1. However, the holograph numbered 4 reads like a different narrative and is an unfinished draft. I refer to the numbered 3 and 4 holographs as separate drafts because they tell a different narrative of 'Ariel'. There are also additional typescripts, which, more or less, resemble the finished version of the poem. A key difference between Plath's handwritten drafts and the final poem is the pace: 'By disrupting and fragmenting these in her revision, Plath creates the illusion of pure energy in motion' (Van Dyne, *Revising Life* 126). In the holographs, Plath used longer lines, which create a slower reading experience, then changed them to shorter lines and em dashes in the final version, imitating the quick movement of the horse riding.

'Ariel' was foreshadowed by Plath's experience of horse riding during her Cambridge years, which she commemorated in 1958 in 'Whiteness I Remember', inspired by the horse called Sam:

> Simplified me: a rider, riding
> Hung out over hazard, over hooves
> Loud on earth's bedrock. Almost thrown, not
> Thrown: fear, wisdom, at one: all colors
> Spinning to still in his one whiteness. (*CP* 103)

The lines portray the horse riding more explicitly than 'Ariel' and separate the two personae, the horse and the rider. Yet, the enjambment 'all colors / Spinning' prefigures the fluid transformation of bodies in 'Ariel'. The recurring sound patterns, such as alliteration and repetition, portray the dynamic and rhythmic motion of the horse riding. In her letter to Gordon Lameyer from 1956, Plath writes about horse riding as an ecstatic and transformative experience: 'Never has every fiber of mind & body been so simply & passionately concentrated' (*L1* 1044). While Sam is rather a mundane name, the title horse of 'Ariel' provided creative possibilities for Plath, alluding to Shakespeare's Ariel and the Pegasus figure from Greek mythology (Clark, *Red Comet* 792). In 'Ariel', there is a sense of flexibility and fluidity, which allows multiplicity, counteracting the gendered entrapment, in poems like 'Virgin in a Tree', written around the same time as 'Whiteness I Remember'.

Plath marks the transformation by the shifting of colours: white is associated with Lady Godiva, recalling 'Whiteness I Remember', red, which has a more dominant presence in the drafts, is linked with fiery burning and rebirth, and dark/black has connotations to stillness. In the poem, Plath uses the slur interchangeably with the darkness. Renée R. Curry argues that Plath identifies whiteness in her poems with racial sameness and the speaker in, for example, 'Whiteness I Remember' 'perceives the power of nature as white' (14; 138). More recently, Murphy notes that Plath's associations of white and black with different characteristics are often ambiguous: in 'Ariel', whiteness is not only Lady Godiva's power but death; she 'ends in a "[s]uicidal," if creative, dissolve of corporeal transformation' (96). Additionally, Maeve O'Brien observes that for Plath, black bodies are deformed and fearful and white bodies are normalised and the centre of her poetry (108). In 'Ariel', the white and the black subjects merge, establishing a hybridity which, while it does not counteract her use of the slur, offers a provocative reading. In her response likewise titled 'Ariel', the poet Karen McCarthy Woolf interrogates Plath's whiteness from a non-white audience's perspective, remarking that 'when you're not Lady / [fucking] // Godiva with milk-white skin,' then, she continues, Plath's words are 'casual, ruthless violence' (52). For Plath, blackness frequently represents danger and dark supernatural powers, which Chapters 4 and 7 discuss in detail.

In 'Ariel', the adverbs and echoes show that the poem is in a continuous movement: 'Then the substanceless blue / Pour of tor and distances' (*CP* 239). From the second stanza, the pace of the poem accelerates, which is highlighted by the short words and allusions. The speaker and the horse blend into each other, which is the first appearance of the process of transformation: 'How one we grow' (*CP* 239). Perloff notes that the poem portrays the 'identification with the animal kingdom [. . .] [a]s the motion accelerates, the speaker cannot distinguish the brown furrow ahead from the brown neck of the horse' ("'Angst' and Animism" 66). Plath's poetic techniques enhance the motion of the transformation: the recurring enjambments create a quick pace, and the internal rhymes stress the merging of the bodies, which echo throughout the poem. The third stanza continues the metamorphosis between the speaker and the horse: 'Splits and passes, sister to / The brown arc' (*CP* 239). The reference to sisterhood stresses female kinship, which is prefigured in naming the horse 'God's lioness', evoking its supernatural power. Plath's gendering of the animal as female shows the influence of *The Tempest*: in the play, Prospero compares the spirit to female mythological creatures, like a nymph and a harpy. The spirit Ariel is a hybrid creature whose change of shape and subsequent liberation imply bodily autonomy. In Plath's 'Ariel', the bond between the human and the animal subject is explicitly gendered, however, it is a compassionate and equal relationship based on fluidity.

The manuscripts of 'Ariel' reveal that Plath initially envisioned a very different relationship between the rider and the animal. The first holograph left out Lady Godiva's figure and focused only on the horse riding. In the second holograph numbered 3, Lady Godiva materialises as marginalia. In the holograph numbered 4, the poem starts with images of death, which Plath then crossed out. There is a tension between the imagery of deceased body parts and the fast-paced reading of the stanza. Here, Plath included several new stanzas portraying the female speaker who undergoes a fiery rebirth, suggesting the transformational powers of horse riding. Plath abandoned the passage by drawing a large wavy pen movement, however, the tercets remain mostly intact and readable. In the erased lines, the description of the poetic persona borrows imagery from Plath's previous poems that portray a fiery transformation. She links the metamorphosis of the season with the transformation of the self to Godiva: 'In a season of burning, I' (MS 'Ariel', 1962 October 27). The dying of red autumn leaves evokes the imagery of 'Witch Burning': 'In the month of red leaves I climb to a bed of fire' (*CP* 135). In the passage, Plath's association of fire with red hair recalls the speaker of 'Lady Lazarus', whereas the movements of rising and burning show similarity to the imagery of 'Fever 103°'. The draft also alludes to John Collier's Pre-Raphaelite painting *Lady Godiva* (1897) in which she rides on a white horse and her naked body is covered with her red hair. In the 1955 British film, *Lady Godiva of Coventry*, directed by Arthur Lubin, Lady Godiva is played by the redhead Maureen O'Hara, which expresses a similar portrayal of Godiva to Collier's painting. The references to Godiva's naked ride suggest 'female rebellion against male perfidy', which evokes 'Lady Lazarus' (Clark, *Red Comet* 793). In the finished version of the poem, Plath emphasised Lady Godiva's association with whiteness, which implies power and the motion of transformation, not a rebirth: 'White / Godiva, I unpeel' (*CP* 239). The verb 'unpeel' recalls the line 'unwrap me hand and foot' from 'Lady Lazarus', alluding to the transformation of the speaker (*CP* 245). Plath's initial exclusion of Lady Godiva from the poem, then her central role in the draft numbered 4, and finally her later merger of human and nonhuman bodies demonstrate that she was hesitant about the boundaries between the self and the other.

In the last section of the poem, the speaker's identity becomes more dominant. Her self-identification with the arrow that flies in the air demonstrates her independence. The rhyming rising vowels of 'now', 'flies', 'I', and 'cry' reinforce the upward movement at the end of the poem (*CP* 239–40). The holograph numbered 3 accentuates the separation of the human and the animal subjects. Plath altered the relationship between the horse and the poetic persona in the second revised typescript dated 27 October 1962, expressing a closer relationship between the rider and her horse. She crossed out the bestial name of the horse, which she first capitalised. The deleted enjambment recalls 'God's lioness', attributing to the animal a supernatural character. Van Dyne suggests that the line breaks in the stanza read as 'a fluid exchange of identities' (*Revising Life* 121). Another instability in the manuscripts is the fluctuating role of the arrow concerning the speaker. In the draft, Plath is more explicit about the metaphorical relationship between riding, rising, and flying. Her shifting references demonstrate her uncertainty about the focus of the poem: whether it should narrate ascending, signalling a rebirth, or centre on horse riding as a metaphor for the fluid transformation. The recurring images of air, flying, and rising movements express that horse riding is a motion that creates a hybrid form between the rider and her horse. 'Ariel' portrays a unique transformation narrative among Plath's poems. The fluid transformation textually and metaphorically breaks the boundaries between human and nonhuman subjects, creating a non-hierarchical bond.

Plath's female contemporaries also engaged with the poetic association between the wild animals, mythological creatures, and women, recognising their shared experiences of confinement and limitations in society. Adrienne Rich's poem 'Aunt Jennifer's Tigers' (1951) links female liberation to the tiger. Rich likewise employs the animal world to reflect on the limited roles and agency of women in the post-war era. 'Aunt Jennifer's Tigers' is written in quatrains with an AABB rhyme pattern that gives a nursery rhyme-like reading to the dark subject matter. Aunt Jennifer's symbolic tigers 'do not fear the men beneath the tree; / They pace in sleek chivalric certainty' (4). The speaker's desire for wildness and freedom is expressed in her artistic creation of the tigers that 'Will go on prancing, proud and unafraid' (4). In 'Planetarium' from 1968, Rich begins her poem: 'A woman in the shape of a monster / a monster in the shape of a woman', suggesting interchangeability with 'woman' and a monstrous animalistic creature (361). Parallel to Rich's poems, Plath's 'Ariel' shows boldness and desire for freedom, associating the female speaker with wild animals. In Anne Sexton's 'In Celebration of my Uterus' (1969), the speaker boldly declares: 'Everyone in me is a bird. / I am beating all my wings' (181). She emphasises a connection between mythological female figures like the *strix* and harpies and women's liberation as a celebration of the female body, suggesting the influence of the second-wave feminist movement. In the posthumously published poem 'Horse', Sexton seeks inspiration from Plath's 'Ariel': '[Y]ou brown furry locomotive /[. . .] a silver spoon. You are a four-footed wing' (507). Here, there is a clear separation between the speaker and the animal, even though she is afraid of the horse which makes her feel 'like a little girl with a papa' (507). The speaker's perception of herself as a little girl and the horse as a 'shark-mouthed man' (507) implies that she projects ambiguous gendered power dynamics to the animal kingdom while comparing the horse's pace to the mythological creature of the Pegasus. In these poems, the relationship between the animals, such as the tiger and the horse, and the speaker expresses respect and compassion, which signifies the possibilities of female autonomy. Plath, Rich, and Sexton challenge the domestic, cultural, and natural boundaries and interrogate the confinement and liberation of both women and animals. Hybridity and the metaphorical exchange of bodies offer new possibilities for the poetic personae.

The supernatural character of the horse in 'Ariel' seeks inspiration from mythological creatures: Hughes linked Plath's poem to the 'Story of Phaethon' from Ovid's *Metamorphoses* in a lecture from 1988, highlighting the poem's origin in classical mythology (Ranger, 'Ovid, Plath, Baskin, Hughes' 9). The Ovidian myth understands horse riding as flying, similar to the rising movements in Plath's poem. In the tale, Phaethon asks his father, Helios, to give him the chariot of light to drive it to heaven. However, he cannot control the winged horses, and the chariot starts to melt as he falls to the ground. The myth ends with the metamorphosis of his sisters into trees because of their grief. Barkan notes that the myth suggests the hybridity between the horse and the rider (34). The mythological origins of 'Ariel' reinforce the fluid supernatural transformation Plath imagined in her drafts. In his retellings of Ovidian myths, Hughes uses images of fiery burning to describe the horse riding into the Sun: 'Now Phaethon saw the whole world / Mapped with fire. He looked through flames / Flame in and flame out, like a fire-eater' (*Tales from Ovid* 38). The lines, in particular the expression of 'fire-eater', recall Plath's 'Lady Lazarus' and manuscripts of 'Ariel'. While 'Ariel' has mythological origins in reimagining the horse as a supernatural creature, unlike Phaethon, the speaker is in control of the horse. Plath focuses on female autonomy by bonding the speaker with her horse: she shifts the culturally negative connotations associated with flying women, such as the night flight of witches, to an affirmative narrative on female autonomy, highlighting the liberatory motion of flying and horse riding.

'Ariel' enhances the association of flying with the freedom of the horse. The last tercet alludes to the merging of bodies in the process of a movement, referring back to the beginning of the poem where the bodies of the rider and the animal merged. By the end of 'Ariel', the motion of transformation reaches the 'cauldron of morning', which concludes the process of metamorphosis (*CP* 240). The word 'cauldron' suggests the merging of bodies. Plath plays with the sonic similarity between the 'Eye' and the 'I' implying the merger of the poetic persona and the Sun. There is fluidity between the human and the nonhuman subjects: we do not know whose 'Eye' is referenced, the rider or the horse. The full stop at the end of the poem reinforces the stillness with which the poem starts. For Plath, the animal world (goatsucker, moth, bee, phoenix, and horse), which she often grants supernatural qualities, provides the possibility of moving away from the restrictions of the female gendered bodily existence. She portrays the fluid boundaries between the human and nonhuman as a counter-narrative to the forces of violent transformation of women, which can entrap them in a confined form. 'Ariel' creates compassion, equality, and fluidity between the subjects, seeking inspiration from the ambiguities of human-nonhuman hybrid shapes, such as the spirit of Ariel and mythological horses. Plath's portrayal of horse riding is figurative, not literal, which links flying to freedom. 'Ariel' narrates the transformation of the rider and the horse into a new form of existence, challenging not only who is considered human but the gendered corporeal existence to which women are assigned. In the poem, the motion *is* a supernatural transformation that creates a new hybrid form.

Plath draws on diverse sources from historical accounts, mythology, literature, and folklore on supernatural transformations that interrogate normative ideas of gender, power, and autonomy. The violent metamorphosis of the girl in 'Virgin in a Tree', the perfected floral body of the woman in 'Edge', and the exploration of animal and human subjects in 'Goatsucker' and 'Ariel' are narratives through which she describes female corporeal transformation, questioning contemporary gender norms. The transformation is either a creation of a new autonomous persona or a gendered entrapment in a vegetal form. The female-centred retellings of Ovidian myths critique the negative connotations attached to accounts of women's lack of bodily autonomy traditionally told by male writers. Plath's narratives about shapeshifting rely on mythological and folkloric sources and question whether women can accomplish bodily, spiritual, and sexual autonomy and power in their gendered bodies. Her prose and letters further give evidence of her varied engagement with and knowledge of superstitions, folkloric beliefs, and the classical myths that she draws on to interrogate gender dynamics and female autonomy. In her poetry, she experiments with the ambiguities of human-nonhuman subjects, challenging fixed boundaries, particularly of womanhood, influenced by narratives of supernatural transformations that depict women's struggle for autonomy. Flying is a recurring movement in these poems, which demonstrates Plath's association of animals, particularly birds and mythological creatures, with supernatural women who defy societal and gender constraints. In Chapter 7, I further examine the question of autonomy, magical power, and the links between flying creatures and ideas of witchcraft in her bee poems.

CHAPTER 7

The Racial Rhetoric of Witchcraft in the Bee Poems

Plath's writings about bees and beekeeping centre on female independence and revival. This chapter examines Plath's employment of elements of witch imagery and the racial rhetoric of witchcraft in her portrayal of the dark flying female creatures struggling for autonomy. Plath wrote her five bee poems between 3 and 9 October 1962, four of which she included in *Ariel* as a sequence. In the poems, the speaker moves from fearing the bees to controlling them, then she develops a kinship with the creatures through their shared experience of female survival. Like 'Poem for a Birthday', the sequence signals a shift in Plath's poetry: she develops a poetic persona in the image of the queen bee, which prefigures the portrayal of autonomous heroines in 'Lady Lazarus' and 'Ariel'. The descriptions of the bees, particularly in the drafts, draw on familiar cultural stereotypes of the witches as the diabolical other and the intertwined relationship between the fear of (racialised) blackness and witchcraft that was revived during the post-war era. In addition to her bee poems, Plath's short stories about beekeeping and the small English village, such as 'Mothers' and 'Charlie Pollard and the Beekeepers', depict community tensions and the ambiguous relationship between the self and the other. Plath demonstrates her awareness of post-war British politics, which she draws on in writing about the bees as the racialised others with ambiguous access to power.

The previous chapters demonstrated Plath's knowledge of the politics of the witch-hunt, her observation that the persecution of witches resembles the twentieth-century racial inequalities, and the literary texts and cultural beliefs on witches as shapeshifting women with flying abilities. The supernatural allusions in Plath's bee poems give evidence of her use of the concepts of white and black magic, knowledge of modern witch-cult theories, and engagement with post-war anxieties about the other. Plath's writings about beekeeping and the village community interrogate fears of the racialised other in the post-war British political and religious landscape. Further, her bee sequence simultaneously subverts and reinforces ideas about the racial rhetoric of witchcraft. By focusing on Plath's writings about the bees and beekeeping, I circle back to ideas from Chapter 1, which outlined her knowledge of the political witch-hunt and awareness of the racial politics of witchcraft.

7.1 Politics and Witchcraft in Post-War Britain

The bees' defiance of oppressive control in Plath's sequence mimics the uprising of marginalised groups; particularly, she seeks inspiration from the political tensions in post-war Britain, McCarthyism, and the revival and prejudices against modern witchcraft. While the war-torn United Kingdom welcomed people after World War II, the increased immigration from the Commonwealth, particularly Indian, Caribbean, and African people, created new political debates. After the Suez Crisis, it was also clear that the British Empire was failing: even moderate Conservatives 'openly embraced decolonisation. This was particularly so in the early 1960s when Harold Macmillan [the Prime Minister] called for the "winds of change" to sweep across the continent of Africa' (Hickson 20). In the 1950s–60s, immigration from Commonwealth countries and Ireland triggered a rise in English nationalism, which parallelled the growing anti-witchcraft sentiment: '[F]ictionalised witch-hunters helped readers consider what was a reasonable level of control and conformity in a greatly changed world, decide which innovations were acceptable and which were not' (Gibson, *Rediscovering Renaissance Witchcraft* 76–77). In the post-war period, the 'immigrant' became increasingly associated with non-white people (Layton-Henry 73): the perception of the other as a racially marked person – unlike a white American like Plath – intertwined with Cold War politics and the racial rhetoric of witchcraft. Plath's writings about beekeeping in the English village community interrogate the boundaries between the self and the other in which the bees, as a metaphor for the other, respond to the racial politics of witchcraft and power. She engages with post-war politics and the colonial roots of anti-witchcraft rhetoric in her portrayal of the bees as dark creatures from Africa who want their freedom, particularly in 'The Arrival of The Bee Box' from the bee sequence and the short story 'Charlie Pollard and the Beekeepers', which I discuss later in detail.

Post-war British discourses of witchcraft exemplify that the racial and gender stereotypes associated with witches in the UK were similar to the United States – as demonstrated in Chapter 1 – with the overemphasis of Tituba's role in retellings of the Salem witch trials. The rhetoric of the

Cold War also reinforced fears and anxieties about the secret gatherings, making the witch-cult hypothesis, which I discuss later in detail, a politically charged concept. Literary witch figures at the time were often characterised by dark features; the 'colour-coded threat, related to the racial rhetoric' was associated with foreignness and Communism (Gibson, *Rediscovering Renaissance Witchcraft* 88). In particular, Dennis Wheatley's horror and occultist novels articulated nationalism and conservative values, in which 'British heroes confront villains and devilish figures whose characteristics resemble those of the "enemy" we all know' (Wiske 100). Wheatley's works – although not exclusively – influenced the imagination of the British public on paganism and black magic. In his renowned novel *The Satanist* (1960), 'devil-worshipping witches fund communists, commit murder, drug and rape women and blackmail public men in an attempt to destroy the British economy and, eventually, cause World War Three' (Gibson, *Rediscovering Renaissance Witchcraft* 79–80). Wheatley alludes to the existence of political and religious secret societies, which sets the novel in the era of surveillance and espionage of the Cold War: 'C. B. [Colonel C. B. Verney] was responsible for keeping tabs on all groups which might be engaged in any anti-social activity, it had included several secret societies that practised Black Magic' (12). *The Satanist* associates black magic with political and sexual nonconformists and the racialised other (Mr Ratnadatta). Wheatley's novels often blend the magical practices of African and Caribbean people, such as Voudou, with Satanism and diabolism, demonstrating the racist and colonial approaches to supernatural concepts and practices. In doing so, he draws on nineteenth-century gothic novels like *Strange Case of Dr Jekyll and Mr Hyde* and *The Picture of Dorian Gray* to oppose 'what is British' with the diabolical other, who are often defeated by Christianity embodied in the Church of England (Wiske 102–4). Wheatley echoes the post-war rhetoric of white Christian superiority in Britain similar to McCarthyism in the United States. Plath's letters, short stories, and poems written in Devon give an account of her disapproval of the exploitation of religious ideas and vocabulary whether it is about the atomic warfare, British colonialism, persecution of marginalised groups, or abuse of institutional power.

In her short story written in 1961–62, 'Mothers', Plath reflects on contemporary tensions in Britain on national identity and immigration and critiques the supremacy of the Church of England. 'Mothers' illustrates her awareness of the exclusionary politics in post-war Britain: even as a white American, Plath experienced being the other in the small English community, foreshadowing her writing about the bees. In the short story,

Plath's alter ego Esther goes to her local church's Mothers' Union; however, she feels alienated in her community: 'If Mrs Nolan, an Englishwoman by her looks and accent, and a pub-keeper's wife as well, felt herself a stranger in Devon after six years, what hope had Esther, an American, of infiltrating that rooted society ever at all?' (*Prose* 479) Plath's description demonstrates the nationalism and xenophobia present in post-war Britain, particularly among small communities. As a white middle-class American, she felt somewhat alienated from the village. 'Mothers' describes the exclusionary community in which women are divided into churchgoers and non-churchgoers; further, divorced women are not supposed to attend the meeting of the Mothers' Union. Plath's unsympathetic portrayal of the villagers originates from the merger between the Anglican Church and the Mothers' Union: 'We don't always meet in church, though. Only when there's new members joining.' (*Prose* 479) The description of the meeting resembles an unsettling baptism; finally, Esther and Mrs Nolan decide they do not want to be part of the exclusionary and unfriendly Union. Plath's short story engages with contemporary colonial discourses about the British Empire, by describing the rector as an Irish man who spent 'years in Kenya, where he had known Jomo Kenyatta', the anti-colonial activist and former president of Kenya, and another church member 'who has been a rubber planter in Malaya', a British colony at the time (*Prose* 480; 483). Unlike Esther and Mrs Nolan, the men with former relations to the British Empire and colonialism are members of the church. It gives evidence of the intersections of English nationalism, the Anglican Church, and colonialism, paralleling the political anxieties of the post-war era. In her letter to Marcia B. Stern in 1961, Plath used a similar language commemorating her experience: 'I started going to Evensong on Sundays as a purely community thing, having asked the Rector (a rather stupid little Irishman who knew Jomo Kenyatta in Africa [. . .] the Anglican church is the church in the community' (*L2* 694). Both Plath's letter and the short story critique the superiority of the Church of England within the smaller community and the larger English society. 'Mothers' ends with a description of the gravestones in the churchyard that 'looked as if their ancient lichens might possess some magical power of phosphorescence' (*Prose* 485). Plath associates dark magical powers with the institutional religion, questioning the authority of the Anglican Church and its exclusionary politics. Her depictions of the cultish church and the unsympathetic rector figure resurface in her writings about the beekeepers' meeting.

Plath draws on the political anxieties of the Cold War concerning secret societies that marked the other as a Devil-worshipping figure who is a threat to Britain's national security. The idea of a secret gathering or religious cult links back to the witch-cult theory popularised by the Egyptologist Margaret Alice Murray during the early twentieth century. Her most well-known book *The Witch-Cult in Western Europe* (1921) builds on the hypothesis that witches participated in a fertility cult during the Middle Ages and early modern period. Murray claimed that witches celebrated the Horned God, who became the Christian representation of the Devil. She established her hypothesis based on manipulated and edited confessions of accused witches from different times and locations in Western Europe and regularly applied her knowledge of native cultures to hypothesise the fertility cult of witches. While Murray's book disregards the social and political context of the early modern period, her description of the 'highly disciplined organisation secretly permeating society' fitted the 1920s, which abounded in conspiracy theories concerning the political groups, such as the Bolsheviks and Zionists (Simpson 92). Even the early suffragettes were viewed as conspiracy groups who formed an underground secret society that alludes to witches (Bearman 379). Beliefs in secret groups and religious cults also resurfaced during the Cold War.

Despite some earlier critics, Murray's hypothesis continued to be widespread for decades, and her 1929 entry on 'Witchcraft' in the *Encyclopaedia Britannica* remained unchanged; it was even reprinted in 1969 (Simpson 89). During her high school years, Plath used the same 14th edition of *Encyclopaedia Britannica* for her paper on Hawthorne's novel on witchcraft laws, which featured Murray's description of the alleged cult of witches. Plath's *WCD* defines witches' sabbath as 'a midnight assembly in which demons, sorcerers, and witches were thought to celebrate their orgies' ('witches' sabbath'). Although she did not underline this definition, the witches' sabbath appears as the page header where she annotated the definition of the witch, suggesting that she likely came across this entry. The dictionary description demonstrates the influence of Murray's hypothesis, particularly the allusion to fertility rituals as 'orgies'. Nancy D. Hargrove argues that Plath's poem 'Vanity Fair', written in 1956, suggests her familiarity with theories of witchcraft, such as the fertility-cult hypothesis, as her poem references a witch's coven (88–89).

The denunciation of Murray's theories from historical scholarship did not mean that her enormous influence had ended. Gerald Gardner, the founder of Wicca, borrowed several ideas from Murray's witch-cult theory; she even wrote the introduction to his book. In Gardner's account, modern pagans organised in covens, where they performed fertility rites, including dances and singing in a circle (*Witchcraft*

Today 20). His allusions often frame religion in the post-war political climate: he argues that one can be a witch and a Christian, which is 'easier than being a Christian and a Communist' and likens the torture of witches to the interrogations of Nazis and Communists (G. B. Gardner, *Witchcraft Today* 112; 121). Gardner's political parallels echo Plath's employment of witch trials as a metaphor for mid-twentieth-century political persecution in 'Lady Lazarus'. The representation of the female beehive in Plath's sequence draws on the discourses of witchcraft in post-war England, implying the subtle influence of Murray's and Gardner's works.

In 1951, the English Act against witchcraft was repealed – created in 1604 – and replaced by the Fraudulent Mediums Act (Purkiss 39). From then on, Gardner started publicly promoting Wicca in newspapers, radio, and in interviews. Plath read articles from *The Observer*, whose poetry editor was Al Alvarez, her friend and literary critic. The articles in the magazine included a piece by Gardner from December 1956 in which he defended present-day witches as 'ordinary people', though he also suggested that the Salem witch trials were not a 'smoke without fire' ('Modern Witches'). In post-war Britain, the Folklore Centre of Superstition and Witchcraft opened in 1949 in the Isle of Man, and then moved to Boscastle, Cornwall, in 1960, as the Museum of Witchcraft, which is still open today (Hutton, *The Triumph of the Moon* 251–52). In an interview with Harriet Rosenstein, Clarissa Roche claimed that Plath had visited the museum ('Roche, part four'). Plath did not document visiting the museum, which is an hour's drive away from the Devon village where she lived with Hughes. In public, Wicca often received hostility, suggesting the perception of witches and witchcraft as a threat to British society (Hutton, *The Triumph of the Moon* 256–57). Devon was a site where a report claimed that witches still practised both black and white magic ('Devon Witches'). Among the clerics, the Roman Catholic Archbishop Dr William Godfrey cautioned against the new arrivals of Irish immigrants with 'many pagan tendencies', continuing that 'the moral outlook [is] totally different in many ways' in England than in Ireland ('Pagan Tendencies'). Such perceptions originated from the Great Famine of the nineteenth century when the Irish immigrants 'brought Irish magic with them', including healing practices and curses (Waters 44). The Archbishop's warning against 'pagan immigrants' also references some of the similar prejudices against African, Indian, Caribbean, and Irish people in England (Fielding 132). With Gardner's initiation, Wicca was emerging at a time when political and religious tensions highlighted the prejudices and racial stereotypes of paganism, reinforcing anxieties about witchcraft and the dark other. Plath's engagement with post-war politics suggests that she drew on contemporary debates and discourses of English nationalism, the other, and changing attitudes towards magic and religion, marking the bees as the foreign and dark other with an ambiguous relationship to witchcraft and power.

Though Plath only indirectly shows awareness of the witch-cult theory, Ted Hughes's poem 'Witches' (1958) explicitly references Murray's ideas. Plath often typed and mailed her husband's manuscripts to publishers: she mentions 'Witches' in her letters, demonstrating her familiarity with it (*L2* 156n; 230n). The poem signals Hughes's knowledge of witchcraft beliefs:

> Once was every woman the witch
> To ride a weed the ragwort road:
> Devil to so whatever she would:
> Each rosebud, every old bitch.
> [...]
> Dancing in Ireland nightly, gone
> To Norway (the ploughboy bridled), (*THCP* 80).

'Witches' describes several popular beliefs about witchcraft, for example, the night rides of witches and sexual encounters with the Devil, which previously had been regarded as dreams, hallucinations, or hysteria of women (*The Witch-Cult* 10; 177). The poem rhymes 'witch' and 'bitch', expressing a misogynistic attitude towards women, however, the simple rhyme scheme reads it as a humorous nursery rhyme. The line, 'To ride a weed the ragwort road', recalls Murray's hypothesis that brooms were a form of sticks 'for going to a Sabbath or for use in the processional dance. The sticks were stalks of the broom-plant, of ragwort, hemp, bean, or any hollow stalk' (*The God of the Witches* 88–89). The poem associates Ireland with witches, particularly their night-flying and dancing. Gardner devotes a chapter to Irish Witchcraft describing a presumed 'ordinary fertility dance' of Alice Kyteler, the first accused witch of Ireland, who was tried for denying the Church and holding a midnight witches' sabbath (*Witchcraft Today* 99). Apart from Ireland, the other geographically specific chapter in Gardner's book is 'Out of the Land of Egypt?', which broadly centres on indigenous and African magical traditions. Gardner's paralleling of Ireland and Egypt as locations associated with magic, particularly naming them as 'primitive', shows his colonial view and emphasises the hostile treatment of Irish and African immigrants in post-war Britain. Hughes singles out Ireland regarding its history of witchcraft, though it also implies his interest in

Ireland's association with Celtic myths. 'Witches' illustrates Hughes's knowledge of the witch-cult hypothesis, presenting the sexualised relationship between the Devil/Horned God and witches.

Plath's knowledge of the political and cultural discourses of witchcraft includes not only post-war America and the McCarthy witch-hunt but also the context of post-war Britain in which the rhetoric of witchcraft and fear of pagans resurfaced, corresponding to xenophobia against immigrants. Plath's short stories likewise demonstrate her engagement with religious and political debates in post-war Britain, critiquing exclusionary politics. In the bee poems, discussed in the next sections, she draws on the racial and gendered politics of witchcraft and interrogates who is the othered in the cultural climate and why. The explicit gendering of the bees as women and allusion to their black mass implies similarities between the beehive and a witch cult.

7.2 Witches' Sabbath in 'The Bee Meeting'

Plath's first poem from the bee sequence describes the speaker's initiation into the beekeepers' meeting. There are five drafts of this poem: one holograph and four revised typescripts, kept at Smith. Plath only made a few revisions in the language and narrative of the manuscripts that are almost identical to the finished version. Critics, such as Perloff and Van Dyne, argue that 'The Bee Meeting' reads as a ritualistic initiation ('The Two Ariels' 15; *Revising Life* 105). Clark notes that the poem narrates a 'Gothic assemblage' where Plath links her 'memories of her shock treatment with medieval sacrificial rite' and seeks inspiration from T. S. Eliot's 'Little Gidding' (1942) and Shirley Jackson's 'The Lottery' (1948) (*Red Comet* 767). Karen Jackson Ford remarks that Nathaniel Hawthorne's 'Young Goodman Brown' influenced Plath's poem, likening the gathering of the beekeepers to the witches' sabbath (142). In the short story about the Salem witch trials, also discussed in Chapter 1, Young Goodman Brown participates in a nightmarish witches' sabbath during which he encounters members of his community who participate in a secret gathering. In Plath's poem, the bees emerge as the dark fearful other; however, by the end of the poem, the speaker questions her presumptions about belonging, community, power, and the other. Among Rosenstein's research papers, Suzette Macedo remarked that Plath compared beekeeping to 'rites, rituals, and purification' (Macedo, Suzette and Helder). The heavily ritualised practice offered Plath ways to reimagine the gathering in her poem as a meeting of a cult.

'The Bee Meeting' starts with the speaker's inability to identify the villagers, who, under their protective clothes, become unfamiliar and strange: 'Who are these people at the bridge to meet me? They are the villagers — / The rector, the midwife, the sexton, the agent for bees' (*CP* 211). The speaker positions herself as the new member of the beekeepers, who is initiated into the group. The recurring question marks in the poem highlight her uncertainty and alienation from the community. Plath describes the beekeepers' masks and specific clothes and colours, likening the villagers to a cult. In 'Charlie Pollard and the Beekeepers', first transcribed in her journals, Plath explicitly associates the protective clothing with the strangeness of the meeting, which she compares to a ritual: 'The donning of the hats had been an odd ceremony. Their ugliness & anonymity very compelling, as if we were all party to a rite' (*J* 658). The 'anonymity' of the masked faces further implies a secret gathering, alluding to Hawthorne's 'Young Goodman Brown'. In her copy, Plath heavily annotated the short story and noted next to the title 'evil is the nature of mankind' (*SP Hawthorne's Short Stories* xxi). Her marginalia focuses on morality and evil, she even wrote the words 'Black mass' in the section when the villagers gather for the sabbath (*SP Hawthorne's Short Stories* 174). Plath's notes and annotations anticipate her description of the beehive in 'Wintering', comparing them to a cultish black mass.

'The Bee Meeting' portrays the speaker as a passive participant in the meeting: 'I am led through a beanfield'; 'They are leading me to the shorn grove, the circle of hives' (*CP* 211). The depiction of the bees as a 'circle of hives' reinforces the ritualistic element of the meeting. It likewise alludes to the ritual magic often performed in a specific shape, such as a circle. The ritualised initiation echoes her short stories about McCarthyism and the politics of exclusion, such as 'Mothers' and 'Initiation'. In the latter, a young girl called Millicent is initiated into a sorority; she decides not to join the group because of their exclusivity. Clark notes that the short story, written in 1952, is set in the McCarthy era during which anyone outside of the status quo was suspicious and considered the enemy of the state (*Red Comet* 120–21). Plath reworked this narrative in 'Mothers', as highlighted earlier, which demonstrates her preoccupation with the politics of exclusion in post-war British society. While Millicent and Esther resist peer pressures, the speaker of the poem accepts the conformism of the group and becomes one of the beekeepers. Throughout the sequence, whiteness is associated with protection from the bees; the colour appears six times in the poem. In the speaker's initiation, she accepts the uneasy conformism of the villagers instead of being the other. The ritualistic initiation in 'The

Bee Meeting' responds to social and political anxieties about otherness in post-war Britain.

Plath contrasts whiteness, which signifies protection and unity, and blackness, which is associated with danger and strangeness: 'black veil', 'black head', 'bean flowers with black eyes' (*CP* 211). The speaker singles out the rector, whose association with blackness suggests his ambiguous figure: 'Which is the rector now, is it that man in black?' (*CP* 211). The line evokes her earlier poem 'Man in Black'; the description also reappears in 'Daddy', which I detailed in Chapter 4. The rector's identification with the ambiguous man in black expresses Plath's uneasy relationship with the Church of England. In the holograph, Plath emphasised the uncertainty of the speaker about the identity of a man in black, further suggesting that the masks hide identities. Her hesitation conveys the surrealism and the dreamlike experience of the bee meeting. Among the village members, the rector is the only clerical figure who is positioned at the top of the hierarchy of the village community. Britzolakis argues that Plath's rector figure blends with the 'surgeon-priest' who wants to perform the sacrificial operation on the speaker, making him the antagonist (96). The hostile description of the rector evokes Plath's late poetry in which priests, doctors, and patriarchal authorities are portrayed as sinister figures. In 'Charlie Pollard and the Beekeepers', Plath further elaborates on the rector's association with the dark colour that defines his relationship with the bees:

> 'See all the bees round the Rector's dark trousers!' whispered the woman. 'They don't seem to like white'. I was grateful for my white smock. [...] 'Maybe they want to join his church', one man, emboldened by the anonymity of the hats, suggested. (*J* 657)

Here, the description shows a similarity to the darkness of the bees in the sequence. The woman warns against the bees' secret society and frames the hive as an underground religious group. The short story implies this organisation is part of the Church of England, which presents the religious institution as ambiguous and unorthodox, similar to the end of 'Mothers'.

In Hughes's poetic response to Plath's bee poems, 'The Bee God', he compares the hive to a religious organisation governed by a male deity – a reference to Plath's father – who not only controls the bees but possesses Plath through the beekeeping: 'But you bowed over your bees / [...] Fanatics for their God, the God of the Bees' (*BL* 150–52). Hughes portrays the bees as dangerous and a cause of the breakdown of their marriage. He also suggests that in 'the nunnery of bees' Plath became an

'Abbess' (*BL* 150). In the poem, the beehive becomes a female-only religious group, a kind of coven. 'The Bee God' evokes Murray's hypothesis, centring the fertility cult on a male deity, the Horned God. Hughes presents similar ideas in his poetry book *Gaudete* (1977), where Lumb, an Anglican clergyman, establishes an unorthodox religious coven in which 'only women can belong to it / They are all in it and he makes love to them all, all the time' (*Gaudete* 114). The reference to lovemaking evokes a fertility cult, in which Lumb is the male figure who, at the end of the poetry book, is killed and replaced by a female deity. In a letter to Leonard Baskin, Hughes described Lumb's participation in a witch cult to advocate his religion, after which he is hunted by men (Bate 333). His depiction of the women in the coven is similar to Plath's bees, whom he calls 'black as flies' and 'birdlike' (*Gaudete* 132). Hughes's poems influenced by Plath's bee sequence reinforce the portrayal of bees as dark supernatural creatures with an ambiguous relationship to power and religious institutions.

In 'The Bee Meeting', the speaker fears the bees, yet she relates to them more than to the beekeepers. She associates herself with the queen bee and links them through the theme of survival: 'She is old, old, old, she must live another year, and she knows it' (*CP* 212). The beehive does not seem to be concerned with her; instead, they are productive workers. The speaker is uncertain about her identity, and this allows her to move between the human and nonhuman worlds. Plath brings the speaker's initiation to the group into parallel with the hunting of the queen bee as a ritualistic ceremony. The villagers' hunt for the queen echoes the ritualistic 'stamping and dancing' in 'Daddy'. In both poems, Plath describes the village community as secluded and violent who penalise the outsider, as highlighted in Chapter 5. In 'The Bee Meeting', the villagers' violence is reinforced by the drumming sound of the alliterative line 'Dream of a duel they will win inevitably' (*CP* 212). The speaker feels empathy towards the queen bee who escapes from the beekeepers. Plath alludes to sacrificial rituals; however, both the queen and speaker survive the beekeepers' meeting. The poetic persona's recurring exhaustion implies confusion in her identity as if she were hunted by the villagers, not the queen bee. The speaker feels lost, even when the nightmarish meeting ends and the villagers return to their usual selves: 'The villagers are untying their disguises, they are shaking hands. / Whose is that long white box in the grove' (*CP* 212). The lines anticipate the white box at the start of the next bee poem, creating a smooth transition in the speaker's relationship with the bees. The 'long white box' imagery also implies a coffin, which continues in 'Stings' associated with the spectral presence of the father figure. The self-identification with a 'magician's girl' suggests the supernatural powers of beekeeping, which I discussed in Chapter 3. 'The Bee Meeting' establishes the parallels between beekeepers' meeting as a religious ceremony in which the speaker's alienation from the village community questions the binary categories, such as human and nonhuman, powerful and powerless, and their association with whiteness and blackness. It anticipates the portrayal of the bees as dark, flying creatures who are explicitly gendered, alluding to witches. 'The Bee Meeting' builds on the cultural and political framework of post-war Britain to interrogate conformity and exclusion among the villagers in which the bees represent the dark and foreign other whom the beekeepers want to control.

7.3 The Racialised Other and Witchcraft in Plath's Bee Metaphor

From the second poem of the sequence 'The Arrival of the Bee Box', Plath's bee metaphor becomes racialised and she associates the bees with darkness and power that the beekeeper cannot conquer. The poem narrates the speaker's ambiguous and hierarchical relationship with the bees in which the bees are referenced as foreign, originating from Africa. 'The Arrival of the Bee Box' exploits the racialised rhetoric of the fear of the other (Chakraborty 1011): darkness and its connotation to diabolism are central identifiers of the beehive and its power. Lynda K. Bundtzen observes that Plath draws on ideas from *The Tempest* in her portrayal of the dark bees as diabolical creatures, such as Caliban and Sycorax, whom the speaker controls (172). The negotiation between freeing or enslaving the bees also mimics Prospero's and Sycorax's use of magic to control Ariel. The poem parallels the racist attitudes towards Africans and Caribbean people during colonialism as both inferior and possessors of diabolical powers. 'The Arrival of the Bee Box' is written in five-line stanzas: each reads like a sentence finishing with a full stop or exclamation point. The closed structure parallels the shut box, in which the speaker keeps the bees. The poem ends with an isolated line that implies the uncertainty of their relationship.

Plath originally titled the poem 'The Arrival of the Bees', which she changed to their box, suggesting the objectification of creatures. The metonym distances the speaker from the bees: instead of them, it is the box that signals danger. The speaker contemplates enslaving the bees whom she perceives as out of control: 'With the swarmy feeling of African hands / Minute and shrunk for export, / Black on black, angrily clambering'

(*CP* 213). The lines evoke the dehumanising practice of slavery by the bees' identification with African slaves. The four-time repetition of the colour black reinforces the speaker's fear of the bees; their otherness is also a source of disgust (R. R. Curry 160). The speaker calls them 'a box of maniacs' (*CP* 213). The line recalls Robert Lowell's poem 'A Mad Negro Soldier Confined at Munich' published in *Life Studies* (1959), which portrays the imprisonment of mentally ill African American soldiers: 'The boys who floored me, two black maniacs, try / to pat my hands. Rounds, rounds! Why punch the clock' (8). While Lowell's phrasing interrogates the racial power imbalance, Plath's expression further dehumanises the bees who are compared to African slaves. Murphy argues that the bee poems emphasise 'the bees' communal blackness, their otherness, and their implicit threat' (94). In the poem, Plath also links 'the dangers of extreme psychological states [i.e., madness] to political issues' (Hicok 169), which interrogates the effects of authority and control on both the bees and the beekeeper. 'The Arrival of the Bee Box' suggests that blackness is a source of power for the bees and it signals danger, recalling supernatural concepts, such as black magic, rooted in the history of colonialism.

In the short story 'Charlie Pollard and the Beekeepers', Plath further links the bees to the other framed within contemporary British politics and identifies the Commonwealth with the lack of resources: 'The blue-coated woman pointed them out. She was from British Guiana, had lived alone in the jungle for 18 years, lost £25 pounds on her first bees there — there had been no honey for them to eat' (*J* 658). The short story suggests that the bees come from a colony who were not productive workers for the woman; they are only used and exploited by the colonial power. Similar to 'Mothers', there are echoes of British colonialism in Plath's writings about the practice of beekeeping in the English village. 'The Arrival of the Bee Box' articulates diverse connotations of darkness, just as in *The Tempest* 'Sycorax can be both witch and Indian woman, both monstrous hag and former resident of Algiers, both native and immigrant to the island' (Purkiss 258). The bees are simultaneously fearful and enslaved, powerless and powerful, which their association with darkness accentuates.

The speaker calls herself 'not a Caesar' and 'owner' but a 'sweet God', which suggests her negotiation of power and identity (*CP* 213). Plath was familiar with the connection between the expansion of colonial power and the fear of diabolism depicted in, for example, *The Tempest*, while the racial rhetoric of witchcraft was present in the post-war era both in the United States and Britain. The poem's engagement with colonial power recalls the opposition between Prospero and his slave Caliban, showing concerns about 'British identity and history' (Wymer 4). In the play, Caliban represents the dark other whose identity is not fixed; he 'has no coherent ethnographic model' (Gilles 197). Paul Brown argues that Caliban's language offers him a source of resistance against white power; he is not only othered through his perceived incomprehensible speech, but it is also his curse 'provoking the master to curse in reply' (61). Caliban and Sycorax are reflections of colonialism and they embody non-European magic, perceived as diabolism (Joseph 129). Shakespeare's play offers an analogy of the speaker's disgust with and annoyance at the bees, which recalls Prospero's treatment of Caliban (Bundtzen 133–34). The speaker's attitude towards the bees parallels the racial rhetoric of witchcraft in early modern literature and during modern British colonialism: she considers liberating the bees, yet she still wants to exercise control over them.

The bees are not only foreign, but they also possess knowledge that the speaker does not know; she calls their language 'furious Latin' (*CP* 213). Latin is a learned language often associated with the educated class, such as scholars, priests, and the early modern magus figure. During the early modern period when Protestants theorised a connection between 'Catholic superstition and magic', Latin-language prayers could be regarded as diabolical practices for which some were prosecuted (Levack, *The Witch-Hunt* 125). The reference to Latin, identified with Catholic prayers, also recalls the anti-Catholic and anti-Irish sentiment present in post-war Britain (Walter 87). In Ireland, Protestant settlers were more likely to make witchcraft accusations: in Catholic beliefs, the 'witch figure was not threatening enough to warrant legal proceeding' even among Catholics, 'professional and semi-professional magical practitioners' continued to exist until the mid twentieth century (Sneddon 129; 146). In Plath's poem, the language of the bees expresses their ambiguity: it is both a source of their otherness, hence dangerous and a form of power. Identifying the bees' language with foreign sounds gestures towards some of the ideas I laid out in Chapter 5 about the language of magic, particularly the foreign origin of spells and magic words. Plath likewise studied Latin in her high school years. In a 1954 letter to her friend Melvin Woody, she remarked that mel 'devilishly enough' means honey in Latin (*L1* 781). Plath's knowledge of Latin words associated with the honey of the bees anticipates their metaphorical Latin in the poem: its foreign origin makes it a source of fear and power, like the language of both Catholic prayers and black magic.

In the second half of 'Arrival of the Bee Box', the speaker becomes more sympathetic towards the bees. She only feels compassion towards them when she 'soothed herself by proclaiming her ownership'; therefore, she takes up the 'white role' (R. R. Curry 160). We can understand whiteness in the poem as the Prosperoean white magic, associating beekeeping with the control of the bees. The bees are hungry for their freedom and food, which the speaker contemplates granting them. She claims she cannot give them sweetness, reinforcing her ambiguous attitude towards the dark creatures. She does not take responsibility for them, yet the pause of the caesura expresses hesitation. The last line suggests an uncertain ending: 'The box is only temporary' (*CP* 213). By questioning the enslaving of the bees, the speaker also examines her power over them, developing a closer relationship with the hive. The poem highlights the tensions in their relationship. 'The Arrival of the Bee Box' portrays blackness as a power of the bees, which the speaker recognises as ambiguous. Plath's poem parallels the colonial imagery of *The Tempest* with its racialised portrayal of witchcraft and contemporary political tension on the dark other, suggesting an ambivalent perception of the bees and their perceived dangerous powers.

The third poem, 'Stings', is a transitional part of the sequence. Plath wrote an initial poem in August, months before the bee sequence, which is considered a separate poem from the autumn 'Stings'. The August manuscript, kept in SCSC, has a different narrative, which is textually similar to 'The Bee Meeting'. The August manuscripts centre on an unnamed figure referred to as 'you' and their relationship to the bees who appear as defeated soldiers. The poem was written in three quatrains and includes four drafts; in the revised typescript numbered 4, Plath starts the poem with a question: 'What honey in you summons these animalcules?' (TS 'Stings', 2 August 1962). Summoning prefigures the supernatural imagery of the sequence, alluding to the invocation of the father in 'The Bee Meeting' and his ghostly presence in 'Stings'. The August manuscripts present several early ideas that Plath later incorporated in the bee poems, such as the dangerous character of the bees, their attraction to hair, and the appearance of black and white coloured clothes. This poem contains fewer explicit supernatural imagery, and like in 'The Swarm', the bees are portrayed as male soldiers, not a group of diabolical flying women.

The revised typescript numbered 5 focuses on the bees' 'suicidal' stinging and ends with resignation and hopelessness: 'Gelded and wingless. Not heroes. Not heroes' (TS 'Stings', 2 August 1962). Here, Plath alludes to the bees as dying soldiers and suggests that it is the task of women to tidy up after the injured bees. The adjectives 'Gelded and wingless' imply castration, which genders the bees as male, demonstrating that Plath initially linked the productive work to housewives, not the bees who appear passive and weak. The typescript depicts the bees as masculine, yet tired and defeated. Plath's bee metaphor is evocative of the bee simile in the *Iliad:* '[B]ut like a swarm of fine-waisted wasps or bees / [. . .] so these men will not, though there's only the two of them, / fall back from the gates while they're killing, or until they are killed' (12.166; 171–72). In Milton's *Paradise Lost,* the Homeric bee-simile reappears associated with the 'winged Heralds' of Fallen Angels: 'Brushed with the hiss of rustling wings. / As bees / In spring-time, when the Sun with Taurus rides' (1.767–69). In her copy of the book, Plath annotated the line referring to bees and noted on the margin 'throngs of angels: bees' (*SP Paradise Lost* 37). Her allusion to the well-recognised simile shows that she sourced her bee metaphor from the male scholarly and literary tradition, as she did in 'The Beekeeper's Daughter', evoking her father's writing on the bees. Plath's initial association of the bees with fallen heroes and angels is opposite to the darkness, diabolism, and danger of the female bees in the evolved sequence, which expresses the diverse supernatural and literary inspirations she draws from.

In the October poem 'Stings', Plath altered the portrayal of the bees from a swarm of defeated male soldiers to productive female workers, reconsidering the gender of her bee metaphor. The manuscripts include one holograph dated 6 October 1962 and two revised typescripts also dated 6 October 1962: the first includes several crossed-out lines and revisions with blank ink and the second is much neater and only has one revision in the final line. The speaker develops a closer bond with the bees who are characterised as female workers: 'Of winged, unmiraculous women, / Honey-drudgers' (*CP* 214). She declares her care for the bees by ornamenting their box: 'With excessive love I enameled it // Thinking "Sweetness, sweetness"' (*CP* 214). Patricia Grisafi argues that the speaker's decoration of the box with her bare hands shows that she is 'now confident with her ability to handle bees' (54). In the Harriet Rosenstein research papers, several interviewees, including Elizabeth Sigmund, highlighted that Plath's painting of the box was an unusual practice in England and the flowers were 'in Austrian style' to which she attributed supernatural powers (Sigmund, 1962–1975 8). These anecdotes further engage with ideas of associating the bees with magical powers and frame beekeeping within a creative-aesthetic practice of ritual magic. As I outlined in Chapter 5, ritual magic often blurs the boundaries between the mundane and the supernatural and reimagines the domestic practices as magical acts performed in the home. In 'Stings', the speaker associates the bees with domestic drudgery. She explicitly calls the bees women, a gendering which likens them to busy workers and blurs the boundaries between housewifery and domestic magical rituals: 'These women who only scurry, / Whose news is the open cherry, the open clover?' (*CP* 214). Plath earlier attributed to the bees the adjective 'unmiraculous', which is the opposite of a miracle, a positive supernatural phenomenon, suggesting the dark magical powers associated with the bees. It also recalls 'Lady Lazarus' in which the speaker dismisses the 'miracle' label, implying a link between the two poems that reject a male authority.

'Stings' contains less racialised imagery of the bees, yet the speaker describes them as dangerous and fearful. She identifies her 'strangeness' with 'dangerous skin' (*CP* 214). Despite being the owner, she wonders if the female bees will accept her. The speaker blames the bees for their otherness, which shows her ambiguous attitude towards their blackness. She names the bees flying black female creatures, suggesting an allusion to witches. The bees' drudgery implies their rushed flying to an assembly similar to the witches' sabbath. 'Stings' furthers the connection between the female bees and darkness, which foreshadows their black mass in 'Wintering', employing the magical connotations of blackness. In the second half of the poem, a third person appears – alluding to the dead father figure – who is watching the scene. The man's sweetness is associated with the bees' honey, which is named the reason for his death: 'The bees found him out, / [. . .] They thought death was worth it, (*CP* 215). Similarly, in 'The Beekeeper's Daughter', the speaker foreshadows the father's sweet death: 'A fruit that's death to taste: dark flesh, dark parings' (*CP* 118). The relationship suggests the ambiguous gender power dynamics between the female bees and the male beekeeper. The bees' attack on the father expresses their dark supernatural power, which is more explicit and diabolical in the draft.

On the second page of the October holograph of 'Stings', Plath depicts the bees' attack on the father as a sinister and diabolical ritual, who is stung seven times: 'And a ~~great~~ big boss on his forehead // Black as the devil & vengeful.' (MS 'Stings', 6 October 1962) The 'boss' has a dual meaning: it alludes to the queen bee and the knob made of metal or wood in ecclesiastical architecture, usually featuring religious iconography or even animals. The North Tawton church is characterised by 'open wagon roofs with moulded ribs, carved bosses and wall-plates' made in the late-fifteenth century early-sixteenth century ('Church of St Peter'). This meaning further highlights the bees' subversion of religion. 'Seven' refers to the seven deadly sins from the Bible; it is a superstitious number, suggesting that the bees' attack on the father is executed with full force due to its magical properties. Among the bees, only female bees can sting since the stinger 'is a modification of the *ovipositor*, the female egg-laying organ' (Capaldi and Butler 142). The attack on the male figure inverts the power relation of the hunting of the queen in 'The Bee Meeting', which expresses a change in the speaker's attitude towards the creatures. The bees are domineering and aggressive and use diabolical powers. Van Dyne reads Plath's portrayal of the male presence in the holograph as a refusal of patriarchal authority (*Revising Life* 109). The beehive not only rejects the men but kills them; it foreshadows Plath's murderous poetic personae, such as Lady Lazarus, who represents the autonomous self. In the holograph of 'Stings', the speaker articulates neither support nor disapproval of the bees' violence against the father. Yet the simile ('Black as the devil') shifts them from the dehumanised slaves to devilish female figures. They are compared to witches and other diabolical creatures, suggesting that the hive is like a witch cult. In the final version of the poem, the father's death and an explanation of why the bees are dangerous are missing. Plath toned down the expressive supernatural language, particularly the allusions to the bees as diabolical and dangerous women.

In the last section of the 'Stings', the poem turns from the attack of the male figure to the speaker's rebirth, as she becomes one with the queen, flying away: 'More terrible than she ever was, red / Scar in the sky, red comet' (*CP* 215). Plath compares the queen bee to a red lioness, signalling a shift from her perceived darkness, central to the hierarchical relationship of ownership, autonomy, and rebirth. The null rhyme ('red' / 'red') highlights the new colour the speaker associates with the bees as a result of her changing attitude. The fiery portrayal of the queen bee parallels the resurrected self in 'Lady Lazarus', the burning virgin in 'Fever 103°', and the speaker from 'Ariel', who merges with the animal in horse riding, which she perceives as flying. As we have seen, in her October poems, Plath frequently associates supernatural women with flying creatures. 'Stings' ends with the escape of the queen bee: 'Over the engine that killed her — / The mausoleum, the wax house' (*CP* 215). Here, Plath returns to the mechanical imagery of the engine, which is evocative of the 'engine' in 'Daddy' that chuffs the speaker 'off like a Jew' (*CP* 223). 'Stings' demonstrates the speaker's kinship to the female bees, which foreshadows the non-hierarchical and gendered human and animal relationship in 'Ariel' ('sister', 'lioness'), linking women's freedom and productive autonomy to the animal world. The manuscripts and the final version of 'Stings' present Plath's explicit and implicit identification of the bees with devilish female creatures, which demonstrate her use of the witch imagery.

Plath wrote 'Wintering', the final poem in the bee sequence, between 8 and 9 October 1962. She redrafted the poem several times, shifting the relationship between the beehive and the speaker from uncertainty to hope. The manuscripts include a holograph and six revised typescripts and from the third typescript, the drafts become tidier. Structurally, the final version of the poem resembles 'Stings', with five-line stanzas and varied punctuation. 'Wintering' focuses on female survival through kinship and collectivism. It also associates the honey production of the bees with their creative-productive work. In the poem, darkness appears as ambiguous; it is linked to the bees and their collective power and the unknown. Plath employs dark gothic imagery to describe the cellar (K. J. Ford 158–59): 'This is the room I could never breathe in. / The black bunched in there like a bat' (*CP* 218). The repetition suggests that darkness is a source of suffocation and danger. It is also a metaphor for the speaker's 'troubled state of mind' (Clark, *Red Comet* 769). The alliterations, such as 'black bunched' and 'bat', reinforce the sense of confinement and link the bees to darkness. Plath continues to compare the bees to gothic supernatural creatures, such as witches and vampires. In the poem, the images of darkness associated with the bees are ambiguous: 'Possession. / It is they who own me' (*CP* 218). The one-word sentence 'Possession' acknowledges the changing power dynamic between the speaker and the bees: it is now the bees who are in control of her. The possession of the speaker is also metaphorical; it evokes the concept of demonic possession, discussed in Chapter 4. The bees represent demonic spirits who enter the human body and can move between worlds.

In 'Wintering', Plath enhances the supernatural imagery, portraying the bees as flying women who gather in a black mass and move between worlds. Their blackness is a source of supernatural power. They become stronger and more resilient together: 'Now they ball in a mass, / Black / Mind against all that white' (*CP* 218). The lines express the tension between the bees and 'all that white'. It suggests a reversal of the power dynamic previously expressed in 'The Bee Meeting', positioning the bees as the dominant group. The references to flying women link the bee poems to 'Goatsucker', 'Lady Lazarus', and 'Ariel', in which Plath relies on the association between flying and freedom to narrate women's autonomy. The speaker alters her previous attitude towards the bees who now defy her control (R. R. Curry 161). In the stanza, Plath changes the word order of the black mass to 'mass, / Black', stressing the colour, which stands alone as a line. The mass suggests the Roman Catholic name for worship, which Plath's poem reimagines as a 'black mass', as Devil worship. Plath's wording is visual, sociological, and theological (Murphy 99). The black mass subverts the imagery of the beekeepers' ritual as a witches' sabbath in 'The Bee Meeting' and alludes to Murray's witch-cult theory. In 'The Swarm', the fourth bee poem that Plath left out of the sequence, she likewise references the beehive as a black mass like soldiers marching in Napoleon's army: 'Mass after mass' (*CP* 216). In the poem, the mass of black bees has political connotations: the bees are not strong enough to defy the authority of the Napoleonic beekeeper (Peel, *Writing Back* 178). The black mass in 'Wintering' further echoes Plath's early identification of racial injustices with the early modern witch-hunt, which I discussed in Chapter 1. Her representation of the bees mimics the figure of the witch reimagined as a metaphor for persecuted groups in 'Lady Lazarus'.

The first draft of 'Wintering' includes an explicit reference to female sexuality in which honey has an ambiguous role: men consume it excessively, alluding to the hedonistic and domineering male sexual desire that Plath portrayed in, for example, 'Virgin in a Tree'. Unlike the male bees who consume it, the female bees produce honey, which helps them to survive the winter. Plath suggests that the female bees have the power to reproduce, recalling her father's scientific knowledge. Parthenogenesis allows small invertebrates, such as bees, to procreate without male fertilisation. For the speaker, the bees offer security for survival. They gather at the tin to collect more sweet syrup, relying on manufactured sweetness: 'It is Tate and Lyle they live on, instead of flowers' (*CP* 218). Plath's reference to the British brand Tate & Lyle has direct links to the slavery of sugar plantations. Although 'both businesses were established after the abolition of slavery. The early nineteenth and early twentieth century British sugar industry was predominantly supplied by Caribbean plantations, founded under colonialism and supported by enslaved labour' (Huxtable et al. 97). The poem describes the bees taking and living on the sugar syrup, which suggests their reclamation of the sweet product to defy their enslavers. Tate & Lyle's Golden Syrup features a picture of a dead lion surrounded by buzzing bees. The illustration references the biblical story when Samson kills a lion and the bees gather around the carcass; it also uses a quotation from the Bible: '[O]ut of the strong came forth sweetness' (Norman 52–54). In February 2024, Tate & Lyle announced the removal of the image and the quotation from their tin syrup, ending their reign as the oldest unchanged brand logo to modernise the company. The reference to the golden syrup product in 'Wintering' gives evidence of Plath's engagement with the religious, political, and cultural context of post-war Britain. The bees are not only resilient creatures, but they also defy the oppressive systems that the beekeepers and slavery kept them in. The bees' explicit identification with female and creative reproduction reinforces the reading of the beehive as a fertility cult.

Plath's speaker notes that wintering is for the 'hanging on for the bees' (*CP* 218). The end of the poem echoes the title, stating that winter is not only a period of survival, but for women, it is a peaceful time of domestic and creative work, like knitting. The relationship between women and winter stresses 'forbearance and equanimity' (K. J. Ford 161). Plath used the expression 'wintering' in two other poems, both written in 1959. 'Point Shirley' narrates the memories of her dead grandmother and shows the association of old maternal figures with domestic work:

> Nobody wintering now behind
> The planked-up windows where she set
> Her wheat loaves
> And apple cakes to cool. (*CP* 110)

The grandmother's knitting and bread-making can be compared to the honey-making of the bees, which associates women with creative-productive work. In 'Electra on Azalea Path', Plath links wintering to the survival of bees: 'It was good for twenty years, that wintering' (*CP* 116). 'Wintering' ends on an uncertain yet hopeful note about whether the bees will survive the winter: 'What will they taste of, the Christmas roses? / The bees are flying. They taste the spring' (*CP* 219). The speaker associates their freedom with the rebirth of nature, which allows productivity, creation, and life. The positive ending moves away from the identification of the bees with danger, diabolism, and death. They free themselves from the restrictive labels and controlling powers. 'Wintering' associates the bees with a domestic creative work as mundane creative practices of magic, suggesting the rejection of harmful prejudices against the dark other and witchcraft.

In the holograph, Plath ended the poem with four questions, implying uncertainty. Here, rejuvenation barely makes an appearance, expressing that the initial ending is less hopeful. The violent imagery echoes the line that the bees 'can only carry their dead' (*CP* 218). Plath alludes to Greek and Roman mythology in which the bees represent the borderland between the gods and humans; they have been linked with divine qualities and were believed to cross between the underworld and the world of the living (Carlson 19). Bryant notes that Plath draws on Edith Sitwell's 'The Bee Oracles', linking the bees to the Delphian oracle that 'arid modern world with ancient powers of prophecy and regeneration' ('Beelines' 204).

'Wintering' concludes the bee sequence throughout which Plath shifts the speaker's relationship with the bees from ownership, fear, and enslavement to kinship based on their shared experience of survival as she develops a closer relationship with the nonhuman world. The depiction of the bees as dark and flying creatures alludes to beliefs about witches and their cult, which reappear in Plath's other poems, particularly those she wrote in October 1962. Their flying helps the bees to achieve autonomy, while their darkness develops into an ambiguous supernatural power.

The bees offer a complex metaphor for Plath; she combines her paternal heritage of beekeeping with sources from mythology and classical literature. The metaphor draws on broader political issues, such as overcoming the oppressive powers of colonisation, the dehumanising practice of othering, and racial injustice. Plath's bee poems and short stories, 'Mothers' and 'Charlie Pollard and the Beekeepers', build on the vocabulary of the racial rhetoric of witchcraft and the exclusionary politics employed in the post-war British discourses of immigration and the fear of the dark other. In the bee poems, particularly in the drafts, Plath deploys supernatural concepts in her portrayal of the diabolical queen, alludes to witches, and identifies the bees with the black mass. She draws parallels between her depiction of the beehive and the racist and racial rhetoric of witchcraft, which was revived during the post-war era. The sequence explores the tensions between the powerful and powerless, the self and the other, and attributes these qualities to the bees. Plath's allusions to Murray's witch-cult hypothesis and ambiguous representation of blackness and magic give evidence of her engagement with post-war discourses and perception of witchcraft rooted in colonialism and xenophobia. Her short stories about the Devon village illustrate the post-war colonial, national, and religious tensions present in Britain. Plath's portrayal of the bees exemplifies the often-contradictory ideas she challenges, subverts, or reinforces in her poetry about witches and witchcraft, such as female power versus powerlessness, martyrdom versus heresy, and the other versus the self. The bee poems express her complex understanding of supernatural concepts circulating in post-war American and British culture and politics.

Conclusion

In October 1956, the month of Sylvia Plath's twenty-fourth birthday, Screamin' Jay Hawkins released the now-classic romantic song 'I Put a Spell on You'. The song describes the use of a magic spell to secure a romantic partner. During the post-war era, beauty products advertised in women's and teen magazines, such as *Seventeen* and *Mademoiselle*, frequently used language that associated female seduction with 'bewitchment'. The films *I Married a Witch* (1942) and *Bell, Book, and Candle* (1958) and Arthur Miller's play *The Crucible* (1953) make a similar connection between female sexuality and witchcraft. Plath echoes the sentiment in a journal entry from January 1953: 'If the French women can be *bewitching* reclining on a divan, so can I' (*J* 160 emphasis added). Her wording demonstrates that the vocabulary of magic is deeply rooted in our culture, language, and thinking, and the themes and concepts related to the supernatural centre on power and its relationship to gender, the self, and the other.

In the post-war era and the early Cold War, the complex and intertwined relationship between gender, power, and magic was highly present from lowbrow to highbrow art and culture. The period likewise saw a rise in the rhetoric of the witch-hunt exploited by the politics of fear and exclusion. The Salem witch trials functioned as a metaphor for the anti-communism of the Cold War and represented a dark time of American history and national memory that evoked the dangers of fanaticism (Adams 150). It is not something that belongs to the superstitious past but is employed as a metaphor and rhetorical tool by politicians, from Senator Joseph McCarthy to contemporary American politics. Plath's interest in the Salem witch trials and her frustration with the injustices of American politics beyond McCarthyism, as well as her well-researched knowledge of the New England witch-hunt and geographical closeness to the village where the trials took place gave her a great understanding of abuse of power by institutions that influenced her later writings. Her high school essay offers evidence of her awareness that the term 'witch-hunt' is a metaphor for the persecution of marginalised groups, foreshadowing the political themes of her mature writing. In *The Bell Jar*, the parallels between Esther's electroshock therapy and the electrocution of the Rosenbergs suggest that gender and political nonconformists are punished in McCarthyist America. The growing number of people placed into asylums and mental hospitals and their torturous treatment during the nineteenth and early twentieth century, including electroshock therapy and insulin treatment that Plath herself underwent, parallels the power dynamics of the witch-hunt in America (Davies 171; 175). Reading Plath comparatively with the defining texts of the New England witch-hunt, such as Hawthorne's novels and Miller's *The Crucible* demonstrates the dangerous perception of female sexuality and its association with attributes of the witch figure in the Puritan American society. Paradoxically, the witch is both the young sensual seducer and the crone with potions and spells, on which literary texts, such as Ovidian tales on mythological women, the Evil Queen in Grimms' fairy tale 'Briar Rose,' and even the ambiguous figure of the witch in *The Crucible*, draw. Plath understood the semantic difference between the two and their distinct roles in society. Nevertheless, both categories show ambivalence towards women and female power, autonomy, and sexuality in a male-dominated society. The witch, particularly in post-war America, is a loaded term that embodies martyrdom, sexual and political nonconformists, and victims of the oppressive and intersecting power of the ecclesiastical, political, and medical authorities.

By employing the conceptual and historical framework of the early modern witch-hunt, this book showcases Plath's engagement with the supernatural and its relation to gender and power. At first glance, her writings do not use direct reference to the witch-hunt as an embodiment of near-present political oppressions and focus on the power dynamics between the prosecuted and the prosecutor. However, in her drafts, she often employs the explicit language of the witch trials. Plath's evident emotional resonance with the early modern persecution of witches and allusions to the subject express her personal and broader political struggles during the post-war era. Her poems understand the witch as a gendered figure, yet she mostly associates the historical witch figure with marginalised groups, encompassing a variety of nonconformists and the other. In Plath's work, the accused witches of the early modern period signify racial injustices and the tyranny of McCarthyism. She represents the witch figure more subtly and symbolically than subsequent second-wave feminist writers and even her contemporary, Anne Sexton, expressing her intellectual and political interest in that historical period and ambiguous martyr-witch figures like Joan of Arc.

Plath's poetry and prose differentiate between the historical witch as a metaphorical embodiment of the victims of political injustices and the literary witch figure, drawing on a variety of historical, mythological, and folkloric sources. In her poems, witches are 'daunted', 'crooked', 'baked into gingerbread', 'burning', 'kindled, and curled', 'angry', and 'wicked' (*CP* 21; 32; 75; 135; 280; 308; 319). The descriptions show that when Plath explicitly names witches, she means the old maternal hag, inspired by the literature of witchcraft like *Macbeth*, fairy tales, and mythological witchlike figures. By unpicking Plath's knowledge and use of witch imagery and her references to witches, this book demonstrates that the concepts have multiple layers and express the contradictory and ambiguous thoughts Plath acquired from literary, cultural, and political discourses. While it is true to some extent that her depiction of evil maternal witches is symbolic of her ambiguous relationship to her mother, Plath's intellectual, political, and literary engagement with the witch figure has been overlooked. She taps into several characteristics of witches that we still see today, such as the maternal hags with inescapable powers in 'The Disquieting Muses' and 'All the Dead Dears', the feminist witch who defies the patriarchal institutions in 'Lady Lazarus', the wrongly prosecuted witch in 'Witch Burning', and the black female bees that allude to the reclamation of power and autonomy by marginalised groups. From her dictionary to literary and historical narratives, Plath's creative and personal writings draw on rich discursive and textual sources that associate the witch with various female figures and powers.

As opposed to witchcraft, magic, a more neutral term, evokes the vocabulary of magical tales and the powerful magus who can control their environment with supernatural powers. For Plath, magic is primarily associated with the father figure, expressing her ambiguous relationship to male power and patriarchal institutions. The self-reference of the magician's girl in 'The Bee Meeting' reveals that paternal magic is protective but also paralysing and domineering. Plath reflects on her ambivalent feelings towards the overpowering presence of her father by referencing the early modern magician Prospero from *The Tempest* and his magical powers. The magician represents the subtle ambiguities of desire and distance in the father-daughter bond and his legacy. Magic expresses the interweaving male dominance of society, which corresponds to a colonial understanding of knowledge and power. While the Prosperoean father is not the authoritarian Nazi from 'Daddy', he embodies aspects of the paternal relationship between Sylvia and Otto Plath that she portrayed in 'The Beekeeper's Daughter' and 'Among the Bumblebees'. Plath reimagines beekeeping as a supernatural power of the father figure whose relationship to bees symbolises the ambiguities of the scholarly and practical aspects of magic. From an ecocritical reading, Plath's depiction of beekeeping is a colonial power, which parallels the postcolonial reading of Shakespeare's play. However, like Prospero from *The Tempest*, Plath's paternal magician is exiled to an island: the island of Winthrop Bay and her childhood memories, where the daughter cannot connect to the domineering father, which she depicted in 'Landscape of Childhood', 'Full Fathom Five', and 'On the Decline of Oracles'. Plath's experimentation with beekeeping and reflections on the paternal inheritance parallel the idea that magic is a learnt power, a scholarly-scientific knowledge, and a praxis. Magic is linked to established norms, conventions, and institutions, and its gendered connotation associates it with dominance and authority.

The intertwined relationship between science, religion, and magic is depicted in Renaissance plays like Marlowe's *Doctor Faustus* in which the Faustian black magician embodies the larger political struggles and harmful consequences that come with unrestricted knowledge and power. Plath's references to diabolism and demonology, including devils, demons, demonic possession, and black magic can only be fully appreciated by looking at the political landscape and poetic reflections on the era torn by wars, the impending presence of the atomic bomb, and murderous ideologies. Post-war poets understood twentieth-century politics, including World War II, McCarthyism, and American capitalism as a dark and wicked time for which the early modern concept of diabolism portrayed in, for example, *Doctor Faustus* provided a vocabulary to write about malice, destruction, immorality, and, even, redemption. The references to the play in the poems by Sitwell, Shapiro, and Berryman express the direct link between the Faust legend and the political events of the twentieth century. Whereas critics from Harold Bloom to Seamus Heaney often treated Plath's writings on the Holocaust that employ emotive language and diabolical imagery as an isolated and personal occurrence, this book gives evidence of the parallels between *Faustus* and the modern Faustian bargain. Poets, atomic scientists, and public discourses equally interrogated the hellish realities of World War II and the Atomic Age. Besides politics, the language of demonology was present in Freudian psychoanalytic theories and anthropological works on demonic possession, which prompted Plath and her contemporaries to interrogate oppressive, often gendered, interpersonal relationships. Her encounters and familiarity with Elizabethan tragedies, modernist poetry, and anthropological and Freudian theories within the post-war climate demonstrate that we cannot reduce the supernatural imagery in her writings to a single and simplified reading. The references to witches, magicians, demons, and devils convey historical, theological, psychoanalytic, and political connotations which she carefully unpicks and engages with. Plath shows awareness of the loaded terms by significantly reducing their presence in the final versions of her poems.

Both black and white magic present contradictions in power, freedom, and agency, especially in the broader context of post-World War II. The bee poems demonstrate the ambiguities of whiteness and blackness as racialised concepts relating to magical power. For example, the bees are portrayed as 'Black on black, angrily clambering' and represent the collective power and kinship of the 'mass / Black' who defy the white mind (*CP* 213; 218). It implies that blackness – identified with witchcraft – is dangerous when it is associated with the other. It is not a coincidence that the criminalisation of magic and the fear of witchcraft occurred when the dominant nations of Europe began to colonise the world. Plath was aware of the echoes of colonialism in the racial rhetoric of witchcraft and interrogates these links in the bee sequence. Yet she fails to create new associations, and the fear of blackness as the power of the bees remains. The speaker of the bee poems 'experiences the self both the colonizer and colonized' (R. R. Curry 161). Plath, like many poets of her time, writes from a white middle-class point of view, disregarding the realities and voices of the marginalised groups, as suggested in her use of the slur in 'Ariel'. However, in her poems like 'Lady Lazarus' and 'Wintering' we see echoes and reflections from Plath's passionate criticism of militarism, warfare, and social and racial injustices.

In the poem 'Frederick Douglass' (1966), written about a murdered black slave, Robert Hayden writes: 'When it is finally ours, this freedom, this liberty, this beautiful / and terrible thing, needful to man as air' (62). The poem starts with a reckoning with freedom and power and ends with hope for a future of racial minorities during the Civil Rights Movement. Hayden's poem parallels Plath's bee sequence in which the bees' power is feared and desired. The enjambment 'beautiful / and terrible thing', which describes the freedom of black people, recalls Plath's 'Elm' wherein the speaker is 'terrified by this dark thing / That sleeps in me' and the frightful freedom of the queen bee in 'Stings': 'Now she is flying / More terrible than she ever was, red' (*CP* 193; 215). Plath's imagery expresses the ambiguities and complexities of power and autonomy and their relation to gender, race, and hierarchy, for which she deploys magic as a metaphor. For Plath, the distinctions between black magic, meaning diabolism and often associated with witchcraft, and white magic, the benevolent supernatural powers, are not so obvious: both white and black magic can be powerful, dangerous, oppressive, and even liberatory. Plath's employment of supernatural concepts is broadly concerned with the intersections of gender, magic, and power that interrogate her personal struggles and political tensions of the post-war era.

The seven chapters discussed what and how Plath knew of the early modern witch-hunt, supernatural figures and magical powers, the ambiguities of white and black magic, folkloric beliefs about witches, mythological sources of magical powers, the intersections of poetry and spellwork, the racial rhetoric of witchcraft, the revival of the metaphor of witch-hunt in both the United States and Great Britain during the post-war period, and her continuous interest in magical themes around gender power dynamics. Poems like 'Witch Burning', 'Fever 103°', 'Daddy', and 'The Bee Meeting' illustrate that the previous so-called 'mythical' and 'occultist' approaches to Plath's poetry have been reductionist. They underestimate that she considered herself 'a damn good high priestess of the intellect' (*L1* 781). Her short stories, such as 'Johnny Panic and the Bible of Dreams', 'Tongues of Stone', 'Charlie Pollard and the Beekeepers', and 'Mothers' centre on the themes of political exclusions, power imbalances between male medical-religious authorities and women, and supernatural practices and draw on the historical witch-hunt and its literary representations and rhetorical presence in the post-war period. Plath's interest in the supernatural is foremost intellectual and a creative exploration, not a belief, which is supported by accounts of interviewees on Plath from the Harriet Rosenstein research papers. Her poems, short stories, novel, and personal writings inform us about vocabulary, themes, and narratives of the supernatural in political, cultural, and literary discourses of the post-war era and early Cold War. Plath's rich literary allusions to and conversations with writers from Ovid, Shakespeare, and Marlowe, to Hawthorne, Miller, and even Wheatley suggest the varied discourses and texts she seeks inspiration from classics to contemporary literature. This book demonstrates that numerous post-war poets from Anne Sexton, John Ashbery, and John Berryman to Edith Sitwell, Elizabeth Bishop, Isabella Gardner, and Ted Hughes, along with Plath, engaged in political and literary representations of the supernatural and the complex relations between gender, power, and magic. Concluding my analysis, post-war literature and politics, particularly in America, were filled with supernatural references. Plath, among many poets, challenged and drew on the rhetoric of politicians and religious authorities, popular retellings of early modern plays, the associations between spellwork and poetry, and the racist and xenophobic prejudices against modern witchcraft that coincided with the fall of the British Empire and the uprising of racial minorities in the United States.

Sylvia Plath and the Supernatural recentres the supernatural themes and creative development of Plath's poetry by looking closely at the original drafts. The manuscripts of 'Lady Lazarus', 'Fever 103°', 'Daddy', 'Burning the Letters', 'Ariel', and 'Sting' all kept at Smith and written in the autumn of 1962, use the witch-hunt as a metaphor. In these drafts, Plath regularly attributes magical powers to language. Though we do not know what her intentions were, the shared language of the October 1962 manuscripts expresses a pattern of emotional resonance and preoccupation with the theme of the prosecution of witches during a specific and emotionally challenging period of Plath's life. As established, she removed supernatural allusions and references from the final versions of her poems, which shows her erasure of the highly charged and often political language. We can only imagine the labels and 'cult' allegations Plath and her readers would have received from the earlier male literary critics if she kept lines alluding to the torturous execution of a witch in 'Lady Lazarus' and the use of expressive spiritual words to dispel spirits in 'Burning the Letters'. Plath's reduction of expressions that relate to female magical power in her poems is a self-censoring practice, suggesting that she was aware of the highly charged connotations of the language she used, which she changed to more metaphorical and less direct references. Her erasures gesture towards a broader cultural phenomenon: despite living in a largely secular society, we attribute magical powers to language, particularly speech acts like curses, exorcisms, oaths, and prayers.

By focusing on Plath's intellectual curiosity and writing craft in her deployment of supernatural narratives, themes, and vocabulary, this book argues that Plath's oeuvre significantly contributes to the post-war literature on the supernatural, particularly concerning gender, power, and magical practices. Her work shows her broad understanding of the culture and politics she lived and the complex histories of magic, as well as the references to magical themes in the works of her contemporaries. While the creative partnership between Hughes and Plath is undeniable, this book demystifies the narrative that Hughes initiated Plath into the world of magic and the occult and shows the varied interests and poetic conversations she partook with post-war writers. Plath's familiarity with topics, such as the early modern witch-hunt and literary representations of magic, is primarily connected to her childhood and young adult years in post-war America. She studied the New England witch-hunt in her high school education and read about the subject as an adult. Many post-war American poets shared Plath's interests in the Salem witch trials, McCarthyism, and Cold War politics; further, the emerging feminist movements reinforced the female-centred retellings of classical stories of witches and magical women. Plath encountered Ovid's *Metamorphoses*, Shakespeare's *Macbeth* and *The Tempest*, Marlowe's *Doctor Faustus*, Goethe's *Faust*, Hawthorne's *The House of the Seven Gables*, and Miller's *The Crucible* during her education in the United States and England. The literary texts across periods offered her a broad understanding of the supernatural and its relation to gender and politics in Western culture and history, which she applied to in her writings.

With the new editions of *The Collected Prose of Sylvia Plath* and *The Poems of Sylvia Plath*, there is more research to be done on less publicised materials that were only accessible in the archives for decades. This book opens doors to the study of the supernatural in Plath's writings with a critical lens, which previously might have caused unease among literary scholars. *Sylvia Plath and the Supernatural* purposefully recentres the discussion on this subject on Plath's wide-ranging knowledge of literature, religion, and history. We cannot deny that our vocabulary is ingrained with the supernatural, originating from long historical, religious, and cultural traditions and that the collective imagination of gender and power relates to magic. Politics, the media, religion, and public discourses deploy them just as much as poets do. Further, the long-standing connection between poetry and magic and the magical powers attributed to language persisted among post-war writers. The increased popularity of poetry readings on BBC radio services, poets performing their own works, and the emergence of Beat poetry as a spontaneous, performative, spiritual countercultural art movement originate from the idea that poetry happens the same way spellwork is made. They share the belief in the power of words. Plath recognised these associations and expressed interest in supernatural narratives, themes, and vocabulary present across history, culture, and literature. The mythological, folkloric beliefs about witches, the fear of the dark other and devils, and the powers of various supernatural figures portrayed in literary texts offered metaphors for mid-twentieth-century concerns regarding women's social status and power, and post-war political tensions.

This book comes at a time when many countries reckon with their role in the witch trials: in 2022, the Scottish Parliament proposed a pardon act to the people accused of witchcraft; however, it was dropped in 2023. In 2024, a petition was created in England to pardon the Pendle witches that reached more than 10,000 signatures, and in Salem, the last person accused in the witch trials was formally pardoned in 2022. It is also time to release Plath from the accusations and false narratives that have persisted for decades. The broader public interest in the histories and literature of witches demonstrates that reassessing Plath's engagement with the subject is timely and necessary. *Sylvia Plath and the Supernatural* bridges the gap between historical studies on the witch-hunt and literary investigation into the occult, offering a broad and large-scale analysis of Sylvia Plath's works through the historical and literary lens of the supernatural. The study of Plath's archives, poetry, prose, letters, and journal entries in conversation with post-war literature and political discourses gives a renewed understanding of the many ways in which the supernatural encompasses and captivates the literary and political imagination.

Bibliography

Ackerman, Diane. *A Slender Thread: Rediscovering Hope at the Heart of Crisis*. New York: Vintage Books, 1998.

Adams, Gretchen A. *The Specter of Salem: Remembering the Witch Trials in Nineteenth-Century America*. Chicago: University of Chicago Press, 2008.

Adelman, Janet. '"Born of Woman": Fantasies of Maternal Power in *Macbeth*'. *Cannibals, Witches, and Divorce: Estranging the Renaissance*. Ed. Marjorie Garber. Baltimore: Johns Hopkins University Press, 1987. 90–121.

Alkalay-Gut, Karen. 'The Dream Life of Ms. Dog: Anne Sexton's Revolutionary Use of Pop Culture'. *College Literature* 32.4 (2005): 50–73.

Altman, Janet Gurkin. *Epistolarity: Approaches to a Form*. Columbus: Ohio State University Press, 1982.

Alvarez, Al. *The Savage God: A Study of Suicide*. London: Bloomsbury, 2002.

Ashbery, John. *Selected Poems*. New York: Penguin Books, 1986.

Ashe, Marie. '*The Bell Jar* and the Ghost of Ethel Rosenberg'. *Secret Agents: The Rosenberg Case, McCarthyism, and Fifties America*. Ed. Marjorie Garber and Rebecca L. Walkowitz. New York: Routledge, 1995. 215–32.

Atwood, Margaret. *Morning in the Burning House*. London: Virago Press, 1995.

Auden, W. H. *The Poet's Tongue: An Anthology*. London: Bell & Sons, 1935.

Axelrod, Steven Gould. *Sylvia Plath: The Wound and the Cure of Words*. Baltimore; London: Johns Hopkins University Press, 1992.

Balitas, Vincent. 'On Becoming a Witch: A Reading of Sylvia Plath's "Witch Burning"'. *Studies in the Humanities* 4.2 (1975): 27–30.

Barkan, Leonard. *The Gods Made Flesh: Metamorphosis and the Pursuit of Paganism*. New Haven; London: Yale University Press, 1986.

Barranger, Milly S. *Margaret Webster: A Life in the Theater*. Ann Arbor: University of Michigan Press, 2004.

Baskin, Esther. *Creatures of Darkness*. Boston: Atlantic Monthly Press, 1962.

Bassnett, Susan. *Sylvia Plath: An Introduction to the Poetry*. 2nd ed. New York: Palgrave Macmillan, 2005.

Bate, Jonathan. *Ted Hughes: The Unauthorised Life*. London: William Collins, 2015.

Beardsworth, Adam. *Confessional Poetry in the Cold War: The Poetics of Doublespeak*. Cham: Palgrave Macmillan, 2022.

Bearman, C. J. 'An Examination of Suffragette Violence'. *The English Historical Review* 120.486 (2005): 365–97.
Beddow, Di. 'Sylvia Plath's Cambridge'. *Bloomsbury Handbook to Sylvia Plath*. Ed. Anita Helle, Amanda Golden, and Maeve O'Brien. London: Bloomsbury, 2022. 53–62.
Behringer, Wolfgang. 'Demonology, 1500–1660'. *The Cambridge History of Christianity*. Ed. R. Po-chia Hsia. Cambridge: Cambridge University Press, 2007. 406–24.
Berryman, John. 'The Wholly Fail'. *Poetry* 75.4 (1950): 191.
Love & Fame. New York: Farrar, Straus & Giroux, 1970.
Black, Monica. *A Demon-Haunted Land: Witches, Wonder Doctors, and the Ghosts of the Past in Post-WWII Germany*. New York: Metropolitan Books, 2020.
Bloch, Nikki. *Patterns of Rape in Ovid's Metamorphoses*. Boulder: University of Colorado, 2014.
Bowen, Elizabeth. *The Demon Lover and Other Stories*. London: Jonathan Cape, 1945.
Brain, Tracy. *The Other Sylvia Plath*. Harlow: Longman, 2001.
'Sylvia Plath and You'. *Sylvia Plath in Context*. Ed. Tracy Brain. Cambridge: Cambridge University Press, 2019. 84–93.
Bren, Paulina. *The Barbizon: The Hotel That Set Women Free*. New York: Simon & Schuster, 2021.
Breslaw, Elaine G. 'Tituba's Confession: The Multicultural Dimensions of the 1692 Salem Witch-Hunt'. *Ethnohistory* 44.3 (1997): 535–56.
Britzolakis, Christina. *Sylvia Plath and the Theatre of Mourning*. Oxford: Oxford University Press, 1991.
Bronfen, Elisabeth. *Sylvia Plath*. 2nd ed. Tavistock: Northcote House, 2004.
Brontë, Charlotte. *Jane Eyre*. Ed. Margaret Smith. Oxford: Oxford University Press, 2020.
Brown, Paul. '"This Thing of Darkness I Acknowledge Mine": *The Tempest* and the Discourse of Colonialism'. *Political Shakespeare: New Essays in Cultural Materialis*. Ed. Jonathan Dollimore and Alan Sinfield. Ithaca; London: Cornell University Press, 1985. 48–71.
Brunner, Edward. *Cold War Poetry*. Urbana: University of Illinois Press, 2001.
Bryant, Marsha. 'Queen Bees: Edith Sitwell, Sylvia Plath & Cross-Atlantic Affiliations'. *Feminist Modernist Studies* 2.2 (2019): 194–211.
'Beelines: Reading Plath through Edith Sitwell and Carol Ann Duffy'. *The Bloomsbury Handbook to Sylvia Plath*. Ed. Anita Helle, Amanda Golden, and Maeve O'Brien. London: Bloomsbury, 2022. 199–209.
Bundtzen, Lynda K. *The Other Ariel*. Stroud: Sutton, 2005.
Burton, Sarah. 'Bedlam and Broomsticks: Representations of the Witch in Nineteenth- and Twentieth-Century Women's Writing'. Doctoral dissertation, Cardiff University, 2006.
Butler, Eliza Marian. *Ritual Magic*. Cambridge: Cambridge University Press, 1949.

Cam, Heather. '"Daddy": Sylvia Plath's Debt to Anne Sexton'. *American Literature* 59.3 (1987): 429–32.

Cardon, Lauren S. 'Plath, Sexton, and the "New Look"'. *Fashioning Character: Style, Performance, and Identity in Contemporary American Literature*. Charlottesville; London: University of Virginia Press, 2021. 27–64.

Carlson, Rachel D. 'The Honey Bee and Apian Imagery in Classical Literature'. Doctoral dissertation. University of Washington, 2015.

Caroll, Robert, ed. *The Bible: Authorized King James Version*. Oxford: Oxford University Paperbacks, 2008.

Castelow, Ellen. *Recycling - A Way of Life in the 1950s and 1960s*. 13 September 2019. www.historic-uk.com/CultureUK/Recycling-1950s-1960s/.

Chakraborty, Sumita. 'Anthropocene Ethics and Its Lapses: Lyric Eros, Racism, and the Example of Sylvia Plath's Bees'. *ISLE: Interdisciplinary Studies in Literature and Environment* 28.3 (2021): 1002–28.

Chamberlin, W. A. 'Longfellow's Attitude toward Goethe'. *Modern Philology* 16.2 (1918): 57–76.

'Christianity vs. Communism'. *The Washington Post*, 22 July 1953: 3.

Christodoulides, Nephie J. 'Medusa/Melusina: The Magic Mirror of Sylvia Plath's "Medusa"'. *The Plath Profiles* 3 (Summer 2010): 247–58.

Church of St Peter. 3 October 2019. https://historicengland.org.uk/listing/the-list/list-entry/1146842.

Clark, Heather. 'P(l)athography: Plath and Her Biographers'. *Sylvia Plath in Context*. Ed. Tracy Brain. Cambridge: Cambridge University Press, 2019. 360–70.

Red Comet: The Short Life and Blazing Art of Sylvia Plath. London: Jonathan Cape, 2020.

'Sylvia Plath: An Iconic Life'. *Women's History Review* (2021): 1–14.

Cohn, Norman. *Europe's Inner Demons*. London: Pimlico, 1993.

Coleridge, Samuel Taylor. *The Complete Poetical Work of Samuel Taylor Coleridge*. Vol. 1. Oxford: Clarendon Press, 1975.

'Communists Decry "Hunt" by Regents'. *New York Times*, 18 June 1953: 17.

Connors, Kathleen. 'Visual Art in the Life of Sylvia Plath'. *The Unraveling Archive: Essays on Sylvia Plath*. Ed. Anita Helle. Ann Arbor: University of Michigan Press, 2007, 65–88.

Corcoran, Miranda. *Witchcraft and Adolescence in American Popular Culture: Teen Witches*. Cardiff: University of Wales Press, 2022.

Corcoran, Neil. *Shakespeare and the Modern Poet*. Cambridge: Cambridge University Press, 2010.

Crowther, Gail. 'Religious Contexts for Plath's Work'. *Sylvia Plath in Context*. Ed. Tracy Brain. Cambridge: Cambridge University Press, 2019. 213–20.

Three-Martini Afternoons at the Ritz: The Rebellion of Sylvia Plath & Anne Sexton. New York: Gallery Books, 2021.

What Cost, Sylvia Plath? 21 July 2021. https://gailcrowther.com/2021/07/21/what-cost-sylvia-plath/.

Crowther, Gail, and Peter K. Steinberg. *These Ghostly Archives: The Unearthing of Sylvia Plath*. Stroud: Fonthill Media, 2017.

Curran, Jane V. 'Goethe's "Helen": A Play within a Play'. *International Journal of the Classical Tradition* 7.2 (2000): 165–76.
Curry, Renée R. *White Women Writing White: H. D., Elizabeth Bishop, Sylvia Plath, and Whiteness*. Westport, CT; London: Greenwood, 2000.
Curry, Walter Clyde. 'The Demonic Metaphysics of Macbeth'. *Studies in Philology* 30.3 (1933): 395–426.
Danet, Brenda, and Bryna Bogoch. '"Whoever Alters This, May God Turn His Face from Him on the Day of Judgment": Curses in Anglo-Saxon Legal Documents'. *The Journal of American Folklore* 105.416 (1992): 132–65.
Davies, Owen. *America Bewitched*. Oxford: Oxford University Press, 2013.
'Davison, Peter and Jane, 1972–1975'. Harriet Rosenstein research files on Sylvia Plath, Manuscript Collection No. 1489. Stuart A. Rose Manuscript, Archives, and Rare Book Library., n.d. Box: 1, Folder: 22.
Deats, Sara Munson. '"Mark This show": Magic and Theater in Marlowe's *Doctor Faustus*'. *Placing the Plays of Christopher Marlowe: Fresh Cultural Contexts*. Ed. Sara Munson Deats and Robert A. Logan. ldershot; Burlington, VT: Ashgate, 2008, 13–24.
'Devon Witches Still Practising'. *The Observer* 13 May 1956: 9.
Dickinson, Emily. *Selected Letters*. Cambridge, MA: Belknap Press of Harvard University Press, 1986.
Durrani, Osman. 'Faust in the Nuclear Age'. *Lives of Faust*. Ed. Lorna Fitzsimmons. Berlin; Boston: De Gruyter, 2011, 477–78.
'19th-century American Fausts'. *Lives of Faust*. Ed. Lorna Fitzsimmons. Berlin; Boston: De Gruyter, 2011, 405–6.
Dyson, Freedman. *Disturbing the Universe*. New York: Basic Books, 1979.
Eberwein, Jane Donahue. '"My Faith Is Gone!" "Young Goodman Brown" and Puritan Conversion'. *Christianity and Literature* 32.1 (1982): 23–32.
'Eisenhower Is Assailed: Jenner Endorsement Brings an Attack from Stevenson Aide'. *New York Times* 10 September 1952: 16.
Elliott, Charlene. 'Purple Pasts: Color Codification in the Ancient World'. *Law & Social Inquiry* 33.1 (2008): 173–94.
Ellis, Jonathan. '"Mailed into Space": On Sylvia Plath's Letters'. *Representing Sylvia Plath*. Ed. Sally Bayley and Tracy Brain. Cambridge: Cambridge University Press, 2011, 13–31.
'Last Letters: Keats, Bishop and Hughes'. *Letter Writing among Poets: From William Wordsworth to Elizabeth Bishop*. Ed. Jonathan Ellis. Edinburgh: Edinburgh University Press, 2015, 231–45.
Emig, Rainer. 'Making War Poetry Contemporary'. *A Companion to Poetic Genre*. Ed. Eric Martiny. Chichester: Wiley-Blackwell, 2012, 543–54.
Encyclopaedia Britannica. 14th ed. Vol. 13. London: Encyclopaedia Britannica, 1932.
Epstein, Andrew. *Beautiful Enemies*. New York: Oxford University Press, 2006.
Evans, Elizabeth Capaldi, and Carol A. Butler. *Why Do Bees Buzz? Fascinating Answers to Questions about Bees*. New Brunswick, NJ; London: Rutgers University Press, 2010.

'Fainlight, Ruth, interview recording, undated (side A); Al Alvarez, interview recording, undated (side B)'. Harriet Rosenstein. Stuart A. Rose Manuscript, Archives, and Rare Book Library, undated. 19 September 2024.

The Faculty of English. 'Sylvia Plath and the Tragedy Paper'. *Cambridge Authors*. 22 July 2009. www.english.cam.ac.uk/cambridgeauthors/sylvia-plath-and-the-tragedy-paper/.

Ferretter, Luke. *Sylvia Plath's Fiction: A Critical Study*. Edinburgh: Edinburgh University Press, 2010.

Fielding, Steven. *Class and Ethnicity: Irish Catholics in England, 1880–1939*. Buckingham; Philadelphia: Open University Press, 1993.

Ford, Karen Jackson. *Gender and the Poetics of Excess*. Jackson: University Press of Mississippi, 1997.

Ford, Mark. *'Lady Lazarus' by Sylvia Plath: A Close Reading*. 2016. www.bl.uk/20th-century-literature/articles/a-close-reading-of-lady-lazarus.

Fowler, Rowena. '"This Tart Fable": Daphne and Apollo in Modern Women's Poetry'. *Thought, Laughing with Medusa: Classical Myth and Feminist*. Ed. Vanda Zajko and Miriam Leonard. Oxford: Oxford University Press, 2008, 381–98.

Frazer, James George. *The Golden Bough: A Study in Magic and Religion*. New York: The Macmillan Company, 1952.

Freud, Sigmund. 'A Seventeenth-Century Demonological Neurosis'. *The Standard Edition of the Complete Psychological Works of Sigmund Freud, Volume XIX (1923–1925)*. Ed. Anna Freud. Vol. 19: The Ego and the Id and Other Works. London: Vintage, 2001, 67–106.

Gage, Matilda Joslyn. *Women, Church and the State*. Memphis: General Books, 2012.

Garber, Marjorie. 'Macbeth: The Male Medusa'. *Shakespeare's Ghost Writers: Literature as Uncanny Causality*. Ed. Garber, Marjorie. New York: Routledge, 1987, 116–65.

Gardner, Gerald B. 'Modern Witches'. *The Observer* 16 December 1956: 2.

Witchcraft Today. New York: Citadel Press, 2004.

Gardner, Isabella. 'The Looking Glass'. *The Sewanee Review* 67.3 (1959): 450–51.

Gibson, Marion. 'Retelling Salem Stories: Gender Politics and Witches in American Culture'. *European Journal of American Culture* 25.2 (2006): 85–107.

Witchcraft Myths American Culture. New York: Routledge, 2007.

Rediscovering Renaissance Witchcraft. Abingdon: Routledge, 2017.

Gibson, Marion, and Jo Ann Esra. *Shakespeare's Demonology: A Dictionary*. London: Arden Shakespeare, 2017.

Gill, Jo. '"Your Story. My Story": Confessional Writing and the Case of Birthday Letters'. *Modern Confessional Writing: New Critical Essays*. Ed. Jo Gill. London; New York: Routledge, 2006, 67–83.

Anne Sexton's Confessional Poetics. Gainesville: University Press of Florida, 2007.

The Cambridge Introduction to Sylvia Plath. Cambridge: Cambridge University Press, 2008.

The Poetics of the American Suburbs. New York: Palgrave Macmillan, 2013.

'"Quite the Opposite of a Feminist": Phyllis McGinley, Betty Friedan and Discourses of Gender in Midcentury American Culture'. *Women's History Review* 22.3 (2013): 422–39.

Gilles, John. 'The Figure of the New World in *The Tempest*'. *'The Tempest' and Its Travels*. Ed. Peter Hulme and William Sherman. London: Reaktion Books, 2000, 180–200.

Goethe, Johann Wolfgang von. *Faust*. 2nd ed. Trans. Eugene Stelzig. New York: Modern Library, 1912.

Golden, Amanda. *Annotating Modernism Marginalia and Pedagogy from Virginia Woolf to the Confessional Poets*. Abingdon; New York: Routledge, 2020.

'Sylvia Plath's Library: The Marginal Archive'. *The Contemporary Poetry Archive: Essays and Interventions*. Ed. Linda Anderson, Mark Byers, and Ahren Warner. Edinburgh: Edinburgh University Press, 2022, 111–23.

Gordon-Bramer, Julia. *The Occult Sylvia Plath: The Hidden Spiritual Life of the Visionary*. Rochester, VT: Destiny Books, 2024.

Graham, Billy. 'Satan's Religion'. *American Mercury August* (1954): 41–6.

Graves, Robert. *The White Goddess: A Historical Grammar of Poetic Myth*. London: Faber and Faber Limited, 1948.

The Complete Poems. Manchester: Carcanet Press, 1999.

Greenblatt, Stephen. *Shakespearean Negotiations: The Circulation of Social Energy in Renaissance England*. Berkley; Los Angeles: University of California Press, 1988.

Greene, Sally. 'The Pull of the Oracle: Personalized Mythologies in Plath and de Chirico'. *Mosaic: An Interdisciplinary Critical Journal* 25.1 (1992): 107–20.

Grisafi, Patricia. *Breaking Down Plath*. Hoboken, NJ: John Wiley & Sons Inc., 2022.

Gryciuk, Sylwia. 'Rivalry, Betrayal, and Exclusion: Traumatic Reenactments and Female Peer Relations in Sylvia Plath's Short Fiction'. *European Association for American Studies* 17.2 (2022): 1–20.

Hall, Daniel. *Hermit with Landscape*. New Haven: Yale University Press, 1990.

Halpin, Jenni G. 'New Physics, New Faust: Faustian Bargains in Physics Before the Atomic Bomb'. *The Palgrave Handbook of Twentieth and Twenty-First Century Literature and Science*. Ed. The Triangle Collective. Cham: Palgrave Macmillan, 2020, 363–73.

Hammer, Langdon. 'Plath's Lives'. *Representations* 75.1 (2001): 61–88.

'Plath's German'. *ELH* 91.1 (2024): 239–62.

Hargrove, Nancy D. *The Journey toward Ariel: Sylvia Plath's Poems of 1956–1959*. Lund: Lund University Press, 1994.

Harrison, Tony. *Selected Poems*. London: Penguin, 1987.

Haven, Samuel Towernew. 'Yale's "Faust": University's Production Will Celebrate Bicentenary of Goethe's Birth'. *New York Times*, 20 March 1950: 1.

Hawthorne, Nathaniel. *Hawthorne's Short Stories*. New York: Vintage Books, 1955.

The House of the Seven Gables. Minneapolis: First Avenue Editions, 2014.

'The Birthmark'. *Young Goodman Brown and Other Tales*. Oxford: Oxford University Press, 2020, 176–92.

Hayden, Robert. *Collected Poems*. New York: W. W. Norton & Co., 2013.

Helle, Anita. 'Reading Plath's Photographs'. *The Unraveling Archives: Essays on Sylvia Plath*. Ed. Anita Helle. Ann Arbor: University of Michigan Press, 2007, 182–210.

Hickson, Kevin. *Britain's Conservative Right since 1945 Traditional Toryism in a Cold Climate*. Cham: Springer International; Palgrave Macmillan, 2020.

Hicok, Bethany. *Degrees of Freedom: American Women Poets and the Women's College, 1905–1955*. Lewisburg: Bucknell University Press, 2008.

Hitchman, Beatrice. '"Minor Scandal": Lesbian Writing Contexts for *The Bell Jar*'. *Sylvia Plath in Context*. Ed. Tracy Brain. Cambridge: Cambridge University Press, 2019, 169–79.

Homer. *The Iliad*. Trans. Peter Green. Oakland: University of California Press, 2015.

Hughes, Ted. *Gaudete*. London: Faber, 1977.

Tales from Ovid. London: Faber & Faber, 1997.

Birthday Letters. London: Faber & Faber, 1998.

Collected Poems. Ed. Paul Keegan. London: Faber & Faber, 2005.

Letters of Ted Hughes. Ed. Christopher Reid. New York: Farrar, Straus and Giroux, 2008.

'"The Critical Forum" Series.' 1978. *Norwich Tapes in the Library of The University of Birmingham*. 15 December 2023. https://ann.skea.com/CriticalForum.htm.

Hungerford, Amy. *Postmodern Belief: American Literature and Religion since 1960*. Princeton: Princeton University Press, 2010.

Hutton, Ronald. *The Triumph of the Moon: A History of Modern Pagan Witchcraft*. Oxford: Oxford University Press, 1999.

The Witch: A History of Fear, from Ancient Times to the Present. New Haven: Yale University Press, 2017.

Jarrell, Randall. 'A Conversation with the Devil'. *Poetry* 78.1 (1951): 1–6.

Johnston, William M. *The Austrian Mind: An Intellectual and Social History 1848–1938*. Berkeley; London: University of California Press, 1972.

Jolly, Margaretta. 'On Burning, Saving and Stealing Letters'. *New Formations* 67 (2009): 25–35.

Jones, Ian. 'The Clergy, the Cold War and the Mission of the Local Church; England ca. 1945–60'. *Religion and the Cold War*. Ed. Dianne Kirby. Gordonsville: Palgrave Macmillan, 2002, 188–99.

Joseph, May. 'The Scream of Sycorax'. *Nomadic Identities*. Vol. 5. Minneapolis: University of Minnesota Press, 1999. 127–40.

Kendall, Tim. *Sylvia Plath: A Critical Study*. London: Faber & Faber, 2001.

Keniston, Ann. *Ghostly Figures: Memory and Belatedness in Postwar American Poetry*. Iowa City: University of Iowa Press, 2015.

Kermode, Frank. 'Introduction' to Shakespeare, William. *The Tempest*. Arden ed. London: Methuen, 1954, xi–xciii.

Kiessling, Nicolas. 'Doctor Faustus and the Sin of Demoniality'. *Studies in English Literature, 1500–1900* 15.2 (1975): 205–11.

King, Francis. *Modern Ritual Magic: The Rise of Western Occultism*. Bridport; New York; Lindfield: Prism Press, 1989.

Klaassen, Frank. 'Necromancy'. *The Routledge History of Medieval Magic*. Ed. Catherine Rider and Sophie Page. Abingdon; New York: Routledge, 2019, 201–11.

Knox, Sara L. 'The Genealogy of Treason: Ethel Rosenberg and the Masculinist Discourse'. *Australasian Journal of American Studies* 12.2 (1993): 32–49.

Kukil, Karen V. *The Fires of Heaven and Hell: Sylvia Plath's 'Fever 103°'*. 6 September 2018. www.faber.co.uk/blog/sylvia-plath-fever-103/.

Larner, Christina. *Enemies of God: The Witch-hunt in Scotland*. London: Chatto and Windus, 1981.

Layton-Henry, Zig. *The Politics of Immigration*. Oxford; Cambridge, MA: Blackwell 1992.

Levack, Brian P. *The Witch-Hunt in Early Modern Europe*. Harlow: Pearson Longman, 2006.

The Devil Within: Possession and Exorcism in the Christian West. New Haven; London: Yale University Press, 2013.

Levin, David. 'Review: Salem Witchcraft in Recent Fiction and Drama'. *The New England Quarterly* 28.4 (1955): 537–46.

Logan, Robert A. '"Glutted with Conceit": Imprints of *Doctor Faustus* on *The Tempest*'. *Placing the Plays of Christopher Marlowe: Fresh Cultural Contexts*. Ed. Sara Munson Deats and Robert A. Logan. Aldershot; Burlington, VT: Ashgate, 2003. 193–208.

Lowe, Peter J. '"Full Fathom Five": The Dead Father in Sylvia Plath's Seascapes'. *Texas Studies in Literature and Language* 49.1 (2007): 21–44.

Lowell, Robert. *Life Studies and for the Union Dead*. New York: The Noonday Press, 1970.

'Lucie-Smith, Edward, interview recording, July 28 [original: audio cassette]'. Box: AV1. Harriet Rosenstein research files on Sylvia Plath, Manuscript Collection No. 1489. Stuart A. Rose Manuscript, Archives, and Rare Book Library, 28 July 1970.

'Macedo, Suzette and Helder'. Rosenstein research files on Sylvia Plath, Manuscript Collection No. 1489. Stuart A. Rose Manuscript, Archives, and Rare Book Library., Box: 2 Folder: 18 1961–1962, 1972–1974.

'Macedo, Suzette and Helder, interview recording, parts three and four'. Harriet Rosenstein Research Files on Sylvia Plath, 1910–2018. Harriet Rosenstein. Stuart A. Rose Manuscript, Archives, and Rare Book Library, Emory University, 1 December 1973.

Macfarlane, Alan. *Witchcraft in Tudor and Stuart England: A Regional and Comparative Study*. Abingdon: Routledge, 1999.

Marlowe, Christopher. *Christopher Marlowe*. London: E. Benn Limited, 1951.

Doctor Faustus. 3rd. ed. Ed. Roma Gill. London: Methuen Drama, 2008.
McCarthy, Joseph. 'Enemies from Within'. 9 Feb 1950. *Digital History*. 20 Oct 2021.
McCort, Jessica. 'Getting Out of Wonderland: Elizabeth Bishop, Sylvia Plath, Adrienne Rich, and Anne Sexton'. Doctoral thesis, Washington University in St. Louis, 2009.
Millar, Charlotte-Rose. *Witchcraft, the Devil, and Emotions in Early Modern England*. Abingdon: Routledge, 2019.
Miller, Amanda L. 'Guttural Vowels and Guttural Co-articulation in Ju|'hoansi'. *Journal of Phonetics* 35.1 (2007): 56–84.
Miller, Arthur. 'The Crucible'. *Plays: One*. London: Methuen, 1988. 225–329.
'Are you now or were you ever . . .?' 17 June 2000. *The Guardian*. www.theguardian.com/books/2000/jun/17/history.politics.
'Why I Wrote The Crucible'. 1996 Oct. 13. *The New Yorker*. 20 October 2021.
Milton, John. *Paradise Lost*. New York: The Odyssey Press, 1935.
Paradise Lost. Minneapolis: Lerner, 1984.
Moses, Kate. 'Sylvia Plath's Voice, Annotated'. *The Unraveling Archive: Essays on Sylvia Plath*. Ed. Anita Helle. Ann Arbor: University of Michigan Press, 2007.
Mowat, Barbara A. 'Prospero's Book'. *Shakespeare Quarterly* 52.1 (2001): 1–33.
Murphy, Jerome Ellison. '"God's Lioness" and God's "Negress": The Feminine and the Figure of the African American in Plath'. *The Bloomsbury Handbook to Sylvia Plath*. Ed. Anita Helle, Amanda Golden, and Maeve O'Brien. London: Bloomsbury, 2022, 93–100.
Murray, Margaret. *The God of the Witches*. London: Faber & Faber, 1952.
The Witch-Cult in Western Europe. Oxford: Clarendon Press, 1962.
Nance, Guinevara A., and Judith P. Jones. 'Doing Away with Daddy: Exorcism and Sympathetic Magic in Plath's Poetry'. *Critical Essays on Sylvia Plath*. Ed. Linda Wagner-Martin. Boston: G. K. Hall, 1984, 125–29.
Nathaniel Hawthorne's Birthplace. 12 October 2024. https://7gables.org/historic-structures/.
Nelson, Deborah. *Pursuing Privacy in Cold War America*. New York; Chichester: Columbia University Press, 2002.
'Plath, History, and Politics'. *The Cambridge Companion to Sylvia Plath*. Ed. Jo Gill. Cambridge: Cambridge University Press, 2006, 21–35.
Norman, Mark. *Telling the Bees and Other Customs*. Cheltenham: The History Press, 2020.
Norton, Mary Beth. *In the Devil's Snare*. New York: Vintage Books, 2002.
Ogden, Daniel. *The Strix-Witch*. Ed. Marion Gibson. Cambridge: Cambridge University Press, 2021.
O'Brien, Maeve. 'Centering Whiteness: Sylvia Plath's Literary Apprenticeship'. *The Bloomsbury Handbook to Sylvia Plath*. Ed. Anita Helle, Amanda Golden, and Maeve O'Brien. London: Bloomsbury, 2022, 101–10.
Orr, Peter. *The Poet Speaks: Interviews with Contemporary Poets*. Ed. Peter Orr. London: Routledge & Kegan Paul, 1966.

Ostriker, Alicia. *Stealing the Language: The Emergence of Women's Poetry in America*. London: Women's Press, 1986.

Ovid. *Metamorphoses: The New, Annotated Edition*. Ed. J. D. Reed. Trans. Rolfe Humphries. Bloomington: Indiana University Press, 2018.

Owens, Yvonne. 'The Saturnine History of Jews and Witches'. *Preternature: Critical and Historical Studies on the Preternatural* 3.1 (2014): 56–84.

'Pagan Tendencies in Britain'. *The Manchester Guardian* 5 April 1956: 2.

Peel, Robin. *Writing Back: Sylvia Plath and Cold War Politics*. Madison, NJ; London: Fairleigh Dickinson University Press; Associated University Presses, 2002.

'The Political Education of Sylvia Plath'. *The Unraveling Archives: Essays on Sylvia Plath*. Ed. Anita Helle. Ann Arbor: University of Michigan Press, 2007, 39–64.

'*The Bell Jar*, the Rosenbergs and the Problem of the Enemy Within'. *Sylvia Plath in Context*. Ed. Tracy Brain. Cambridge: Cambridge University Press, 2019, 203–12.

Perloff, Marjorie. '"Angst" and Animism in the Poetry of Sylvia Plath'. *Journal of Modern Literature* 1.1 (1970): 57–74.

Perry, Laura. 'Plath and the Culture of Hygiene'. *Sylvia Plath in Context*. Ed. Tracy Brain. Cambridge: Cambridge University Press, 2019, 191–200.

Peters, Edward. *The Magician, the Witch, and the Law*. Philadelphia: University of Pennsylvania Press, 1978.

Phillips, Victoria. 'Cold War Modernist Missionary: Martha Graham Takes Joan of Arc and Catherine of Siena "Behind the Iron Curtain"'. *Dancing the Cold War An International Symposium*. Ed. Lynn Garafola. Columbia University, 2017, 54–64.

Martha Graham's Cold War: The Dance of American Diplomacy. New York: Oxford University Press, 2020.

Plath, Otto. *Bumblebees and Their Way*. New York: Macmillan, 1934.

Plath, Sylvia. 'TS "Stings", 2 August 1962'. Sylvia Plath Collection, Mortimer Rare Book Collection, Smith College Special Collections, Smith College, Northampton. Item: 3 Folder: 245 Box: 13. https://findingaids.smith.edu/repositories/3/archival_objects/162626.

'TS "Stings", 2 August 1962'. Sylvia Plath Collection, Mortimer Rare Book Collection, Smith College Special Collections, Smith College, Northampton. Item: 4 Folder: 245 Box: 13. https://findingaids.smith.edu/repositories/3/archival_objects/162627.

'MS "Stings", 6 October 1962'. Sylvia Plath Collection, Mortimer Rare Book Collection, Smith College Special Collections, Smith College, Northampton. Item: 5 Folder: 245 Box: 13. https://findingaids.smith.edu/repositories/3/archival_objects/162628.

'MS "Ariel", 27 October 1962'. Sylvia Plath Collection, Mortimer Rare Book Collection, Smith College Special Collections, Smith College, Northampton. Item: 3 Folder: 15 Box: 6. https://findingaids.smith.edu/repositories/3/archival_objects/161359.

'MS "Burning the Letters", undated'. Sylvia Plath Collection, Mortimer Rare Book Collection, Smith College Special Collections, Smith College, Northampton: item: 1 Folder: 41 Box: 7.

'MS "Lady Lazarus", undated'. Sylvia Plath Collection, Mortimer Rare Book Collection, Smith College Special Collections, Smith College, Northampton. Item: 1 Folder: 129 Box: 10. https://findingaids.smith.edu/repositories/3/archival_objects/162072.

'TS "Daddy", undated'. Sylvia Plath Collection, Mortimer Rare Book Collection, Smith College Special Collections, Smith College, Northampton. Item: 2 Folder: 61 Box: 9. https://findingaids.smith.edu/repositories/3/archival_objects/161699.

'"Fever 103°" audio'. Plath: Plath Reads Plath. An Interview: Sylvia Plath Talks with Peter Orr of the British Council. Smith College: British Council, 1975. cassette. Sylvia Plath Collection, Mortimer Rare Book Collection, Smith College Special Collections, Smith College Northampton. https://findingaids.smith.edu/repositories/3/archival_objects/164135.

Magic Mirror: The Study of Double in Two of Dostoevsky's Novels. Llanwddyn, Powys: Embers Handpress, 1989.

Letters Home: Correspondence 1950–1963. Ed. Aurelia Plath. London: Faber, 1990.

The Bell Jar. London: Faber & Faber, 2001.

The Unabridged Journals of Sylvia Plath. Ed. Karen V. Kukil. New York: Anchor Books, 2002.

Ariel: The Restored Edition. London: Faber, 2004.

The Collected Poems. Ed. Ted Hughes. New York: HarperCollins, 2008.

'The Disquieting Muses'. *Spoken Word: Sylvia Plath*. London: British Library. London, 2010.

The Letters of Sylvia Plath Volume I: 1940–1956. Ed. Peter K. Steinberg and Karen V. Kukil. London: Faber, 2017.

The Letters of Sylvia Plath: Volume II: 1956–1963. Ed. Karen V. Kukil and Peter K. Steinberg. London: Faber & Faber, 2018.

The Collected Prose of Sylvia Plath. Ed. Peter K. Steinberg. London: Faber & Faber, 2024.

'The House of the Seven Gables; Project. Holograph with instructor's comments. 24 p. For English 21'. Plath mss. II, 1932–1977. Lilly Library, Indiana University, Bloomington. Folder: 1 Box: 10. https://webapp1.dlib.indiana.edu/findingaids/view?doc.view=entire_text&docId=InU-Li-VAC4841.

Plumly, Stanley. 'Popular Beliefs Accepted by Churchmen'. *Materials Toward a History of Witchcraft*. Ed. Henry Charles Lea. Vol. 1. Philadelphia: University of Pennsylvania Press, 1939.

'What Ceremony of Words'. *Ariel Ascending: Writings about Sylvia Plath*. Ed. Paul Alexander. New York: Harper & Row, 1985, 13–25.

Purkiss, Diane. *The Witch in History: Early Modern and Twentieth-century Representations*. London: Routledge, 1996.

'Radio and Television: WNYC to Carry "BBC Playhouse" Series, Starting Wednesday with "Dr. Faustus"'. *New York Times* 4 July 1949: 24.

Rákóczi, Basil Ivan. *The Painted Caravan*. The Hague: L. J. C. Boucher, 1954.

Ramazani, Jahan. *Poetry of Mourning: The Modern Elegy from Hardy to Heaney*. Chicago: Chicago University Press, 1994.

Ranger, Holly. 'Ovid, Plath, Baskin, Hughes'. *Ted Hughes Society Journal* 7.2 (2019): 7–24.

'"My Tree Stays Tree": Sylvia Plath and Ovid's Daphne'. *International Journal of the Classical Tradition* 27.2 (2020): 215–37.

Rankovic, Catherine. *Aurelia Plath and 'The Case for Chastity'*. 21 December 2021. https://aureliaplath.blogspot.com/2021/12/aurelia-plath-and-case-for-chastity.html.

Reed, Isaac. 'Why Salem Made Sense: Culture, Gender, and the Puritan Persecution of Witchcraft'. *Cultural Sociology* 1.2 (2007): 209–34.

Reumann, Miriam G. *American Sexual Character*. Berkeley: University of California Press, 2005.

Rich, Adrienne Cecile. *Collected Early Poems: 1950–1970*. New York: W. W. Norton & Company, 1993.

Roberts, Neil. *A Companion to Poetic Genre*. Ed. Erik Martiny. Chichester: Wiley-Blackwell, 2012.

Robinson, Kathrine. 'The Law of Similarity and the Law of Contact: Sylvia Plath, Ted Hughes, and Sympathetic Magic'. *Bloomsbury Handbook to Sylvia Plath*. Ed. Anita Helle, Amanda Golden, and Maeve O'Brien. London: Bloomsbury, 2022, 165–76.

'Roche, Clarissa, Interview Recording, Part Three'. Harriet Rosenstein Research Files on Sylvia Plath, 1910–2018. Harriet Rosenstein. Stuart A. Rose Manuscript, Archives, and Rare Book Library, Emory University, 20 November 1973.

'Roche, Interview Recording, Part Four, Undated'. Harriet Rosenstein Research Files on Sylvia Plath. Harriet Rosenstein. Emory University Archives, Stuart A. Rose Manuscript, Archives, and Rare Book Library, Emory University, n.d.

Rogers, Harold. 'Faust and the Devil'. *The Christian Science Monitor*, 12 October 1950: 4.

Roper, Lyndal. *Oedipus and the Devil: Witchcraft, Sexuality, and Religion in Early Modern Europe*. London: Routledge, 1994.

Witch Craze: Terror and Fantasy in Baroque Germany. New Haven; London: Yale University Press, 2004.

Rose, Jacqueline. *The Haunting of Sylvia Plath*. 2nd ed. London: Virago, 1991.

Rosenthal, Bernard. 'Dark Eve'. *Salem Story: Reading the Witch Trials of 1692*. Cambridge: Cambridge University Press, 1993, 10–31.

Rowland, Antony. *Tony Harrison and the Holocaust*. Liverpool: Liverpool University Press, 2001.

Salem Witch Museum. *Proctor's Ledge Memorial*. 12 January 2020. https://salemwitchmuseum.com/locations/proctors-ledge-memorial/.

Sawyer, Robert. 'Shakespeare and Marlowe: Re-Writing the Relationship'. *Critical Survey* 21.3 (2009): 41–58.

Scheerer, Constance. 'The Deathly Paradise of Sylvia Plath'. *The Antioch Review* 34.4 (1976): 469–80.

Segal, Charles. 'Ovid's Metamorphic Bodies: Art, Gender, and Violence in the "Metamorphoses"'. *A Journal of Humanities and the Classics* 5.3 (1998): 9–41.

Sexton, Anne. *The Complete Poems*. Boston; New York: Mariner Book, 1999.

Shakespeare, William. *The Complete Plays and Poems of Shakespeare: A New Text*. Ed. William Allan Neilson and Charles Jarvis Hill. Boston: Houghton Mifflin Company, 1941.

The Tempest. Ed. Anne Barton. Harmondsworth: Penguin, 1968.

Macbeth. Ed. A. R. Braunmuller. Cambridge: Cambridge University Press, 1997.

'Antony and Cleopatra'. *The Complete Works of William Shakespeare*. New York: Rock Point, 2019, 924–64.

Shapiro, Karl. 'The Progress of Faust'. *The New Yorker*, 11 May 1946: 28.

Sharpe, J. A. 'Witchcraft and Women in Seventeenth-Century England: Some Northern Evidence'. *Continuity and Change* 6.2 (1991): 179–99.

Sharps, Katrina. *The Secret Lives of Nightjars*. May 2019. www.bou.org.uk/the-secret-lives-of-nightjars/.

Sharrock, Alison. 'Gender and Transformation: Reading, Women, and Gender in Ovid's Metamorphoses'. *Metamorphic Readings: Transformation Language, and Gender in the Interpretation of Ovid's Metamorphoses*. Ed. Alison Sharrock, Daniel Möller, and Mats Malm. Oxford: Oxford University Press, 2020, 33–53.

'Noua . . . corpora: New Bodies and Gendered Patterns in the Metamorphoses'. *Dictynna* 17 (2020): 1–26.

Shaw, Tony. '"Martyrs, Miracles and Martians": Religion and Cold War Cinematic Propaganda in the 1950s'. *Religion and the Cold War*. Ed. Dianne Kirby. Gordonsville: Palgrave Macmillan, 2002, 211–31.

Sheehan, Dan. *Sylvia Plath's Tarot Deck Just Sold for $200,000*. 21 July 2021. https://lithub.com/sylvia-plaths-tarot-deck-just-sold-for-200000/.

'Shook, Margaret, interview recording'. Harriet Rosenstein Research Files on Sylvia Plath, 1910–2018. Harriet Rosenstein. Stuart A. Rose Manuscript, Archives, and Rare Book Library, Emory University, n.d.

Showalter, Elaine. *Sister's Choice: Tradition and Change in American Women's Writing*. Oxford: Clarendon, 1991.

'Sigmund, Elizabeth Compton, 1962–1975'. Harriet Rosenstein research files on Sylvia Plath, Manuscript Collection No. 1489. Stuart A. Rose Manuscript, Archives, and Rare Book Library, Emory University, n.d.

'Sigmund, Elizabeth Compton, Interview Recording, Part Two, Undated'. Harriet Rosenstein. Stuart A. Rose Manuscript, Archives, and Rare Book Library, Emory University, n.d.

'Sigmund, Elizabeth Compton, Interview Recording, Part Five, Undated'. Harriet Rosenstein. Stuart A. Rose Manuscript, Archives, and Rare Book Library, Emory University, n.d.

Simpson, Jacqueline. 'Margaret Murray: Who Believed Her, and Why?' *Folklore* 105 (1994): 89–96.

Sitwell, Edith. *Collected Poems*. New York: Vanguard Press, 1954.

Smith, Gay. *Lady Macbeth in America: From the Stage to the White House*. New York: Palgrave Macmillan, 2010.

Sneddon, Andrew. *Witchcraft and Magic in Ireland*. London: Palgrave Macmillan, 2015.

Sofer, Andrew. 'How to Do Things with Demons: Conjuring Performatives in *Doctor Faustus*'. *Theatre Journal* 61.1 (2009): 1–21.

Spencer, Luke. *The Poetry of Tony Harrison*. New York; London: Harvester Wheatsheaf, 1994.

Stein, William B. *Hawthorne's Faust: A Study of the Devil Ardietype*. Gainesville: University of Florida Press, 1953.

Steinberg, Peter K. 'Sylvia Plath's Circus in Three Rings'. *Sylvia Plath Info Blog*. 1 March 2017. https://sylviaplathinfo.blogspot.com/2017/03/sylvia-plaths-circus-three-rings.html.

'The Education of Sylvia Plath, Smith College 1954–1955'. *Sylvia Plath Info Blog*. 7 December 2017. https://sylviaplathinfo.blogspot.com/2017/12/the-education-of-sylvia-plath-smith_7.html.

'Sylvia Plath: Film Buff'. 15 October 2018. https://sylviaplathinfo.blogspot.com/2018/10/sylvia-plath-film-buff.html

Steiner, Rudolf. *The Genius of Language: Observations for Teachers*. New York: Anthroposophic Press, 1995.

Stockholder, Kay. '"Within the Massy Entrailes of the Earth": Faustus's Relation to Women'. *'A Poet and a Filthy Play-maker': New Essays on Christopher Marlowe*. Ed. Kenneth Friedenreich, Roma Gill, and Constance B. Kuriyama. New York: AMS Press, 1988, 203–19.

Stokes, Raymond G., Roman Köster, and Stephen C. Sambrook. 'Rationalization Measures'. *The Business of Waste: Great Britain and Germany, 1945 to the Present*. Cambridge: Cambridge University Press, 2013, 49–86.

Struck, Peter T. 'Speech Acts and the Stakes of Hellenism in late Antiquity'. *Magic and Ritual in the Ancient World*. Ed. Marvin Meyer and Paul Mirecki. Vol. 141. Leiden; Boston; Köln: Brill, 2002, 386–403.

Tavárez, David. 'Ritual Language'. *The Cambridge Handbook of Linguistic Anthropology*. Ed. N. J. Enfield, Paul Kockelman, and Jack Sidnell. Cambridge: Cambridge University Press, 2014, 516–36.

Thomas, Keith. *Religion and Decline of Magic: Studies in Popular Beliefs in 16th and 17th Century England*. Harmondsworth: Penguin, 1973.

Tonge, Mildred. 'Black Magic and Miracles in *Macbeth*'. *The Journal of English and Germanic Philology* 31.2 (1932): 234–46.

Tunc, Tanfer Emin. 'The Healer and the Witch: Sexuality and Power in Arthur Miller's THE CRUCIBLE'. *The Explicator* 71.4 (2013): 266–70.

Tunstall, Lucy. 'Vision and Visual Art in Sylvia Plath's Ariel and Last Poems'. Doctoral dissertation. University of Exeter, June 2015.

'Plath and the Lyric'. *Sylvia Plath in Context.* Ed. Tracy Brain. Cambridge: Cambridge University Press, 2019, 94–104.

Twiddy, Iain. 'Plath and the Pastoral'. *Sylvia Plath in Context.* Ed. Tracy Brain. Cambridge: Cambridge University Press, 2019, 105–14.

University of Cambridge. 'English Tripos. Part II'. *Tragedy Paper 1957.* 29 May 1957. www.english.cam.ac.uk/cambridgeauthors/wpcontent/uploads/2009/07/tragedypaper1957.pdf.

Van Duyne, Emily. *Loving Sylvia Plath.* New York: W. W. Norton & Company, 2024.

Van Dyne, Susan R. '"Fueling the Phoenix Fire": The Manuscript of Sylvia Plath's "Lady Lazarus"'. *Sylvia Plath.* Ed. Harold Bloom. New York; Philadelphia: Chelsea House, 1989, 133–47.

Revising Life: Sylvia Plath's Ariel Poems. London: University of North Carolina, 1993.

Vaughan, Virginia Mason. '"Something Rich and Strange": Caliban's Theatrical Metamorphoses'. *Shakespeare Quarterly* 36.4 (1985): 390–405.

Vendler, Helen. 'Ashbery's Aesthetic: Reporting on Fairfield Porter and Saul Steinberg'. *Harvard Review* 22 (2002): 81–96.

Coming of Age as a Poet: Milton, Keats, Eliot, Plath. Cambridge, MA; London: Harvard University Press, 2004.

Vernel, H. S. 'The Poetics of the Magical Charm: An Essay in the Power of Words'. *Magic and Ritual in the Ancient World.* Vol. 141. Ed. Paul Mirecki and Marvin Meyer. Leiden; Boston; Köln: Brill, 2002, 105–58.

Wagner, Erica. *Ariel's Gift: Ted Hughes, Sylvia Plath, and the Story of Birthday Letters.* London: Faber, 2001.

Wagner-Martin, Linda. *Sylvia Plath: A Biography.* London: Chatto & Windus, 1988.

Walter, Bronwen. *Outsiders Inside: Whiteness, Place and Irish Women.* London: Routledge, 2001.

Waterman, Hillary. 'Herbs & Verbs: How to Do Witchcraft for Real'. 25 October 2017. https://daily.jstor.org/herbs-verbs-how-to-do-witchcraft-for-real/.

Waters, Thomas. *Cursed Britain: A History of Witchcraft and Black Magic in Modern Times.* New Haven: Yale University Press, 2020.

Webster's New Collegiate Dictionary. 2nd ed. London; Springfield, MA: G. Bell & Sons Ltd.; G. & C. Merriam Co., 1949.

Weston, L. M. C. 'The Language of Magic in Two Old English Metrical Charms'. *Neuphilologische Mitteilungen* 86.2 (1985): 176–86.

Wheatley, Dennis. *The Satanist.* New York: Ballantine Books, 1972.

Whittemore, Reed. 'Hester Prynne'. *The Kenyon Review* 7.3 (1945): 449.

Winder, Elizabeth. *Pain, Parties, Work: Sylvia Plath in New York, Summer 1953.* New York: HarperCollins, 2014.

Wiske, Gina. 'Horrors and Menaces to Everything Decent in Life: The Horror Fiction of Dennis Wheatley'. *Creepers: British Horror and Fantasy in the*

Twentieth Century. Ed. Clive Bloom. London; Boulder: Pluto Press, 1993, 99–110.

Woolf, Karen McCarthy. 'Ariel'. *After Sylvia*. Ed. Sarah Corbett and Ian Humphreys. Rugby: Nine Arches Press, 2022, 52–53.

Woolf, Virgnia. *The Waves*. Hertfordshire: Wordsworth Classics, 2000.

Wylder, Edith. 'Emily Dickinson's Punctuation: The Controversy Revisited'. *American Literary Realism* 36.3 (2004): 206–24.

Wymer, Rowland. '*The Tempest* and the Origins of Britain'. *Critical Survey* 11.1 (1999): 3–14.

Young, Serinity. *Women Who Fly: Goddesses, Witches, Mystics, and other Airborne Females*. Oxford: Oxford University Press, 2017.

Zivley, Sherry Lutz. 'Sylvia Plath's Transformations of Modernist Paintings'. *College Literature* 29.3 (2002): 35–56.

Index